T0137212

Artificial Intelligence: Foundations, Theory, and Algorithms

Series Editors

Barry O'Sullivan, Cork, Ireland
Michael Wooldridge, Oxford, United Kingdom

More information about this series at http://www.springer.com/series/13900

Stefano Mariani

Coordination of Complex Sociotechnical Systems

Self-organisation of Knowledge in $\mathcal{MoK}$

 Springer

Stefano Mariani [ID]
Dipartimento di Informatica - Scienza e
    Ingegneria (DISI)
Università di Bologna
Bologna
Italy

ISSN 2365-3051   ISSN 2365-306X   (electronic)
Artificial Intelligence: Foundations, Theory, and Algorithms
ISBN 978-3-319-83659-1   ISBN 978-3-319-47109-9   (eBook)
DOI 10.1007/978-3-319-47109-9

© Springer International Publishing AG 2016
Softcover reprint of the hardcover 1st edition 2016
This work is subject to copyright. All rights are reserved by the Publisher, whether the whole or part
of the material is concerned, specifically the rights of translation, reprinting, reuse of illustrations,
recitation, broadcasting, reproduction on microfilms or in any other physical way, and transmission
or information storage and retrieval, electronic adaptation, computer software, or by similar or dissimilar
methodology now known or hereafter developed.
The use of general descriptive names, registered names, trademarks, service marks, etc. in this
publication does not imply, even in the absence of a specific statement, that such names are exempt from
the relevant protective laws and regulations and therefore free for general use.
The publisher, the authors and the editors are safe to assume that the advice and information in this
book are believed to be true and accurate at the date of publication. Neither the publisher nor the
authors or the editors give a warranty, express or implied, with respect to the material contained herein or
for any errors or omissions that may have been made.

Printed on acid-free paper

This Springer imprint is published by Springer Nature
The registered company is Springer International Publishing AG
The registered company address is: Gewerbestrasse 11, 6330 Cham, Switzerland

To my beloved wife, Alice
To our beloved daughter, Asia
To our beloved yet-to-come newborn :)

Foreword

Modern societies are organised around a number of (interdependent) complex systems. Logistic and supply chains, transportation networks, health services, energy systems, financial markets, and smart cities are just a few examples. These systems are inherently *sociotechnical* and involve interactions between infrastructures, man-made processes, natural phenomena, multiple stakeholders, and human behaviour. Also, their dynamic arises from interaction of a population of self-interested agents, coordinating/competing locally with one another as well as with their environment. Normally there is no centralised control structure dictating how individuals should behave, and local agent-to-agent interaction often leads to the emergence of global self-organised behaviour.

For instance, in road network infrastructures with traffic light controllers, road-side units, and a communication network between intersections (the technical part), drivers (the human/social component of the system) are self-interested autonomous entities that cannot be directly controlled by a central planner, but rather take decisions according to their own utility function—for instance, minimisation of their travel-time. In traffic networks, queues and congestions arise as system emergent behaviours. In order to avoid them, no centralised control can be exploited: instead, single suggestions based on traffic data harvested by either sensors or road-side units could be provided to drivers, who in turn might choose to change their current plans.

Sociotechnical systems are heavily knowledge-intensive. For the first time in the history of mankind, we have access to data sets of unprecedented scale and accuracy about infrastructures, processes, natural phenomena, and human behaviours. Global systems rely on the Internet of Things, where each object is connected and generates data. Extracting useful knowledge from such an enormous amount of data is essential to design effective control strategies, as well as to construct efficient strategic and tactical planning tools.

In the last 5 years, my research has been focussed on the design and implementation of decision support tools deciding on such complex systems. While traditional modelling techniques have always relied on domain expert knowledge, the complexity of sociotechnical systems calls for a new modelling paradigm where a relevant part of the model is learned from data harvested by sensors, producing observations from heterogeneous data sources. Organising data, clustering them according to their relevance for a specific topic, and extracting modelling components from them constitute a cornerstone of empirical model learning.

This book, written by a young and extremely talented researcher, is about studying and engineering coordination mechanisms in knowledge-intensive sociotechnical systems that are heavily affected by the scale, unpredictability, non-determinism, and amount and pace of data they rely on. All the above features imply challenges that can be approached via a paradigm shift in the coordination perspective: accordingly, the book defines new techniques supporting programmable, self-organising, situated coordination.

The main idea behind self-organising coordination takes inspiration from the socio-cognitive theory of action, and proposes an intriguing concept of $\mathcal{M}$olecules of $\mathcal{K}$nowledge ($\mathcal{MoK}$). The $\mathcal{MoK}$ model is built around a biochemical metaphor where information sources are continuously and spontaneously enriched via information chunks that autonomously aggregate on the basis of user interaction, and gain or lose relevance as time flows. This way, data may become organised information autonomously, guided by coordination mechanisms seamlessly integrating knowledge. In addition, data behave as continuously alive entities, by re-organising themselves spontaneously, and by evolving themselves to better meet the ever-changing needs of the system they describe.

The $\mathcal{MoK}$ metaphor has a potentially tremendous impact on a number of fields: from information gathering in the Internet to distributed control strategies relying on heterogeneous data sources; from predictive systems extracting models from observation to prescriptive systems where data and observation are essential to characterise the system and learn model components.

Also, by adopting an engineering perspective, the $\mathcal{MoK}$ metaphor poses a number of interesting and far from trivial challenges. Along with the model, the book proposes a well-detailed middleware layer for knowledge management applications. The original implementation of the $\mathcal{MoK}$ middleware is built upon the TuCSoN coordination infrastructure for distribution issues, and the ReSpecT language for spatio-temporal awareness and adaptiveness. The middleware supports programmable coordination for dealing with unpredictable and adaptive behaviour and uncertain data, enables the emergence of self-organisation, and supports both mutual and peripheral awareness thanks to situatedness.

I have known Stefano Mariani during his Ph.D. thesis, as I was at the internal reviewing committee. I have been immediately impressed by the intriguing ideas proposed in his research activity, by the deep technological foundations they relied on, and by the forward-looking vision of his Ph.D. work.

Stefano Mariani's book is an excellent contribution to the field of knowledge management in environments where non-determinism, unpredictability, uncertainty, and complexity make traditional coordination mechanisms no longer usable. It proposes an exciting model, covers engineering aspects, and attempts to discern future directions in a fast-moving and innovative field.

Bologna, Italy   Michela Milano
July 2016

Preface

This book stems from the author's own Ph.D. thesis, with the goal of providing a coherent and comprehensive view over a paradigm shift in computational information management systems, going toward self-organisation of information pieces, interpreted as living entities spontaneously adapting to users' needs according to their behaviour. The purpose is to provide graduate students, junior and senior researchers, information systems designers, and knowledge practitioners in general with a novel perspective over knowledge and information management, supported by practical reference guidelines, models, mechanisms, and technologies to exploit during design of their system.

The book is thus structured to gracefully introduce the reader to the coordination perspective over complex sociotechnical systems, by discussing a few examples of such a sort of systems, namely distributed first, self-organising then, finally pervasive ones. Once the reader is more familiar with the aforementioned approaches to coordination, she is presented a comprehensive model for self-organising coordination of knowledge-intensive sociotechnical systems, which is thoroughly described and discussed in both theoretical and technological aspects.

The research landscape that the contents of this book conceptually belong to is at the crossroads between multi-agent systems, nature-inspired self-organisation, situated coordination, and sociotechnical systems. Accordingly, the more technical contents take as a reference agent-oriented models, considering also human agents, where coordination occurs through environment mediation, thus in a setting where agents' actions are always situated in a virtual or physical environment, and where such an environment is able to spontaneously enact computational processes supporting and promoting self-organisation of the agents ensemble.

Cesena, Italy   Stefano Mariani
June 2016

Acknowledgements

This book belongs not only to me but also to all the researchers and professionals I had the pleasure to work with during my life in the University of Bologna.

I wish to thank Prof. Andrea Omicini for his supervision during my whole research activity: he is a constant and endless source of invaluably precious suggestions, criticism, and inspiration, as well as a wonderful person to share random thoughts with. I wish to thank Prof. Michela Milano for writing the foreword to this book, and for her enthusiasm regarding $\mathcal{MoK}$.

I wish to thank Profs. Mirko Viroli and Alessandro Ricci for sharing with me many enlightening discussions, as well as many launch breaks: they may be unaware of this, but their research work has always been a reference for me. I wish to thank Danilo Pianini, Sara Montagna, and Andrea Santi for the wonderful time we had in the APICe lab, and for all the precious discussions we shared. A special mention goes to Roberta Calegari for being so efficient in fixing tuProlog issues for the benefit of TuCSoN.

I wish to thank all the brilliant students I had the pleasure to supervise for their thesis and graduate projects, from whom I have learnt as much as I have taught. A special mention goes to Michele Pratiffi, Mattia Occhiuto, Giulio Crestani, Gianluca Spadazzi, Giacomo Dradi, Luca Santonastasi, Matteo Fattori, Matteo Francia, Giovanni Ciatto, Michele Bombardi, Lorenzo Forcellini Reffi.

Last but not least, I owe everything I have to my family: my wife Alice constantly supports me and helps me in every single important decision, and our daughter Asia has been fundamental to refresh my energies when the work to do was just too much. My parents, too, always supported me, and constantly demonstrated their care and pride about my research work, while my brother has been always available for taking a break from work.

Cesena, Italy
June 2016

Stefano Mariani

Contents

Chapter 1
Introduction

Abstract This chapter explains the context of the book and offers a brief overview of its structure.

1.1 Introduction

Knowledge-Intensive Environments (KIE) are workplaces in which sustainability of the organisation long-term goals is influenced by, if not even dependant on, the evolution of the knowledge embodied within the organisation itself [1]. Being knowledge an organised combination of data, procedures, and operations, continuously interacting and evolving according to human users practice and (learnt) experience, KIE are usually computationally supported by *Sociotechnical Systems* (STS), that is, systems in which cognitive and social interaction is mediated by information technology, rather than by the natural world (alone) [3].

The modern information technology landscape is increasingly pervaded by these kind of systems, mostly due to the astonishing amount of data available nowadays, and to the unprecedented participation of end users in the applications they use everyday—think about, e.g., social networks, crowdsourcing platforms, online collaboration tools, and the like.

By definition, both KIE and STS are heavily interaction-centred, thus, they inevitably need to deal with *coordination issues* to harness the intricacies of runtime dependencies between the data and the agents (either software or human) participating the system [2]. However, engineering effective coordination is far from trivial, mostly due to a few peculiarities of KIE and STS: *unpredictability* of human behaviour, *scalability* of the technological infrastructure, *size* of the amount of data, information, and knowledge to handle, *pace* of knowledge production and consumption, and of users interaction.

For these reasons, this book discusses the issue of engineering knowledge-intensive STS from a *coordination perspective*, dealing with the aforementioned issues at the infrastructural level, with the goal of promoting *user-driven self-organisation of knowledge*, by leveraging self-organising coordination mechanisms,

© Springer International Publishing AG 2016
S. Mariani, *Coordination of Complex Sociotechnical Systems*,
Artificial Intelligence: Foundations, Theory, and Algorithms,
DOI 10.1007/978-3-319-47109-9_1

an architecture for situated pervasive systems, and a cognitive model of social action. Accordingly, the content of the book is articulated as follows:

- Chapter 2 reviews the literature about coordination of distributed systems
- Chapter 3 focusses coordination of self-organising systems, by describing nature-inspired approaches to coordination, among which a chemical-inspired approach dealing with the well-known local versus global issue by engineering coordination laws as *artificial chemical reactions*. Simulations illustrate the expressiveness reach of the approach in practice, while formal definition of the coordination primitives exploited as basic implementation bricks helps grounding the approach on the theoretical side
- Chapter 4 reviews the literature about coordination of pervasive systems, with particular emphasis on a distributed, *situated architecture* for coordination in pervasive Multi-Agent Systems (MAS), supporting engineering of the aforementioned coordination laws, implemented by extending an existing coordination infrastructure. The coordination language exploited by the infrastructure is accordingly extended, too, so as to handle the novel abstractions, enabling, and promoting *situated coordination*
- Chapter 5 focusses coordination of sociotechnical systems, by describing a few research works trying to bring socio-cognitive models of action within computational models, among which the *Behavioural Implicit Communication* (BIC) model of social action, whose abstractions and mechanisms are integrated into the (chemical-inspired, situated) computational framework described so far, so as to leverage the concept of tacit messages to enable *user-driven coordination*
- Chapter 6 describes the *Molecules of Knowledge* model (*MoK*) for *self-organisation of knowledge* in knowledge-intensive STS
- Chapter 7 discusses the *MoK* technology, describing both a prototype middleware implementing the core model, and a complete ecosystem featuring accessory functionalities
- Chapter 8 reports on simulations of the computational and interaction model of *MoK*, performed so as to evaluate its expressive reach
- Chapter 9 reports on early deployments of the *MoK* technology in selected use cases, showcasing the kind of adaptive and self-organising behaviour it can achieve

Chapters are further arranged in two parts: Part I includes Chaps. 2–5, Part II Chaps. 6–9. This reflects the complementary nature of the research works presented in Part I w.r.t. the *MoK* model described in Part II. There, in fact, *(i)* the chemical-inspired approach to self-organising coordination is the reference framework used to implement *MoK* coordination laws as artificial chemical reactions, *(ii)* the situated architecture for pervasive MAS provides the runtime for execution of *MoK* coordination laws, while the situated language is exploited to implement *MoK* artificial chemical reactions, and *(iii)* BIC principles drive the self-organising coordination process according to users interactions.

Part III concludes the book with some final remarks.

1.2 Organisation of Chapters

The book is organised in three parts

- Part I describes the three complementary research works contributing to scientifically ground the $\mathcal{MoK}$ model, and design & implement $\mathcal{MoK}$ infrastructure
- Part II describes the $\mathcal{MoK}$ model and technology
- Part III concludes providing final remarks and a glimpse of what could follow in the research landscape comprising $\mathcal{MoK}$-like systems

Here follows a thorough description of the Chapters within each Part.

1.2.1 Part I

Part I starts with Chap. 2, providing a review of the literature regarding tuple-based coordination for distributed systems, focussed on the models and technologies which mostly relate to $\mathcal{MoK}$.

Then, Chap. 3 describes the chemical-inspired approach to coordination in self-organising systems and the research works that mostly influenced its conception:

- Section 3.1 overviews a few selected bio-inspired patterns for self-organisation
- Section 3.2 describes two chemical-inspired approaches to self-organising coordination which influenced the one described in Sect. 3.3
- Section 3.3 describes an interpretation of chemical-inspired coordination relying on custom kinetic rates, in place of the law of mass action, for artificial chemical reactions implementing coordination laws
- Section 3.4 describes uniform coordination primitives, that is, a probabilistic extension to LINDA coordination primitives, as the basic mechanisms on top of which chemical-inspired coordination laws can be implemented, showcasing its expressiveness

Chapter 4 is dedicated to the issue of coordination of pervasive systems, thus, describes an architectural approach to deal with it:

- Section 4.1 reviews the literature to frame the issue from an historical perspective, analysing the evolution of the meta-models and architectures proposed during time, then describes the architecture taken as a reference for the remainder of the book, along with its meta-model
- Section 4.2 discusses the different facets of situated coordination
- Section 4.3 elaborates on how the architecture supports environmental situatedness from the infrastructural point of view
- Section 4.4 focusses on temporal situatedness from a linguistic point of view
- Section 4.5 elaborates on how the architecture supports spatial situatedness from the linguistic point of view

Finally, Chap. 5 discusses how it is possible to take advantage of some of the peculiar traits of knowledge-intensive STS to promote coordination of sociotechnical systems driven by users interactions:

- Section 5.1 presents the main challenges of such a kind of systems, and how they can be dealt with from a coordination perspective
- Section 5.2 reviews the research efforts which tried to integrate socio-cognitive theories of action within a computational framework for designing MAS
- Section 5.3 reports on a survey of the (inter-)actions means provided by a few real-world STS, to connect the aforementioned theories of action with real-world widely used systems

1.2.2   Part II

Part II starts with Chap. 6, decorated with cross-reference which thoroughly describes the $\mathcal{MoK}$ model for self-organisation in knowledge-intensive STS:

- Section 6.1 motivates the novel approach to coordination promoted by $\mathcal{MoK}$
- Section 6.2 presents the core abstractions which the model revolves around
- Section 6.3 describes $\mathcal{MoK}$ computational model, that is, $\mathcal{MoK}$ reactions, what they are meant for, and how they work
- Section 6.4 describes the interaction model of $\mathcal{MoK}$, that is, how users' interactions affect the self-organising coordination process
- Section 6.5 discusses the information model of $\mathcal{MoK}$, that is, the issue of measuring similarity between pieces of information, for the sake of promoting semantic-driven coordination, while keeping the system efficient

Then, Chap. 7 describes the $\mathcal{MoK}$ technology:

- Section 7.1 describes a prototype of the $\mathcal{MoK}$ core model, developed as a middleware running on top of the TuCSoN infrastructure, and implemented in the ReSpecT language, also reporting on an early evaluation through deployment within a news management scenario
- Section 7.2 instead, reports on an ongoing effort to implement a full-fledged $\mathcal{MoK}$ ecosystem, encompassing also functionalities such as information harvesting, knowledge discovery, persistency, and the like

Chapter 8 reports on simulations of the $\mathcal{MoK}$ model:

- Section 8.1 simulates $\mathcal{MoK}$ computational model in order to evaluate the extent to which $\mathcal{MoK}$ reactions achieve the desired emergent behaviours
- Section 8.2 focusses instead on $\mathcal{MoK}$ interaction model, evaluating the extent to which users' interactions can drive $\mathcal{MoK}$ coordinative behaviour toward their needs

Finally, Chap. 9 reports on exemplary deployments of $\mathcal{MoK}$ technology meant to showcase how it achieves the two main goals of the $\mathcal{MoK}$ model—that is, aggregation and smart diffusion of information:

- Section 9.1 describes a document clustering scenario in which $\mathcal{MoK}$ aggregation reaction exploits different $\mathcal{F}_{MoK}$ similarity measures to aggregate similar information
- Section 9.2 discusses a news management scenario in which the $\mathcal{MoK}$ model is tailored to the business domain and the resulting model is exploited to enable smart diffusion of news items

1.2.3 Part III

Part III concludes the book, by providing final remarks.

References

1. Bhatt, G.D.: Knowledge management in organizations: Examining the interaction between technologies, techniques, and people. J. Knowl. Manag. **5**(1), 68–75 (2001)
2. Malone, T.W., Crowston, K.: The interdisciplinary study of coordination. ACM Comput. Surv. **26**(1), 87–119 (1994). doi:10.1145/174666.174668
3. Whitworth, B.: Socio-technical systems. Encyclopedia of Human Computer Interaction pp. 533–541 (2006)

Part I
Coordination of Complex
Sociotechnical Systems

In the first part of this book the engineering challenges posed by three different but related kinds of complex systems are discussed from a coordination perspective. Then novel approaches to deal with them are described. In particular, the focus is on *distributed* (Chap. 2), *self-organising* (Chap. 3), *pervasive* and (Chap. 4), *sociotechnical* (Chap. 5) systems.

Each chapter contributes an ingredient to the $\mathcal{MoK}$ model described in Part II of this book, namely:

- the approach dealing with self-organisation through *uniform primitives* and *artificial chemical reactions* with custom-defined kinetic rates (Chap. 3) is the ground upon which $\mathcal{MoK}$ *reactions* are conceived and designed
- the situated architecture and language presented in Chap. 4 is exploited to implement the prototype of the $\mathcal{MoK}$ middleware on TuCSoN coordination infrastructure, using the extended ReSpecT language
- the theory of *behavioural implicit communication* discussed in Chap. 5, in particular the notion of *tacit message*, is used as the conceptual ground upon which $\mathcal{MoK}$ *user-centred* self-organisation mechanisms are conceived and designed— *enzymes*, *traces*, and *perturbation* actions in particular

Chapter 2
Coordination of Distributed Systems

Abstract This chapter provides an overview of those approaches to coordination of distributed systems (programmable in Sect. 2.1, probabilistic in Sect. 2.2) which directly motivated, inspired, and influenced the approach to coordination in self-organising systems proposed in Chap. 3. A brief argumentation on why the approaches are all tuple-based, and on which benefits this brings [24], is provided as a preparatory background, describing the seminal LINDA model [11] which almost all the described approaches are built on top of.

2.1 Tuple-Based Coordination

LINDA has been proposed by David Gelernter in [11] as a distributed programming language exploiting the notion of *generative communication*—introduced in the same paper. Nevertheless, it is suddenly recognised by Gelernter himself as a full-fledged computational model whose implications go beyond distributed communication. In fact, LINDA is nowadays mostly considered a *coordination model* [6], rather than merely a distributed programming language.

The LINDA language consists of three primitives: `out`, `in`, `rd`. Respectively, they allow processes to produce, consume, and observe *tuples* stored in a *tuple space*. Tuples are named, ordered collections of heterogeneous, typed values and/or variables—usually, tuples containing some variables are called *templates* (or, anti-tuples). A tuple space is the abstract computational environment in which LINDA programs are executed, thus, it includes tuples as well as processes using LINDA primitives.

The semantics of LINDA primitives is what makes the LINDA language particularly suitable to be used as a coordination model: whereas the `out` primitive always puts a tuple in the tuple space, `in` and `rd` *attempt* to get one—respectively, withdrawing it or not. In fact, if a tuple *matching* the variables (possibly) used in the `in` or `rd` primitive is found that tuple is returned and the caller process may continue execution; otherwise, the caller process is *suspended* until a matching tuple becomes available. This execution semantics is often referred to as LINDA *suspensive semantics*, and is

© Springer International Publishing AG 2016   9
S. Mariani, *Coordination of Complex Sociotechnical Systems*,
Artificial Intelligence: Foundations, Theory, and Algorithms,
DOI 10.1007/978-3-319-47109-9_2

one of its distinguishing features enabling coordination policies to be programmed solely on top of the LINDA language.

In his paper Gelernter does not further specifies `out` semantics. Much more recently, [4] distinguishes two admissible semantics regarding actual tuple insertion in the tuple space w.r.t. to the producer process, deeply affecting the computational expressiveness of the LINDA model. In the following, it is always assumed the *ordered semantics* of `out` primitive—as well as of any other insertion primitive which could be mentioned.

What enables the suspensive semantics is the primary contribution of Gelernter's paper, that is, *generative communication*. In generative communication, the data items communicated—that is, the tuples—live independently w.r.t. their producers, since they are (possibly, persistently) stored by the tuple space. This also enables uncoupling in space and time: in fact, sender (receiver) processes need not to know when and where receivers (senders) will be executing in order to successfully communicate.

The last distinguishing feature of the LINDA model is the *associative access* to data. In fact, interacting processes need not to know the address where a tuple is stored to access it: they simply have to know their name and content—even partially thanks to variables. This enables a third form of uncoupling: reference uncoupling (called communication orthogonality in [11]), w.r.t. both tuples and senders/receivers.

LINDA appears well suited for supporting coordination in systems featuring, e.g.: *(i)* distribution, by relying on multiple tuple spaces installed on networked hosts; *(ii)* openness, thanks to its uncoupling facilities; *(iii)* incomplete information, handled by associative access. Knowledge-intensive sociotechnical systems (STS) enjoy all these features, nevertheless have many more which cannot be dealt with effectively by LINDA as it is; in particular, *uncertainty* and *unpredictability*, and the need for *adaptiveness*.

For this reason, the following sections review some coordination models and infrastructures, either inspired to LINDA or implementing LINDA in interesting ways, all having in common the goal of dealing with the aforementioned shortcomings—some by looking at natural metaphors for implementation, some by extending the model.

2.1.1 On Distribution

As described in previous section, LINDA has been originally conceived as a language for decorating concurrent/parallel programs running on a *shared memory* model. Thus, a *single* global tuple space was sufficient for the task of coordinating interacting *co-located* processes. As soon as LINDA potential to become a full-fledged coordination for *distributed* processes was recognised, the need for working with *multiple* tuple spaces, possibly spread among networked hosts arose.

Many research works since then proposed either LINDA extensions, implementations, or brand new models featuring multiple tuple spaces distributed over a network: Gelernter himself [12], Ciancarini with the PoliS model [5], KLAIM [7] and LIME [23] also adding mobility-related aspects, are just a few examples. In the following, another contribution is described for it is exploited in Chap. 4 as the infrastructure supporting situated coordination: TuCSoN [20].

2.1.1.1 TuCSoN

TuCSoN [20] is a model for the coordination of *distributed* processes, as well as of autonomous agents, extending in a number of ways the basic LINDA model. In TuCSoN, an extension of tuple spaces called tuple centres [19] can be spread *(i)* over *multiple machines* connected in a network, or *(ii)* on the same machine provided they belong to different TuCSoN nodes, which are, essentially, containers of locally available tuple centres—each TuCSoN nodes sharing a host must be reachable on a different network address.

Focussing on the distribution perspective, TuCSoN extends the basic LINDA model by:

- assigning *globally unique* IDs to tuple centres
- allowing processes to invoke TuCSoN primitives—LINDA primitives plus many others—*remotely*, that is, from network reachable hosts
- allowing processes to exploit *any number* of local or remote tuple centres for coordinating with other processes, simultaneously
- allowing tuple centres themselves to invoke TuCSoN primitives on each other, wherever they are—locally available or remotely reachable
- supporting role-based access control policies [27] for dealing with privacy and security issues

It is worth to note that, in any distributed setting, it is fundamental that coordination primitives are designed and implemented to be *asynchronous by default*, that is, to avoid *coupling* control flow of the invoker process with network waits. Differently from LINDA in fact, where the network is not considered thus absence of a matching tuple when a getter primitive is invoked is the only cause of suspension for processes, in TuCSoN network level issues may cause unexpected suspension at the application level, e.g., because a network link breaks during invocation of a getter primitives, which is then bound to wait *indefinitely* for a result.

For these reasons, TuCSoN adopts a *two-steps semantics* w.r.t. primitives execution:

Invocation —The request of the operation is sent to the target tuple centre, wherever it is—remote or local

Completion—The response of the operation is sent back to the invoker process, wherever it is—remote or local

Any TuCSoN primitive undergoes these two steps, so as to *(i)* detect as early as possible network issues, and *(ii)* decouple synchronism of invocation as chosen by the invoker process from synchronism of the underlying implementation as designed in TuCSoN.

2.2   Programmable Coordination

As far as adaptiveness is a main concern, a natural solution to support it is to allow some degree of *programmability* of the coordination machinery, e.g., enabling inter- acting agents to change the coordination laws, or even the coordination medium to change them itself, at run-time. Among the many existing approaches to program- mable coordination, here follows description of those which proven to be particularly influential for the model described in Chap. 3: LGI [16], GAMMA [2], ReSpecT [18], and TOTA [15].

It should be noted that LGI is not tuple based, but message-based, and that GAMMA is a model for specification of programs based on multiset rewriting, not a coordination model. Nevertheless, a few reasons motivate their inclusion in the section:

- LGI is among the first examples of programmable coordination machinery
- LGI can be easily implemented in a tuple space-based setting, by mapping messages to tuples
- GAMMA embeds a notion of programmability in the reaction abstraction, allowing arbitrary manipulation of the multiset data structure
- GAMMA too can be easily implemented in a tuple space-based setting, being tuple spaces themselves multisets
- GAMMA reaction model may be interpreted as a coordination model where transformation rules locally enact some coordination policies based on the contextual information provided by data items in the multiset

2.2.1   LGI

LGI (Law Governed Interactions) [16] is a message-based coordination model for open distributed systems providing system designers with the ability to program and enforce *coordination policies* on agents interactions, called *laws*. LGI design is based on four fundamental software engineering principles:

Enforcement—A coordination policy for an open group needs to be *enforced*
Decentralisation—The enforcement mechanism should *not* require central control
Separation—Coordination policies should be *explicitly* reified, and enforced by a
   single mechanism flexible enough to implement a wide range of policies
Incrementality—It should be possible to deploy and enforce a policy *incrementally*,
   at run-time, *without* affecting agents and activities not subject to it

An LGI system is called an $\mathscr{L}$-group $\mathscr{G}$, which is a four-tuple $\mathscr{G} = \langle \mathscr{L}, \mathscr{A}, \mathscr{CS}, \mathscr{M} \rangle$ where:

$\mathscr{L}$—Is the *law of the group*, that is, an explicit and enforced set of "rules of engage-
   ment" between members of the group
$\mathscr{G}$ —Is the set of *agents* belonging to $\mathscr{G}$
$\mathscr{CS}$—Is a set of *control states*, mutable, and subject to $\mathscr{L}$, one per member of the
   group
$\mathscr{M}$—Is the set of messages—called $\mathscr{L}$-messages—that can be exchanged between
   members of $\mathscr{G}$ under law $\mathscr{L}$

Laws are defined on precise *events*—such as sending and arrival of $\mathscr{L}$-messages—and meant to enforce some effect—the *ruling* of the event. Events subject of laws are called *regulated events*. Laws are global because all members of group $\mathscr{G}$ are subject to them, but defined locally for each member, so that:

• each law regulates only events happening locally
• ruling of events depend on the event itself and on the local control state of the
   agent
• ruling of events may trigger only local operations

A control state $\mathscr{CS}$ is maintained by LGI for each agent in the group, whose seman-tics is defined by the laws of the $\mathscr{L}$-group. The control state is meant to track any information relevant for the purpose of law enforcement, thus coordination—such as the role of the agent, communication tokens, etc. The control state is *not* accessible to agents, but only to LGI *controllers* $\mathscr{C}$, whom any agent is assigned to as soon as it participates in a LGI-governed system, which are LGI components in charge of enforcing laws—thus, of the coordination process.

   Interaction and coordination in LGI are based on message passing and mediated by controllers, thus among the possible regulated events there are:

sent(h,m,y)—Occurring whenever a $\mathscr{L}$-message m sent by agent h to agent y
   arrives at $\mathscr{C}_h$
arrived(x,m,h)—Occurring whenever a $\mathscr{L}$-message m sent by agent x arrives at
   $\mathscr{C}_h$

Given such events, laws may exploit a few *primitive operations* to affect the state of interaction:

Operations on $\mathscr{CS}$—Updating the control state of the agent involved in the event
Operations on $\mathscr{L}$-messages—Forwarding and delivering messages on behalf of the
interacting agents

The role of enforcement belongs to controllers and amounts to ensure that *(i)* any
exchange of $\mathscr{L}$-messages *conforms* to law $\mathscr{L}$, and *(ii)* the *effects* of events regulation
are carried out.

Controllers evaluate laws for each compliant event, and carry out the corresponding event ruling *atomically*, so that the sequence of primitive operations implementing
the ruling *does not* interleave with those of any other event occurring locally. LGI
laws are expressed by means of *event-condition-action* rules, implemented in Prolog.

Summing up, LGI represents a first successful attempt at injecting programmability in a coordination model, and provides design principles with are widely recognised
in subsequent models.

2.2.2 GAMMA

GAMMA [2] is a formal model for specifying programs as *multiset transformers*,
ensuring correctness of the programs despite *sequentiality* or *parallelism* of the computational model executing them.

GAMMA rationale is that a program should be derived in a high-level language
with no *accidental sequentiality*—that is, sequentiality not related to the logic of the
program, but to the underlying computational model eventually adopted for actual
execution. This way, such a high-level language can be implemented on either sequen-
tial, concurrent, distributed, or parallel machines.

GAMMA relies on a single data structure, the *multiset*, and provides a single operator, the Γ operator, which may be intuitively defined by resorting to a *chemical
metaphor*: a computation is a succession of *reactions* which consume elements of
the multiset and produce new ones according to specific rules. The computation ends
when no more reactions can occur. If one or several reactions may trigger on several
subsets at the same time, the choice which is made among them is not deterministic.
If the reactions hold for several *disjoint* subsets, the reactions can also be carried out
simultaneously. Thus, GAMMA programs may contain implicit parallelism

The Γ operator relies on the following basic operations on multisets:

union —the number of occurrences of an element in $M_1 + M_2$ is the sum of its
number of occurrences in M_1 and M_2
difference —the number of occurrences of an element in $M_1 - M_2$ is the difference
of its number of occurrences in M_1 and M_2
oneof(M) —yields one arbitrarily selected element of M

Reactions are pairs of closed functions of the form (R, A) enacting the following
effect on multiset M: *replace* in M a subset of elements $\{x_1, \ldots, x_n\}$ such that

R$\{x_1, \ldots, x_n\}$ by the elements of A$\{x_1, \ldots, x_n\}$. Namely, R is the set of action *pre-conditions*, whereas A is the set of action *post-conditions*, in terms of data items present in the multiset.

Being reactions defined in terms of closed functions, they have a purely *local* effect: they replace in the multiset the consumed elements by the produced elements, *independently* of the rest of the multiset. So execution of a GAMMA program can be interpreted as a chaotic process involving several subsets of the multiset in several reactions at any given time.

Summing up, GAMMA represents a first successful attempt at injecting non-determinism and parallelism in computational processes execution.

2.2.3 Tuple Centres and ReSpecT

ReSpecT (Reaction Specification Tuples) is a *logic-based* language for the coordination of complex software systems [18]. ReSpecT promotes a coordination model providing *tuple centres* [19] as programmable, general-purpose coordination media [6]. The behaviour of ReSpecT tuple centres is programmed through the ReSpecT first-order logic language.

A tuple centre is a tuple space enhanced with the possibility to program its behaviour in response to interactions. First of all, coordinated entities (ReSpecT agents, henceforth, or simply agents) can operate on a ReSpecT tuple centre in the same way as on a standard LINDA tuple space: by exchanging tuples—which are first-order logic terms, in the case of ReSpecT—through a simple set of coordination primitives. Accordingly, a tuple centre enjoys all the many features of a tuple space mentioned in Sect. 2.1, that is, generative communication, associative access, and suspensive semantics.

Then, while the basic tuple centre model is independent of the type of tuple, ReSpecT tuple centres adopt logic tuples—both tuples and tuple templates are essentially Prolog facts—and *logic unification* is used as the tuple-matching mechanism. Since the overall content of a tuple centre is a multiset of logic facts, it has a twofold interpretation as either a collection of messages, or a (logic) *theory of communication* among agents, thus promoting in principle forms of reasoning about communication.

Finally, a tuple centre is a *programmable* tuple space, so as to add programmability of the coordination medium as a new dimension of coordination. While the behaviour of a tuple space in response to interaction events is *fixed*—so, the effects of coordination primitives are fixed—the behaviour of a tuple centre can be *tailored* to the system needs by defining a set of *specification tuples*, or *reactions*, which determine how a tuple centre should react to incoming/outgoing events. While the basic tuple centre model is not bound to any specific language to define reactions, ReSpecT tuple centres are programmed through the ReSpecT logic-based specification language.

The **ReSpecT** coordination language is a logic-based language for the specification of the behaviour of tuple centres. As a behaviour specification language, **ReSpecT** *(i)* enables the definition of computations within a tuple centre, called *reactions*, and *(ii)* makes it possible to associate reactions to *events* occurring in a tuple centre. So, **ReSpecT** has both a *declarative* and a *procedural* part. As a specification language, it allows events to be declaratively associated to reactions by means of specific logic tuples, called *specification tuples*, whose form is `reaction(E,R)`. In short, given a event Ev, a specification tuple `reaction(E,R)` associates a reaction $R\theta$ to Ev if $\theta = mgu(E, Ev)$—where mgu is the most general unifier, in Prolog terminology. As a reaction language, **ReSpecT** enables reactions to be procedurally defined in terms of sequences of logic reaction *goals*, each one either succeeding or failing. A reaction as a whole succeeds if all its reaction goals succeed, and fails otherwise. Each reaction is executed sequentially with a *transactional semantics*: so, a failed reaction has no effect on the state of a tuple centre.

All the reactions triggered by an event are executed before serving any other event: so, agents perceive the result of serving the event and executing all the associated reactions altogether as a single transition of the tuple centre state. As a result, the effect of a coordination primitive on a tuple centre can be made as complex as needed by the coordination requirements of a system.

Generally speaking, since **ReSpecT** has been shown to be Turing-equivalent [9], any computable coordination law could be encapsulated into a **ReSpecT** tuple centre. This is why **ReSpecT** can be assumed as a general-purpose *core* language for coordination: a language that could be used to represent and enact policies and rules (laws) for coordination in systems of any sort.

Summing up, **ReSpecT** is a coordination language supporting programmability of coordination primitives and laws, allowing run-time modifications of the semantics of primitives, as well as run-time adjustment of coordination laws, thus enabling and promoting *adaptiveness* of the overall coordination logic.

2.2.4 TOTA

Tuples On The Air (TOTA) [15] is a programming model and middleware for supporting *adaptive context-aware activities* in pervasive and mobile computing scenarios—in particular, the development of those *nature-inspired, self-organising coordination* schemes (e.g., ant foraging, flocking) that are increasingly finding useful applications in modern distributed systems [1, 3, 21].

The key idea in TOTA is to rely on *spatially distributed tuples*, propagated across a network on the basis of application-specific rules. As will be apparent at the end of the TOTA model description, it is quite a strong departure from the original LINDA model, although being still tuple-based—e.g., no suspensive semantics. In particular, rather than to *enforce* coordination, TOTA is meant to *enable* (context-aware) coordination, to be actually programmed and supported at the application level.

In the TOTA middleware, all interactions between agents take place in a *fully uncoupled* (in space, time, reference) way via tuple exchanges. However, there is not any notion like a centralized shared tuple space as in original LINDA. Rather, a tuple can be injected into the network from any node and, after cloning itself, can diffuse across the network according to tuple-specific *propagation rules*. Once a tuple is spread over the network, it can be perceived as a single distributed data structure called *tuple field*—made up by all the tuples created during the propagation of the injected tuple—to draw an analogy with physical fields (e.g., gravitational), which have different values (in TOTA, tuples) at different points in space (in TOTA, network nodes).

On the one hand, the middleware takes care of propagating the tuples and adapting their values in response to the dynamic changes that can (possibly) occur in the network topology. On the other hand, agents can exploit a simple API to define and inject new tuples in the network and to *locally sense* nearby tuples as well as associated *events* (e.g., arrival and dismissing of tuples). This ultimately enables agents to perform *context-aware coordinated activities*.

To support this idea, TOTA assumes the presence of a peer-to-peer network of possibly mobile nodes, each running a local instance of the TOTA middleware. Each TOTA node holds references to a limited set of *neighbour nodes* and can *communicate directly* only with them. The structure of the network, as determined by the neighbourhood relations, is automatically maintained and updated by the nodes to support dynamic changes, either due to nodes' mobility or to their birth/death.

TOTA tuples T can be defined at the application level and are characterised by a *content* C, a *propagation rule* P and a *maintenance rule* M, hence $T = \langle C, P, M \rangle$:

Content C   —An ordered set of typed elements representing the information conveyed by the tuple.

Propagation rule P   —Determines how the tuple should be distributed across the network—ultimately determining the "shape" of the field. Propagation typically consists of a tuple *(i)* cloning itself, *(ii)* being stored in the local tuple space, then *(iii)* moving to neighbour nodes—recursively. However, different kinds of propagation rules can determine the "scope" of the tuple—e.g., the distance at which such tuple should be propagated, the spatial direction of propagation, etc.—and how such propagation can be affected by the presence or the absence of other tuples in the system. In addition, the propagation rule can determine how the tuple's content C should change during propagation—thus tuples are not necessarily distributed replicas.

Maintenance rule M   —Determines how a tuple should react to *events* occurring in the environment—including flow of time. On the one hand, maintenance rules can preserve the proper spatial structure of tuple fields despite network dynamics— thanks to TOTA middleware constantly monitoring network topology and the income of new tuples, eventually re-propagating tuples. On the other hand, tuples can be made *time-aware*, e.g., to support temporary tuples or tuples that slowly "evaporate"—in the spirit of pheromones [21].

From the architectural viewpoint, the TOTA middleware supporting the above model is constituted by three main parts:

TOTA API   —The main interface between the application agents and the middleware. It provides functionalities to let application agents inject new tuples in the system, retrieve tuples, and place subscriptions to tuple-related and network-related events to the *event interface*.

Event Interface   —The component in charge of *asynchronously* notifying the application agents about subscribed events, like the income of a new tuple or the fact that a new node has been connected/disconnected to the node's neighbourhood.

TOTA Engine   —In charge of receiving tuples injected from the application level, sending them to neighbour nodes according to their propagation rule, and updating/re-propagating them according to their maintenance rule. To this end, this component continuously monitors network reconfiguration, the income of new tuples, and possibly other events.

As regards TOTA API, here follows a deeper explanation of three TOTA primitives— for the others, in particular regarding reading specific instances of field tuples, (un)subscription to events, and tuple deletion, refer to [15]:

inject   —Used to inject a tuple in the TOTA network.

read   —Accesses the *local* tuple space and returns a collection of the tuples present in the tuple space which match the tuple *template* passed as parameter. A template is a TOTA tuple in which some of the content elements can be left uninitialised (null). These null elements are the formal parameters of traditional LINDA models. Shifting to OO pattern-matching, a template tuple $Tmpl$ and a tuple T match if and only if the following holds:

- $Tmpl$ is an instance of either the class of T or one of its superclasses; this extends the LINDA model [13] according to object orientation by supporting match also between tuples of different types, provided they belong to the same class hierarchy
- the non-null elements of $Tmpl$ that represent primitive types (int, char, boolean, etc.) have the same value of the corresponding elements in T and the non-null, non-primitive elements (objects) of $Tmpl$ are equal—in their serialised form—to the corresponding ones of T

readOneHop   —Returns a collection of the tuples present in the tuple spaces of the node's one-hop neighbourhood that match the template tuple.

Notice both read and readOneHop operations are *synchronous* and *nonblocking*— no suspensive semantics *by default*[1]: they return either all the tuples matching the given template or the empty set if no matching tuples are found.

---

[1]It is still possible to realize blocking operations using the event-based interface: an agent may simply subscribe to a specific tuple and wait until the corresponding reaction is triggered to resume its execution—more on this in [15].

Summing up, TOTA is a novel programming model loosely inspired by LINDA, extending OO tuples with embedded "executable" code system designers may exploit to build *distributed computational fields* with the aim of supporting context-awareness—mostly, *spatial-awareness*—at the application level, so as to enable adaptive, spatial-sensitive, self-organising coordination among application agents. To support this vision, [15] elaborates on a couple of examples regarding crowd steering toward POIs and routing to meet-up in a museum scenario.

Some of the mechanisms programmed by means of TOTA tuples in such case studies are very similar to those bio-inspired mechanisms already known in the literature: the meeting task, involving agents attracted towards each other, is similar to those chemotaxis mechanisms allowing bacteria to move in a coordinated way [17, 21], whereas the routing mechanism involved in POIs discovery is instead similar to ant-based routing [3], where ants follow pheromone trails to reach food. This effectively demonstrates the effectiveness of the TOTA middleware in supporting self-organising—mostly field-based—coordination.

2.3 Probabilistic Coordination

A natural solution to account for *unpredictability* and *uncertainty* is to embrace *stochasticity* by tolerating probabilistic rather than deterministic computations and decision making. Among the many existing stochastic approaches to coordination—e.g., digital pheromones [22], biochemical tuple spaces [26], probabilistic pi-calculus [14], probabilistic and stochastic KLAIM [8, 10]—here follows description of the two which proven to be particularly influential for the model proposed in Chap. 3: pKLAIM [10] and SwarmLinda [25].

2.3.1 *p*KLAIM

pKLAIM [10] is a probabilistic extension to KLAIM [7], a *kernel language* for formal modelling of interactions among *mobile agents* distributed in a network—and coordinating by putting and consuming tuples in nodes.

> Understanding the details of KLAIM and pKLAIM is outside the scope of this section, thus only the way pKLAIM exploits probability is discussed here.

pKLAIM introduces probabilities in KLAIM at different levels:

- at the *local* level, that is, considering network nodes in isolation:

  – probabilistic *parallel* and *choice* operators allow processes to express probabilistic behaviours

- probabilistic *allocation environments* associate distributions on physical sites (network nodes) to logical localities—which means, logical names used in processes specifications are probabilistically assigned to network nodes at runtime
- at the *global* level, that is, considering the network of distributed agents and nodes as a whole:
  - a *discrete time* variant of pKLAIM considers a *probability* associated with each node, indicating the *chance* that the process at that node will be selected for execution
  - a *continuous* time variant, instead, associates a *rate* to each node, determining how *often* the node is active—that is, able to perform action transitions

As far as the discrete time execution model is considered, the update principle simulates a *global scheduler*: at every time step one node is scheduled for execution according to probabilities the nodes' probabilities. In case of continuous time semantics, state transitions do not occur regularly like in the discrete case, but the time between state transitions is *exponentially distributed*—that is, driven by a Poisson process. This way, each node can trigger a network update *independently*, at any given time, with a certain probability.

Summing up, pKLAIM provides a probabilistic coordination mobile for mobile agents, where their actions are executed probabilistically according to a number of dimensions, such as intrinsic probability of action, local schedulers (choice and parallel composition), allocation environments.

2.3.2 SwarmLinda

SwarmLinda [25] is the proposal of a scalable implementation of the LINDA model based on *swarm intelligence* techniques, drawing inspiration from ant colonies [21].

One can understand the world of SwarmLinda as a terrain (network of tuple spaces) in which ants (tuple templates) search for food (tuples), leaving pheromone trails upon successful matches, indicating the *likelihood* that further matches for that template are available. Ants look for food in the proximity of the anthill (the caller process); when found, the food is brought to the anthill[2] and a trail is left so that other ants can know where the food is.

Digital ants behave according to the following rules:

1. spread the scent of the caller process in the node it is interacting with and its neighbourhood, to represent the anthill
2. check for a matching tuple: if a match is found, return to the anthill leaving scent for the template matched at each step (tuple space traversed); if no match is found, check the 1-hop neighbourhood for traces of the desired scent

---

[2]The ants know the way back to the anthill because *(i)* they have a short memory of the last few steps they took and *(i)* the anthill has a distinctive scent.

3. if no desired scent is found, *randomly* choose a neighbour space to continue search
4. if a desired scent is found, move one step towards that scent and start over

The key to scalability lies in the *local* nature of ants perceptions: they carry out local searches solely, and inquire direct neighbours only. Furthermore, *probabilistic non-determinism*—necessary for supporting adaptiveness and fault-tolerance [25]—is achieved by adding a small random factor to each scent: this enables paths other that the one with the strongest scent to be chosen.

This results in the *emergence* of application-specific paths between tuple producers and consumers. Moreover, given that scents are *volatile* thanks to an evaporation mechanism, the paths found can dynamically adapt to changes in the system—e.g., when consumers or producers join, leave or move, or in case of failures in nodes hosting tuple spaces.

Besides tuples searching, ant colonies inspiration is also used to partition tuple spaces dynamically, that is, in brood sorting [21]. In nature, ants are able to sort different kinds of things kept in the anthill, such as food, larvae, eggs, etc., and do so in spite of the amount of each type, thus being very scalable. In SwarmLinda, tuples are the things to sort and the ant is the active process representing an `out`, thus:

1. upon execution of an `out`, start visiting the nodes
2. observe the *kind* of tuples the nodes store, that is, the template they match
3. store the tuple in the node if nearby nodes store tuples matching the same template, considering a small random factor
4. if nearby nodes do not contain similar tuples, randomly choose whether to drop or continue to carry the tuple to another node

To guarantee convergence to meaningful partitions, certain conditions must be satisfied: *(i)* for each time the process decides not to store the tuple, the random factor will tend to $\varepsilon \approx 0$ so as to increase the chance of storing the tuple in next steps; *(ii)* the likelihood of locally storing the tuple is calculated probabilistically, based on the kinds of objects in the ant's memory, that is, if most of them are similar to the one being carried, the likelihood to deposit the tuple increases.

Summing up, SwarmLinda is a nature-inspired implementation of the LINDA model, accounting for *uncertainty* and *unpredictability*—e.g., of tuples' location and of agents' interactions—by embracing probability in the mechanisms supporting tuples searching and storage. *Adaptiveness* is enabled in turn, by leveraging *stochasticity* in both resource-to-consumer paths formation and tuples partitioning.

References

1. Babaoglu, O., Canright, G., Deutsch, A., Caro, G.A.D., Ducatelle, F., Gambardella, L.M., Ganguly, N., Jelasity, M., Montemanni, R., Montresor, A., et al.: Design patterns from biology for distributed computing. ACM Trans. Auton. Adapt. Syst. (TAAS) **1**(1), 26–66 (2006)
2. Banâtre, J.P., Métayer, D.L.: The gamma model and its discipline of programming. Sci. Comput. Program. **15**(1), 55–77 (1990). doi:10.1016/0167-6423(90)90044-E

3. Bonabeau, E., Dorigo, M., Theraulaz, G.: Swarm Intelligence. Oxford (1999)
4. Busi, N., Gorrieri, R., Zavattaro, G.: On the expressiveness of linda coordination primitives. Inf. Comput. **156**(1), 90–121 (2000)
5. Ciancarini, P.: Polis: a programming model for multiple tuple spaces. In: Software Specification and Design, 1991., Proceedings of the Sixth International Workshop on, pp. 44–51 (1991). doi:10.1109/IWSSD.1991.213078
6. Ciancarini, P.: Coordination models and languages as software integrators. ACM Comput. Surv. **28**(2), 300–302 (1996). doi:10.1145/234528.234732
7. De Nicola, R., Ferrari, G., Pugliese, R.: KLAIM: A kernel language for agent interaction and mobility. IEEE Trans. Softw. Eng. **24**(5), 315–330 (1998). doi:10.1109/32.685256
8. De Nicola, R., Latella, D., Katoen, J.P., Massink, M.: StoKlaim: A stochastic extension of Klaim. Tech. Rep. 2006-TR-01, Istituto di Scienza e Tecnologie dell'Informazione "Alessandro Faedo" (ISTI) (2006). http://www1.isti.cnr.it/~Latella/StoKlaim.pdf
9. Denti, E., Natali, A., Omicini, A.: On the expressive power of a language for programming coordination media. In: 1998 ACM Symposium on Applied Computing (SAC'98), pp. 169–177. ACM, Atlanta, GA, USA (1998)
10. Di Pierro, A., Hankin, C., Wiklicky, H.: Probabilistic KLAIM. In: R. De Nicola, G.L. Ferrari, G. Meredith (eds.) Coordination Models and Languages, LNCS, vol. 2949, pp. 119–134. Springer, Berlin, Heidelberg (2004). doi:10.1007/978-3-540-24634-3
11. Gelernter, D.: Generative communication in Linda. ACM Trans. Program. Lang. Syst. **7**(1), 80–112 (1985). doi:10.1145/2363.2433
12. Gelernter, D.: Multiple tuple spaces in LINDA. In: Parallel Architectures and Languages Europe (PARLE'89), LNCS, vol. 366, pp. 20–27. London, UK (1989)
13. Gelernter, D., Carriero, N.: Coordination languages and their significance. Commun. ACM **35**(2), 97–107 (1992). doi:10.1145/129630.129635
14. Herescu, O.M., Palamidessi, C.: Probabilistic asynchronous pi-calculus. CoRR **cs.PL/0109002** (2001)
15. Mamei, M., Zambonelli, F.: Programming pervasive and mobile computing applications: The TOTA approach. ACM Trans. Softw. Eng. Methodol. (TOSEM) **18**(4), 15:1–15:56 (2009). doi:10.1145/1538942.1538945
16. Minsky, N.H., Ungureanu, V.: Law-Governed interaction: A coordination and control mechanism for heterogeneous distributed systems. ACM Trans. Softw. Eng. Methodol. (TOSEM) **9**(3), 273–305 (2000). doi:10.1145/352591.352592
17. Nagpal, R.: Programmable self-assembly using biologically-inspired multiagent control. In: Proceedings of the First International Joint Conference on Autonomous Agents and Multiagent Systems: part 1, pp. 418–425. ACM (2002)
18. Omicini, A.: Formal ReSpecT in the A&A perspective. Electron. Notes Theor. Comput. Sci. **175**(2), 97–117 (2007). doi:10.1016/j.entcs.2007.03.006
19. Omicini, A., Denti, E.: From tuple spaces to tuple centres. Sci. Comput. Program. **41**(3), 277–294 (2001). doi:10.1016/S0167-6423(01)00011-9
20. Omicini, A., Zambonelli, F.: Coordination for Internet application development. Auton. Agent. Multi-Agent Syst. **2**(3), 251–269 (1999). doi:10.1023/A:1010060322135
21. Parunak, H.V.D.: "Go to the ant": Engineering principles from natural agent systems. Ann. Oper. Res. **75**(0), 69–101 (1997). doi:10.1023/A:1018980001403. Special Issue on Artificial Intelligence and Management Science
22. Parunak, H.V.D., Brueckner, S., Sauter, J.: Digital pheromone mechanisms for coordination of unmanned vehicles. In: Castelfranchi, C., Johnson, W.L. (eds.) 1st International Joint Conference on Autonomous Agents and Multiagent Systems, vol. 1, pp. 449–450. ACM, New York, NY, USA (2002). http://dx.doi.org/10.1145/544741.544843
23. Picco, G.P., Murphy, A.L., Roman, G.C.: LIME: Linda meets mobility. In: 21st International Conference on Software Engineering (ICSE'99), pp. 368–377. ACM Press, New York, NY, USA (1999). doi:10.1145/302405.302659
24. Rossi, D., Cabri, G., Denti, E.: Tuple-based technologies for coordination. In: Omicini, A., Zambonelli, F., Klusch, M., Tolksdorf, R. (eds.) Coordination of Internet Agents: Models, Technologies, and Applications, Chap. 4, pp. 83–109. Springer (2001)

25. Tolksdorf, R., Menezes, R.: Using Swarm Intelligence in Linda Systems. In: Omicini, A., Petta, P., Pitt, J. (eds.) Engineering Societies in the Agents World IV, LNCS, vol. 3071, pp. 49–65. Springer (2004). doi:10.1007/b98212. 4th International Workshops (ESAW 2003), London, UK, 29-31 Oct. 2003. Revised Selected and Invited Papers
26. Viroli, M., Casadei, M.: Biochemical tuple spaces for self-organising coordination. In: Fiel, J., d, Vasconcelos, V.T. (eds.) Coordination Languages and Models, LNCS, vol. 5521, pp. 143–162. Springer, Lisbon, Portugal (2009). doi:10.1007/978-3-642-02053-7
27. Viroli, M., Omicini, A., Ricci, A.: Infrastructure for RBAC-MAS: An approach based on Agent Coordination Contexts. Appl. Artif. Intell. Int. J. 21(4–5), 443–467 (2007). doi:10.1080/08839510701253674. Special Issue: State of Applications in AI Research from AI*IA 2005

Chapter 3
Coordination of Self-organising Systems

Abstract In this chapter a novel approach to coordination in self-organising systems is described, which rethinks the basis of chemically inspired coordination, from both the engineering standpoint of coordination laws and primitives design, and from the scientific standpoint of relative linguistic expressiveness. Accordingly, first of all state of art literature regarding nature-inspired coordination is reviewed (Sects. 3.1 and 3.2), then the well-known local versus global issue in self-organising systems is dealt with by engineering coordination laws as artificial chemical reactions with custom kinetic rates (Sect. 3.3). After this, the impact of uniform coordination primitives on self-organising systems is discussed, experiments on their applicability are reported, and their formal semantics is defined (Sect. 3.4).

3.1 Bio-Inspired Self-organisation Patterns

Self-organising mechanisms are often inspired by the natural world, in particular by biological systems, which show appealing characteristics such as *robustness* and *resilience*, *adaptiveness* to environmental change, and *expressiveness* of the global behaviours supported despite simplicity of the local mechanisms engineered [20].

In [20], the authors surveyed the literature regarding self-organising mechanisms, with the goal of compiling a catalogue of bio-inspired self-organising design patterns promoting reusability—pretty much like object-oriented design patterns do. As a result, the patterns depicted in Fig. 3.1 are detected and related to each other in a *compositional hierarchy* consisting of three layers:

Basic mechanisms —Can be used to form more complex patterns, but *cannot* be further decomposed into smaller ones

Composed patterns —Mechanisms obtainable as a *composition* of some basic mechanisms, and which in turn can serve as *building blocks* for higher level ones

High-level patterns —Patterns *directly* supporting complex self-organising emergent behaviours, showcasing how to exploit basic and composed patterns

© Springer International Publishing AG 2016

S. Mariani, *Coordination of Complex Sociotechnical Systems*,
Artificial Intelligence: Foundations, Theory, and Algorithms,
DOI 10.1007/978-3-319-47109-9_3

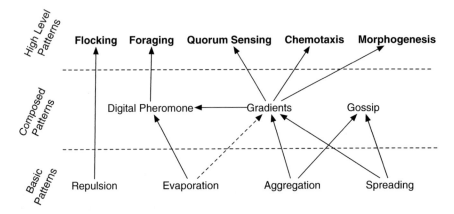

Fig. 3.1 Bio-inspired self-organising design patterns according to [20]. (Dashed) *Arrows* indicate (optional) composition

In the following sections, each basic pattern is briefly described, also thanks to transition rules adopting a chemical-like notation:

- data items are modelled as tuples $\langle L, C \rangle$ where L is data location and C is its content
- transition rules are of the kind

$$\text{name} :: \langle L_1, C_1 \rangle, \ldots, \langle L_n, C_n \rangle \xrightarrow{r} \langle L'_1, C'_1 \rangle, \ldots, \langle L'_m, C'_m \rangle$$

  where

  – the left-hand side specifies which tuples are pre-conditions for the rule to apply, and should be removed as an effect of its execution
  – the right-hand side specifies which tuples are the effect of rule execution, thus should be put in the given location
  – rate r is the *rate* indicating the frequency at which the rule is to be scheduled for execution

> Focus is on *basic* patterns solely because the interest here is in the *minimal* mechanisms enabling general-purpose self-organising coordination. Furthermore, basic patterns only are considered in the research work discussed in Sect. 3.3—for the same reason.

3.1.1 Spreading

Spreading causes a *copy* of a given data item to be sent to neighbours and *recursively* propagated over the network from node to node. This way, information spreads progressively keeping the constraint of *local only* interaction—only neighbourhoods interact. Spreading usually proceeds as follows: someone initiates the spreading process, then information spreads over the network, finally the process ends when the information reaches all the nodes in the network.

Spreading may be represented by the following chemical-like transition rule:

$$\texttt{spreading} :: \langle L, C \rangle \xrightarrow{r_{spr}} \langle L_1, C_1 \rangle, \ldots, \langle L_n, C_n \rangle$$

where

$$(L_1; \ldots; L_n) = v(L), (C_1; \ldots; C_n) = \sigma(C, L)$$

Function $v(L)$ determines which neighbours of L are included in the spreading, while function $\sigma(C, L)$ computes the (*possibly*) novel information content—information *may* change while spreading.

3.1.2 Aggregation

Aggregation *reduces* the amount of information by synthesising more concise information. Aggregation relies on a *fusion operator* locally processing data to synthesise novel information. Such a fusion operator can be, e.g. filtering, merging, transforming, and the like.

Aggregation may be represented by the following chemical-like transition rule:

$$\texttt{aggregation} :: \langle L, C_1 \rangle \ldots, \langle L, C_n \rangle \xrightarrow{r_{aggr}} \langle L, C'_1 \rangle \ldots, \langle L, C'_m \rangle$$

where

$$(C'_1; \ldots; C'_m) = \alpha(C_1; \ldots; C_n)$$

Function $\alpha(C_1; \ldots; C_n)$ is the aggregation function reducing the input set.

3.1.3 Evaporation

Evaporation progressively reduces *relevance* of information—according to whichever notion of "relevance". Accordingly, more recent information becomes more relevant than older information.

Evaporation may be represented by the following chemical-like transition rule:

$$\texttt{evaporation} :: \langle L, C \rangle \xrightarrow{r_{ev}} \langle L, C' \rangle$$

where

$$C' = \varepsilon(C)$$

Function $\varepsilon(C)$ is required to decrease relevance of C at each application of the rule.

3.1.4 Repulsion

Repulsion uniformly distributes agents or information in a region of space, moving entities from regions with higher density to regions with lower density. To apply repulsion each entity must know its position and position of its neighbours.

Repulsion may be represented by the following chemical-like transition rule:

$$\texttt{repulsion} :: \langle L, C \rangle, \langle L_1, C_1 \rangle \ldots, \langle LC_n, C_n \rangle \xrightarrow{r_{rep}} \langle L', C \rangle, \langle L_1, C_1 \rangle \ldots, \langle LC_n, C_n \rangle$$

where

$$L' = \rho(\{\langle L, C \rangle, \langle L_1, C_1 \rangle \ldots, \langle LC_n, C_n \rangle\})$$

Function $\rho(\{\langle L, C \rangle, \langle L_1, C_1 \rangle \ldots, \langle LC_n, C_n \rangle\})$ computes the new location of the entity to repel.

3.1.5 Other Patterns

Many other biological-inspired mechanisms for self-organisation, either basic or not, can be found in state of art literature such as [13, 19, 21, 36, 48, 50]. Here two of them are defined, for they are subject of Sect. 3.3.

3.1.5.1 Feed

Feed increases relevance of information—according to whichever notion of "relevance". Accordingly, the more information is fed the more it becomes relevant. To some extent, the feed pattern is dual to the evaporation pattern, although it is not necessarily—nor usually—based on time, but on explicit feeding items.

Feed may be represented by the following chemical-like transition rule:

$$\texttt{feed} :: \langle L, C \rangle, \langle L_f, C_f \rangle \xrightarrow{r_{feed}} \langle L, C' \rangle$$

where

$$C' = \delta(C)$$

Function $\delta(C)$ is required to increase relevance of C at each application of the rule.

3.1.5.2 Activation/Inhibition

Activation (inhibition) changes the state of information so as to flag it as "enabled" ("disabled")—whatever this means. Accordingly, when information is enabled (disabled) it is (not) allowed to either do something on its own or be manipulated by active entities—e.g. agents. Similarly to the feed pattern, activation (inhibition) needs explicit activator (inhibitor) items to apply.

Activation may be represented by the following chemical-like transition rule:

$$\texttt{activation} :: \langle L, C \rangle, \langle L_a, C_a \rangle \xrightarrow{r_{act}} \langle L, C' \rangle$$

where

$$C' = \gamma(C)$$

Function $\gamma(C)$ is required to flag as enabled C.

Dually, inhibition may be represented by the following chemical-like transition rule:

$$\texttt{inhibition} :: \langle L, C \rangle, \langle L_i, C_i \rangle \xrightarrow{r_{inh}} \langle L, C' \rangle$$

where

$$C' = \omega(C)$$

Function $\omega(C)$ is required to flag as disabled C.

3.2 Nature-Inspired Coordination

Nature-inspired approaches to coordination usually leverage both stochasticity and programmability of the coordination machinery, so as to better cope with adaptiveness and unpredictability/uncertainty. The following sections report on the two models which influenced the coordination approach proposed in this chapter: bio-chemical tuple spaces [49] and SAPERE [54].

3.2.1 Biochemical Tuple Spaces

Biochemical Tuple Spaces (henceforth BTS) are a *stochastic, chemical-inspired* extension of LINDA tuple spaces first, then of the whole LINDA model [49]. Chemical inspiration stems mainly from two considerations: on the one hand, coordination models are increasingly required to tackle *self-** properties as inherent systemic properties, rather than peculiar aspects of individual coordinated components [55]; on the other hand, among the many plausible natural metaphors available, the chemical one appears particularly interesting for the complexity of the stochastic behaviours it enables, despite simplicity of its foundation [51].

The essential idea behind the BTS model is to equip each tuple with a *concentration* value, seen as a measure of the pertinency/activity of the tuple: the higher it is, the more *likely* and *frequently* the tuple will influence system coordination. Concentration of tuples is dynamic, and evolves driven by programmable *chemical-like rules* installed into the tuple space, affecting concentrations over time *exactly* as chemical substances evolve within chemical solutions [26].

Accordingly, primitive out now injects a given concentration of a tuple, possibly increasing the concentration of identical tuples already in the space. Primitive in either entirely removes a tuple, if no concentration is specified, or decreases the concentration of an existing tuple of the given amount. Primitive rd just reads tuples instead of removing them. Also the matching function μ changes w.r.t. LINDA, so as to return 0 if tuple τ does not match template τ', 1 if they completely match, and any value in between to represent partial matching.

From the infrastructural standpoint, a BTS-coordinated system is a set of tuple spaces networked in some *topological* structure, defining the neighbourhood of each space. Interaction between tuple spaces is mediated by a chemical-like law that fires some tuples to a tuple space in the neighbourhood *picked probabilistically*. Links ($\rightsquigarrow$) between tuple spaces (σ and σ') allow tuples movement according to a *markovian rate* r, representing the average movement frequency: $\sigma \stackrel{r}{\rightsquigarrow} \sigma'$. Markovian rates follow the argument of [26] stating that chemical reactions can be simulated as Continuous-Time Markov Chains (CTMC)[1] [8], and are also exploited for both primitives and chemical laws execution.

As regards execution of chemical-like reactions, expressed as rewriting rules of the form $[T_i \stackrel{r}{\rightarrow} T_o]$—meaning reactants T_i should be transformed into products T_o with a markovian rate r— the following is worth noticing:

- in the general case where a tuple set T is found that is not equal to T_i, but it rather matches T_i, $\{T / T_i\}$ could provide more solutions

---

[1] Actually, the BTS model is an *hybrid* CTMC/DTMC model, since instantaneous transitions are allowed; please, refer to [49] for a thorough explanation.

- being one transition allowed *for each* different solution of substitutions $\{T_i/T\}$, one is to be chosen *probabilistically* depending on the matching function
- accordingly, the actual markovian rate of reaction execution is given by $\mu(T_i, T) * G(r, T, T|S)$, which computes the transition rate according to Gillespie's algorithm [26]

The $G(\cdot, \cdot, \cdot)$ function is $r * count(T, T|S)$, where function $count(T, S)$ counts how many different combinations of tuples in T actually occur in S, namely:

$$count(o, S) = 1, \quad count(\tau\langle n\rangle \oplus T, \tau\langle m\rangle \oplus S) = \frac{m(m-1)\dots(m-n+1)}{n!} * count(T, S)$$

Summing up, the rate of execution is influenced by three factors: its intrinsic markovian rate r, the matching function μ, and the relative concentration of involved reactants G.

As regards LINDA primitives extension, BTS operations semantics states that:

- primitive `out` is pretty much similar to LINDA `out`
- primitive `rd` reads a matching tuple with greater concentration than the one specified, where the *likelihood* of choosing a particular tuple among the matching ones depends on the *ratio* between concentrations of τ' and τ—namely, the higher the concentration of a tuple, the more it is likely to read it
- primitive `in` functioning is identical to `rd` but for the destructive semantics

In conclusion, the BTS model promotes self-organisation in multi-agent systems by leveraging a (bio-)chemical metaphor to extend the LINDA model toward a fully stochastic and programmable coordination model.

3.2.2 SAPERE

SAPERE (Self-aware Pervasive Service Ecosystems) [54] was a EU STREP Project funded within the EU 7 FP.[2] SAPERE takes as ground the LINDA model, then follows the pioneer work of approaches like ReSpecT [38] regarding supporting programmability of coordination laws, but taking a different stance inspired to the laws of nature observed in *natural ecosystems*, to promote self-organisation of services in pervasive computing scenarios. SAPERE is inspired to the Biochemical Tuple Space model presented in Sect. 3.2.1, although with some notable differences—e.g. the chemical concentration mechanisms exactly mimicking chemical dynamics is not mandatory in SAPERE.

SAPERE considers modelling and architecting a *pervasive* service environment as a non-layered *spatial* substrate, made up of networked SAPERE nodes, laid above the actual network infrastructure. This substrate embeds the basic laws of nature (*Eco-Laws* in SAPERE terminology) that rule the activities of the system.

Users can access the ecology in a decentralised way to consume and produce data and services. Any individual (e.g. devices, users, and software services) has an

---

[2]FP7-ICT-2009.8.5: Self-awareness in Autonomic Systems.

associated semantic representation inside the ecosystem called *Live Semantic Annotation* (LSA). LSA are handled as living, *dynamic* entities, capable of reflecting the current situation and context of the component they describe. LSA may be used to encapsulate data relevant to the ecology, *reify* events, act as *observable* interfaces of components, and ultimately be the basis for enforcing *semantic* and *self-aware* forms of dynamic interaction—for both service aggregation/composition and data/-knowledge management.

Eco-laws define the basic policies to rule sorts of *virtual chemical reactions* among LSA, thus enforcing dynamic concept-based (e.g. semantic and goal-oriented) networking, composition, and *coordination* of data and services in the ecosystem, to establish bonds between entities, produce new LSA, and diffuse LSA in the networked world.

More specifically, each SAPERE node embeds a so-called *LSA-space*, in which self-adaptive coordination mechanisms take place so as to mediate the interaction between components. Whenever a component approaches a node, its own LSA is automatically injected into the LSA-space of that node, making the component part of that space and of its *local coordination dynamics*.

LSA are semantic annotations with same expressiveness as standard frameworks like RDF. An LSA *pattern P* is essentially an LSA with some variables in place of some values—similarly to LINDA templates—and an LSA *L* is said to match the pattern *P* if there exists a substitution of variables to values that applied to *P* gives *L*. Differently from LINDA, the *matching* mechanism here is *semantic* and *fuzzy* [37].

Besides the LSA-space, each node embeds the set of eco-laws ruling the activities of the ecosystem. An eco-law is of the kind $P_1 + \cdots + P_n \xrightarrow{r} P'_1 + \cdots + P'_m$ where: *(i)* the left-hand side (reagents) specifies patterns that should match the LSA $L_1, \ldots, L_n$ to be extracted from the space; *(ii)* the right-hand side (products) specifies patterns of LSA which are to be inserted back in the space; and *(iii)* rate expression *r* is a numerical positive value indicating the *average frequency* at which the eco-law is to be fired.

In other words, SAPERE models execution of the eco-laws as a CTMC (Continuous-Time Markov Chain) transition with Markovian rate *r*. An eco-law is applied as follows: *(i)* iteratively, one reagent pattern P_i is *non-deterministically* extracted from the eco-law, a matching LSA L_i is found, and the resulting substitution is applied to the remainder of the eco-law; *(ii)* when iteration is over, products form the set of LSA to be inserted back in the space. As far as *topology* is concerned, the framework imposes that an eco-law applies to LSA belonging to the same space, and constrains products to be inserted in that space or in a *neighbouring* one (to realise space–space interaction).

Summing up, the SAPERE project proposed a model, a middleware, and a methodology for the engineering of pervasive services ecosystems, in which the *stochasticity* of interactions and computations, the *programmability* of the coordination laws, and aspects related to *semantic matching* and *context awareness* are of prominent relevance to enable and promote self-organisation and adaptiveness.

3.3 Chemical Reactions as Coordination Laws

This body of work is used as the ground upon which the custom kinetic rates of the chemical-like coordination laws in the $\mathcal{MoK}$ model discussed in Part II of this book are designed—in particular, see Sect. 6.2 of Chap. 6.

A foremost issue while engineering *self-organising systems* is the *local versus global* issue: how to link the *local* mechanisms, through which the components of the system interact, to the *emergent, global* behaviour exhibited by the system as a whole [2].

Existing approaches to face the issue are based on simulation [23], parameter tuning [24], (approximate) model checking [9], or bio-inspired design patterns [20]. Simulation investigates the behaviour of the system prior to real-world deployment; parameter tuning helps improving the performance (according to whatever definition) of the single mechanisms; (approximate) model checking enables formal verification of expected global behaviours; design patterns assist programmers in deploying the correct self-organising solutions according to the problem to solve.

Nevertheless, these approaches may be not enough, especially if used separately: simulation may not be able to accurately reproduce real-world contingencies; parameter tuning may lead to sub-optimal settings; model checking may be impractical for the complexity of the problem at hand; design patterns give no guarantees about quality of solutions.

For these reasons, an integrated approach to deal with the local versus global issue in self-organising systems is needed: *(i)* rely on design patterns to design the local mechanisms by implementing them as *artificial chemical reactions*; *(ii)* go beyond the *law of mass action* [8] by engineering *custom kinetic rates* reflecting the emergent, global behaviour desired; *(iii)* simulate-then-tune loop to adjust the dynamics of the (artificial) chemical system obtained so as to achieve the emergent, global behaviour desired.

Having that a given natural system—in this case, chemical solutions—works properly by relying on a given set of parameters—e.g. concentration, rate, stoichiometry, etc.—each of which having a given set of functional dependencies with others—e.g. the law of mass action—does not necessarily mean that the same sets of parameters and functional dependencies will work for an artificial system drawing inspiration from the natural one.

Similar considerations can be done for other natural metaphors: most notably, the ant colony optimisation approach to distributed optimisation, in which the original ant colony metaphor is indeed just a metaphor, not the actual implementation [18].

3.3.1 Selected Patterns Encoding

Among the possible approaches to face the local versus global issue, one is to rely on *bio-inspired design patterns*. As the name suggests, the concept is similar to design patterns in OO programming: recurrent solutions to recurrent problems are modelled and encapsulated as architectural best practices to promote design reuse—and code reuse, ultimately. As explicitly stated in [20] (e.g. Fig. 3.4 therein), patterns are often decomposable into atomic, non further decomposable patterns: the focus is precisely on these.

State of art literature regarding design patterns and basic mechanisms enabling self-organisation—consider [13, 19, 21, 36, 48, 50]—leads to identification of the following set of basic patterns—in what follows, the term "information" is used, but can be replaced with "process", "component", anything which can be subject of self-organisation:

Decay—The decay pattern (aka evaporation, or cleaning) destroys information. Usually, it destroys a finite amount of information as time passes (e.g. evaporation of pheromone scent)

Feed—The feed pattern (aka reinforcement) increases information relevance. Usually, this means increasing information quantity (e.g. pheromone deposit over other pheromone)

Activation/Inhibition—The activation pattern changes information status depending on external stimuli—the same holds for the dual inhibition pattern. Usually, this means some sort of stimulus triggers some sort of response (e.g. neurones activation in the brain), possibly changing some of the information attributes

Aggregation—The aggregation pattern fuses information together. Fusion can be filtering (e.g. new info replaces old), merging (e.g. related news synthesised into a single story), composing (e.g. building a list from separate values), transforming (e.g. summing, averaging, etc.), etc.

Diffusion—The diffusion pattern (aka spreading, or propagation) moves information within a topology. Diffusion can destroy moved information, resembling some sort of migration, or not, resembling replication

Repulsion/Attraction—The repulsion pattern drifts apart information—dually, attraction approaches information instead. Usually, repulsion considers topological information to spread information fairly

Each of these patterns[3] is modelled as a chemical reaction, then engineered in different ways so as to obtain different global behaviours, finally simulated with the BioPEPA tool to show the effects of custom rates on the emergent, global self-organising behaviour obtained.

---

[3]Except repulsion/attraction, that has been left out since it can be engineered on top of diffusion.

Among the existing frameworks and tools allowing simulation of chemical reactions, either born in biochemistry [1] or in the multi-agent systems community [34], BioPEPA [11] is used.

BioPEPA [11] is a language and tool (Eclipse plugin at http://groups.inf.ed. ac.uk/pepa/update/ update site) for the simulation of biochemical processes. It is based on PEPA [27], a process algebra aimed at performance analysis, extended to deal with the typical features of biochemical networks, such as stoichiometry, compartments and kinetic laws. The most appealing features of BioPEPA are:

- the possibility to define custom kinetic laws by designing *functional rate expressions*
- the possibility to define stoichiometry (how many molecules of a given kind participate) and role played by the species (reactant, product, enzyme, etc.) involved in a given reaction
- the possibility to define topologies of compartments among which reactants may move
- its theoretical roots in CTMC semantics [28]—behind any BioPEPA specification lies a stochastic labelled transition system modelling a CTMC

Rate expressions are defined as mathematical functions involving reactants concentrations (denoted with the reactant name and dynamically computed at run-time) and supporting:

- mathematical operators, e.g. `exp` and `log` functions
- built-in common kinetic laws, e.g. the law of mass action (denoted with keyword `fMA`)
- time dependency through variable `time`, increasing according to the current simulation time step

In summary, BioPEPA allows to: model self-organisation primitives as chemical reactions, simulate them using different stochastic simulation algorithms—the choice is Gillespie's algorithm [26]—tune rates according to simulation results.

3.3.2 Custom Kinetic Rates

The self-organisation patterns listed in Sect. 3.1.1 are now modelled as artificial chemical reactions representing the local mechanisms, then encoded in the BioPEPA language to finally simulate the emergent, global behaviour achievable. While doing so, custom kinetic rates are engineered in different ways, and BioPEPA plots resulting from simulations are compared to highlight how changes in the local mechanisms affect the global behaviour.

Each of the following experiments is performed using the Gillespie stochastic simulation algorithm provided by BioPEPA. Each of the following plots is directly generated from BioPEPA as a result of the correspondent experiment, consisting of 100 Gillespie runs.

Nothing changes from run to run, they are necessary due to the stochastic aspects embedded in the simulation algorithm, and aimed at showing more regular trends—it should be noticed, however, that single runs plots are really similar. In each chart, the *x*-axis plots the time steps of the simulation, whereas the *y*-axis plots the concentration level of the reactants expressed as units of molecules.

The codebase tracking the BioPEPA specifications used in the examples is publicly available under LGPL license at http://bitbucket.org/smariani/mok-biopepa.

3.3.2.1   Decay

The decay pattern can be represented as an artificial chemical reaction as follows:

$$data \xrightarrow{r_{decay}} \bot$$

meaning that a certain unit of *data* disappears at a pace given by r_{decay}—this is the local mechanism. The reaction can be encoded in BioPEPA as follows:

```
1  DECAY_CONSTANT = 0.5;
2  r_decay = [fMA(DECAY_CONSTANT)];  // kinetic rate
3  data = (r_decay, 1) <<;           // chemical reaction
```

meaning that species *data* participates in decay chemical reaction as a reactant ($<<$), thus being consumed, with stoichiometry 1, thus one unit of *data* is involved. The rate (*r_decay*) follows the usual law of mass action (fMA) [8].

Simulations of the above BioPEPA specification lead to the plots depicted in Fig. 3.2, showing the global behaviour achieved—that is, the behaviour of the whole population of *data* items.

As shown, implementing the decay self-organisation pattern (the local mechanism) as an artificial chemical reaction with a kinetic rate following the law of mass action, leads to a fast-then-slow decay (the emergent, global behaviour), which is independent of the quantity of data to decay (compare middle plot to bottom plot), and whose timing can be tuned by changing the rate constant (compare top plot to middle plot).

But: what if the aforementioned trend is not the best to suit the needs of the application at hand? What if the self-organising system should display a different trend, e.g. an opposite slow-then-fast decay? Maybe also sensitive to the quantity of information to decay? A time-dependant custom kinetic rate can be encoded as follows:

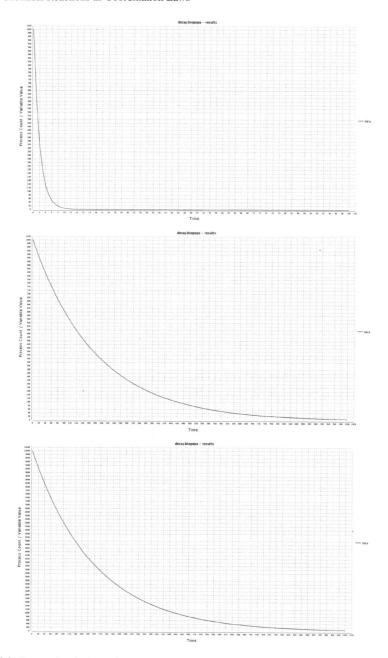

Fig. 3.2 Decay chemical reaction with usual law of mass action rate [30]. In the *middle* plot the rate constant is decreased w.r.t. the *top* plot (from 0.5 to 0.005), thus time needed to complete decay increases accordingly (from 100 simulation steps of *top* plot to 1,000 steps of *middle* plot). In the *bottom* plot data quantity is increased w.r.t. previous plots (from 1,000 units to 10,000) but decay time remains the same (still 1,000 time steps)

```
1 DECAY_CONSTANT = 0.5;
2 r_decay = [fMA(DECAY_CONSTANT) + H(data) * time/data];
3 data = (r_decay, 1) <<;
```

where time is the BioPEPA variable tracking simulation time steps and H(·) is the Heaviside step function,[4] whose value is 0 for negative arguments and 1 for positive ones (0 arguments are usually associated to 0)—useful to avoid meaningless negative rates.

Simulations of the above custom kinetic rate are depicted in Fig. 3.3. As shown, decay has now a completely different trend w.r.t. the plain fMA-driven rate of Fig. 3.2: actually, the opposite, slow-then-fast trend. Furthermore, whereas decreasing the rate constant still leads to a delay in decay completion (compare top plot with middle plot), changing the quantity of *data* to decay now affects decay time proportionally (compare middle plot to bottom plot).

The reason for this behaviour twist lies in the new factors added to the kinetic rate expression: direct proportionality to time and inverse proportionality to *data*. Thus, while time passes decay slows down, whereas while quantity of data to decay decreases decay becomes faster. It should be noted that, in order to keep independency of data quantity, factor $\frac{1}{data}$ can be removed from the rate expression.

This demonstrates the extreme flexibility and accurate controllability that custom kinetic rates provide to engineers of self-organising systems: adding/removing factors to the local mechanism (the reaction manipulating each *data* item) leads to a well-defined change in the emergent, global behaviour achieved (the evolution of the whole population of *data* items), tackling the local versus global issue.

Discussing why it could be useful to switch from the trend depicted in Fig. 3.2 to that of Fig. 3.3 in a real-world application is out of the scope of this section, and is done, although in a more specific scenario, in Part II of this book—specifically, in Sect. 6.2 of Chap. 6. Nevertheless, giving some clues is undoubtedly useful.

Imagine to exploit self-organisation patterns in, e.g. an information management application, in which novel data can be produced and consumed anytime, without knowing *when* a given piece of information may become interesting for some of the co-workers. There, shifting to the slow-then-fast trend exhibited by the custom, time-dependant kinetic rate is better.

The reason is that, exactly because it is not known in advance when information will become relevant, it is unreasonable to decay it as soon as it is put in the shared collaboration space: it is better to start with a slow decay so as to give co-workers the opportunity to find the information, then, only if after a while nobody manifested interest, the decay process can be safely quickened to get rid of (potentially) useless information.

---

[4]http://en.wikipedia.org/wiki/Heaviside_step_function.

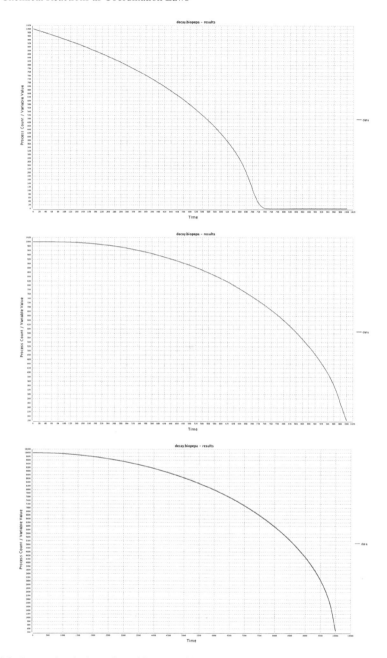

Fig. 3.3 Decay chemical reaction with custom kinetic rate [30]. In the *middle* plot the rate constant is decreased w.r.t. the *top* plot (from 0.5 to 0.005), thus time needed to complete decay increases accordingly (from $\approx$700 simulation steps of *top* plot to over 1,000 steps of *middle* plot). In the *bottom* plot data quantity is increased w.r.t. previous plots (from 1,000 units to 10,000) and decay time increases proportionally (over 10,000 time steps)

3.3.2.2 Feed

The feed pattern for self-organisation can be represented as an artificial chemical reaction as follows:

$$data + food \xrightarrow{r_{feed}} data + data$$

meaning that if *food* is present then *data* can be increased at a pace given by r_{feed}—the local mechanism. The reaction can be encoded in BioPEPA as follows, if the law of mass action only should influence the kinetic rate:

```
1 FEED_CONSTANT = 0.5;
2 r_feed = [fMA(FEED_CONSTANT)];
3 // same rate name ==> same chemical reaction
4 data = (r_feed, 1) >>; // product (1 unit produced)
5 food = (r_feed, 1) <<; // reactant (1 unit consumed)
```

Or as follows, if a time-dependant kinetic rate is preferred (only changes are reported):

```
r_feed = [fMA(FEED_CONSTANT) + H(food) * time/food];
```

Simulations focussing on the above BioPEPA specifications lead to the plots depicted in Fig. 3.4. As shown, similarly to what happened in the case of decay, shifting to a custom kinetic rate twists the global behaviour achieved, that is, the growing trend exhibited by the whole population of *data* items: basically, with the usual law of mass action the trend is fast-then-slow, whereas for the $\frac{time}{food}$-dependant rate, the trend is the opposite.

But, conversely to decay, acting on the rate constant or on the quantity of data to feed has the same effect both in the case of the fMA-driven kinetic rate and of the custom one: a lower rate leads to a slower feeding process, whereas a higher quantity of data does not affect time taken to complete the process.

The reason for this difference at the level of emergent behaviour—that is, the change in the population dynamics—can be once again explained in terms of the local mechanisms level—changing the reaction rate: whereas for the custom decay proportionality of the kinetic rate was to *data*, for the custom feed primitive proportionality is to *food*.

Once again, the global behaviour can be directly put in a causal relationship with the local mechanisms.

3.3.2.3 Activation/Inhibition

The activation pattern can be represented as an artificial chemical reaction as follows:

$$data + on \xrightarrow{r_{activation}} on + data\_on$$

meaning that if *on* is present then *data* becomes *data_on*, due to activation, at a pace given by $r_{activation}$—the local mechanism. The dual inhibition pattern is similar:

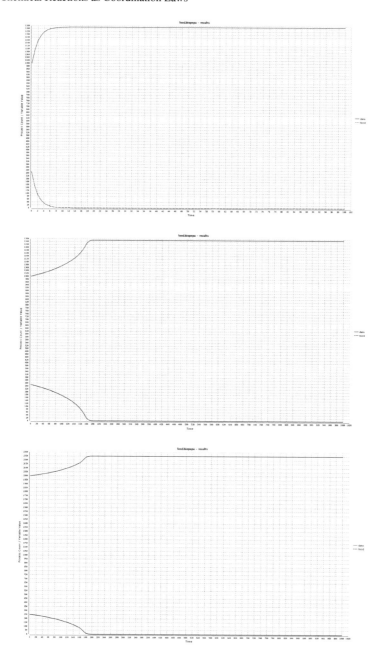

Fig. 3.4 Feed chemical reaction with fMA-only (*top* plot) and custom kinetic rate (*middle and bottom plots*) [30]. fMA-only rate is sensitive to rate constant change and to data quantity likewise decay; custom kinetic rate, too (*bottom* plot has twice the data of *middle* plot but saturation time is the same), due to its inverse proportionality to *food*, not *data*. Changing *food* affects saturation time of both rate expressions

$$data + \textit{off} \xrightarrow{r_{\textit{inhibition}}} \textit{off} + data\_\textit{off}$$

Since also the trends exhibited by the two complementary patterns are dual, the focus is on either one: activation. The corresponding reaction is then encoded in BioPEPA according to three different kinetic rates—usual fMA-only, *data_on*-dependant, and *data*-dependant—as follows:

```
1  ACTIVATION_CONSTANT = 0.5;
2  r_activation = [fMA(ACTIVATION_CONSTANT)];
3  data = (r_activation, 1) <<;
4  on = (r_activation, 1) (+); // activator enzyme (not consumed)
5  data_on = (r_activation, 1) >>;
6  // inhibition ==> replace (+) with (-)
```

```
r_activation = [fMA(ACTIVATION_CONSTANT) + H(data) * time/data_on];
```

```
r_activation = [fMA(ACTIVATION_CONSTANT) + H(data) * time/data];
```

Simulations of the above BioPEPA specifications are depicted, respectively, in Figs. 3.5, 3.6, and 3.7. As shown, three different emergent, global behaviours arise, that is, the dynamics exhibited by the whole population of *data* and *data_on* items, in terms of both the exhibited trend and how involved parameters affect it.

First of all, Fig. 3.5 shows that a fMA-driven activation reaction is dependant on the rate constant as well as on the quantity of the activator enzyme (*on*), but not on the quantity of the reactant to activate (*data*). This is in contrast to what happened for the feed pattern, in which changing the reactant (*food*) affected time taken to complete the feeding process.

It should be noted that comparison is between *food* and *data*, not with *on* as could be done intuitively. The reason is that, although *food* and *on* play a similar role in the artificial chemical reaction, that is, that of activators, they have a different chemical nature: *food* is a *reactant*, being consumed by the reaction, whereas *on* is an enzyme, not altered by it. This difference is taken into account by the simulation algorithm provided by BioPEPA, and affects the outcome of the simulation accordingly.

In Fig. 3.6, not only the emergent, global behaviour changes, but also sensitivity to the parameters involved in kinetic rate computation: dependency on the quantity of the activator enzyme is lost (*on*), while direct proportionality to the quantity of data undergoing the activation process is experienced.

This is the first time that a *product* of the artificial chemical reaction in process is put in its kinetic rate computation. This is something impossible to find in chemistry as it is in the natural world, but something to take advantage of in *artificial* chemical reactions. As a side note, this is the true power of custom kinetic rates: to be free from the natural world's constraints.

Finally, as far as Fig. 3.7 is concerned, whereas the trend is completely different from both previous plots, sensitivity to parameters is the same as that of Fig. 3.6: independency of the enzyme, direct proportionality to *data*.

It should be noted that direct proportionality is w.r.t. time taken to complete the activation process, not to the kinetic rate dynamically computed. In fact, being *data*

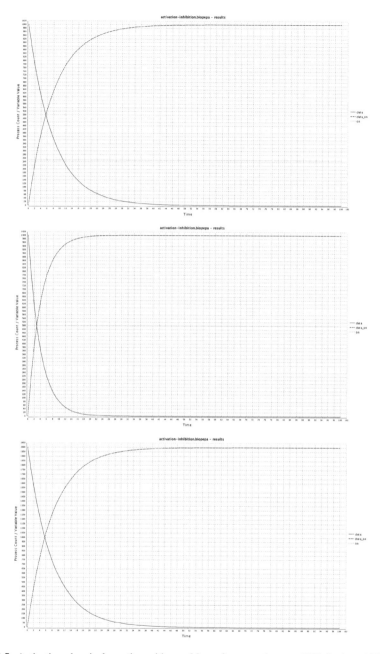

Fig. 3.5 Activation chemical reaction with usual law of mass action rate [30]. In the *middle* plot the activator enzyme quantity (*on*) is twice that of the *top* plot, causing a faster activation process (almost time step 6 in *top* plot, around time step 3 in *middle* plot). In the *bottom* plot *data* quantity is twice that of the other plots, but activation time is the same as that of *top* plot: thus, conversely w.r.t. reactant *food* in the feed pattern, the quantity of reactant *data* here does not affect timing. Acting on the rate constant speeds up or slows down the process as usual

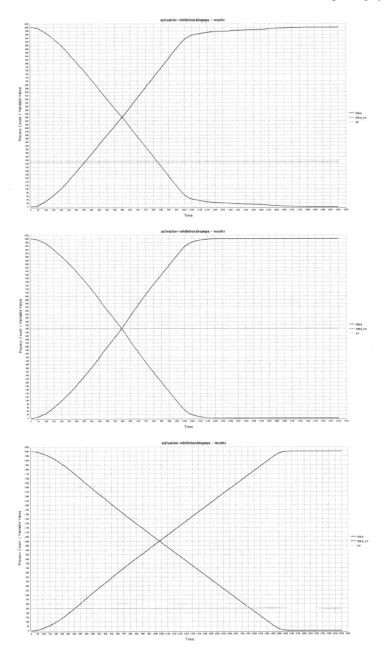

Fig. 3.6 Activation chemical reaction with time and *data_on*-dependant kinetic rate [30]. Besides the exhibited trend being completely different w.r.t. that of Fig. 3.5, also sensitivity to parameters changes: increasing the activator enzyme quantity no longer affects the activation process time (*middle* plot has twice *on* than *top* plot, but crossing time step is still ≈600), whereas increasing the quantity of data to activate does (*bottom* plot has twice *data* than *top* plot, thus time taken until the crossing point increases to ≈1050). Acting on the rate constant speeds up or slows down the process as usual

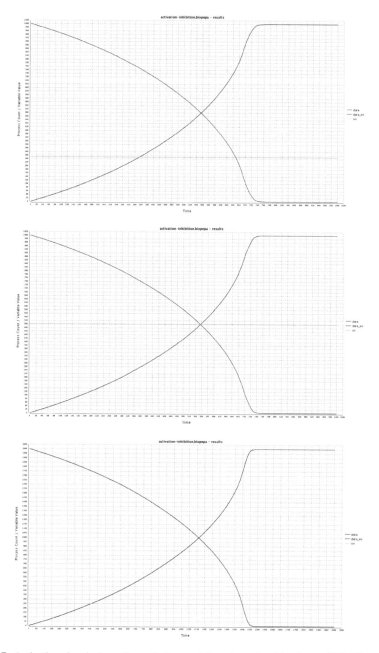

Fig. 3.7 Activation chemical reaction with time and *data*-dependant kinetic rate [30]. Whereas the emergent, global behaviour achieved is different from both previous ones, sensitivity to parameters is the same as for that in Fig. 3.6: increasing the activator enzyme quantity does not affect the activation process time (*middle* plot has twice *on* than *top* plot, but crossing time step is still ≈560), whereas increasing the quantity of data to activate does (*bottom* plot has twice *data* than *top* plot, thus time taken until the crossing point increases to over 1100). Acting on the rate constant speeds up or slows down the process as usual

the denominator of the rate expression, starting the process with a higher value implies term `time` is divided by a greater number, thus the factor added to the fMA factor is smaller, likewise the whole kinetic rate.

Furthermore, denominator *data* is slowly decreasing due to conversion to *data_on*, while `time` is increasing: this leads to a numerator increasing and a denominator decreasing, which explains the faster activation after some time has passed.

3.3.2.4 Aggregation

The aggregation pattern for self-organisation can be represented as an artificial chemical reaction as follows:

$$part^1 + part^2 \xrightarrow{r_{aggregation}} whole$$

meaning that if both parts composing a whole are available, those parts ($part^1$ and $part^2$) should be consumed to produce *whole*, at a pace given by $r_{aggregation}$—the local mechanism.

Aggregation reaction can then be encoded in BioPEPA according to three different kinetic rates—usual fMA-only, time and $\frac{1}{whole}$ dependency, time and $\frac{1}{part^1}$ dependency ($part^2$ will be identical)—as follows:

```
1  AGGREGATION_CONSTANT = 0.0005;
2  r_aggregation = [fMA(AGGREGATION_CONSTANT)];
3  part1 = (r_aggregation, 1) <<;
4  part2 = (r_aggregation, 1) <<;
5  whole = (r_aggregation, 1) >>;
```

```
r_aggregation = [fMA(AGGREGATION_CONSTANT) + H(part1) * H(part2)
                 * time/whole];
```

```
r_aggregation = [fMA(AGGREGATION_CONSTANT) + H(part1) * H(part2)
                 * time/part1];
```

Simulations of the above custom kinetic rates under different settings are depicted, respectively, in Figs. 3.8, 3.9, and 3.10.

As shown, the exhibited trends are almost identical to those of the activation pattern; nevertheless, sensitivity to reactant change is not always in line with those results.

Figure 3.8 shows the same trend as Fig. 3.5, but the effect of increasing (decreasing) quantity of reactant *data* is counter-intuitive: while in Fig. 3.5 timing was independent of *data*, and in subsequent plots of Figs. 3.6 and 3.7 dependency had the form of a direct proportionality, here increasing (decreasing) *data* decreases (increases) time taken to aggregate parts into *whole*. This is the first time that inverse proportionality of time w.r.t. the quantity of the reactant involved in the reaction is experienced.

As far as Figs. 3.9 and 3.10 are concerned, both the exhibited trend and the local mechanisms' parameters effect on the emergent, global behaviour achieved is the same as that of Figs. 3.6 and 3.7, respectively.

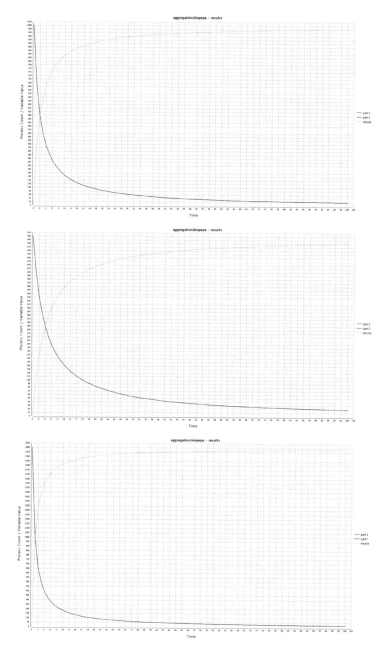

Fig. 3.8 Aggregation chemical reaction with usual law of mass action rate [30]. In the *middle* plot the two reactants *part*[1] and *part*[2] are half w.r.t. the *top* plot, causing a slower aggregation process (time step 2 in *top* plot, time step 4 in *middle* plot). In the *bottom* plot instead, their quantity is twice that of the *top* plot (2000 units), thus aggregation time faster (half time w.r.t. *top* plot). Acting on the rate constant speeds up or slows down the process as usual

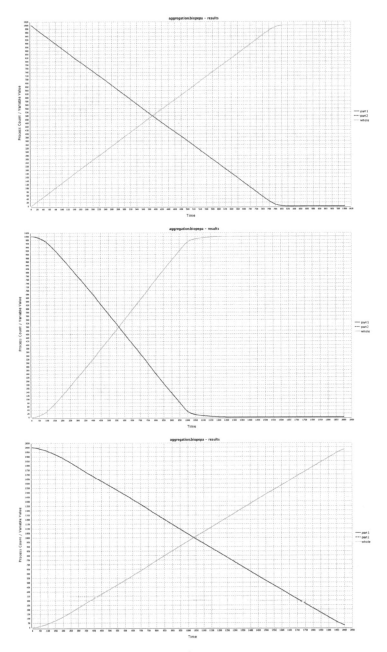

Fig. 3.9 Aggregation chemical reaction with $\frac{time}{whole}$-dependant kinetic rate [30]. Besides the emergent, global trend exhibited, also sensitivity to parameters is very different w.r.t. Fig. 3.8: now increasing the reactants quantity (*bottom* plot has twice parts than *middle* plot) increases time taken to complete aggregation (from slightly more than 550 time steps in *middle* plot, to almost 1050 in *bottom* plot). Instead, acting on the rate constant speeds up or slows down the process as usual (*top* plot has rate constant 0.5 with crossing point at $\approx$390 time steps, whereas *middle* plot rate constant is 0.005 thus crossing point gets delayed to over 550 time steps)

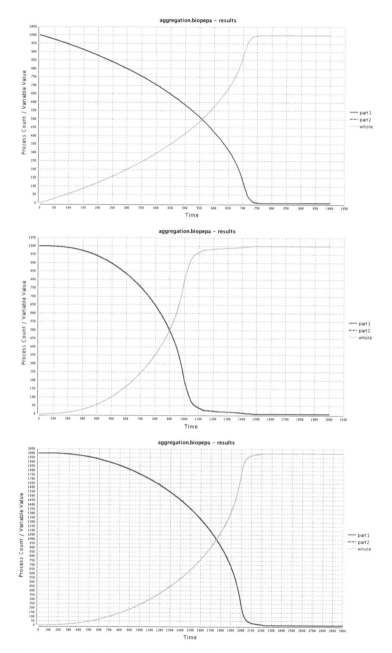

Fig. 3.10 Aggregation chemical reaction with $\frac{time}{part^1}$-dependant kinetic rate [30]. Although the behaviour shown is yet again different from both previous ones, parameters of the local mechanism (the aggregation reaction) have the same effect on the emergent, self-organising behaviour achieved, as described for Fig. 3.9. In particular, *middle* plot has a slower rate than *top* plot, thus time scale almost doubles, and *bottom* plot has twice parts than *middle* plot, thus, again, time scale almost doubles

This is another consequence of the nice controllability property of custom kinetic rates in artificial chemical reactions: being the role played by *whole* in the aggregation pattern the same as that played by *data_on* in activation—that is, *products* of the reaction—as well as the role played by *part*[1] and *part*[2] in aggregation the same as that played by *data* in activation—that is, *reactants*—it is reasonable to expect for them both the same global behaviour to emerge and the same sensitivity to parameters.

3.3.2.5   Diffusion

The diffusion pattern for self-organisation can be represented as an artificial chemical reaction as follows:

$$data_{c'} \xrightarrow{r_{diffusion}} data_{c''} \mid data_{c'''}$$

meaning that one piece of *data* is withdrawn from compartment c' and put into either compartment c'' or c''', chosen probabilistically,[5] at a pace given by $r_{diffusion}$—the local mechanism.

Diffusion reaction can be encoded in BioPEPA according to the following kinetic rates—usual **fMA**, equal-distribution driven by source compartment, dual to **fMA**, and equal-distribution driven by destination compartment—as follows:

```
1  // topology definition (c2<---c1--->c3)
2  location c1 : size = 1, type = compartment;
3  location c2 : size = 1, type = compartment;
4  location c3 : size = 1, type = compartment;
5
6  diff_const = 0.0005;
7  // usual fMA
8  r_diffusion = [fMA(diff_const)];
9  data = (r_diffusion[c1->c2], 1) (.) data
10          + (r_diffusion[c1->c3], 1) (.) data;
```

```
// equal-distribution driven by source compartment
r_diffusion = [fMA(diff_const) * (data@c1 - data@c2)];
```

```
// dual to fMA
r_diffusion = [fMA(diff_const) * (data@c2 + 1)];
```

```
// equal-distribution driven by destination compartment
r_diffusion = [fMA(diff_const) * H(data@c1 - data@c2)
               * (data@c2 + 1)];
```

Simulations of the above custom kinetic rates are depicted in Figs. 3.11 and 3.12.

As shown, the **fMA** kinetic rate (Fig. 3.11, top) exhibits a fast-then-slow global (emergent) trend, where *data* from its origin compartment is eventually depleted. The equal-distribution custom rate, instead, (Fig. 3.11, bottom) does not deplete the

---

[5]How the destination compartment is chosen is not relevant here.

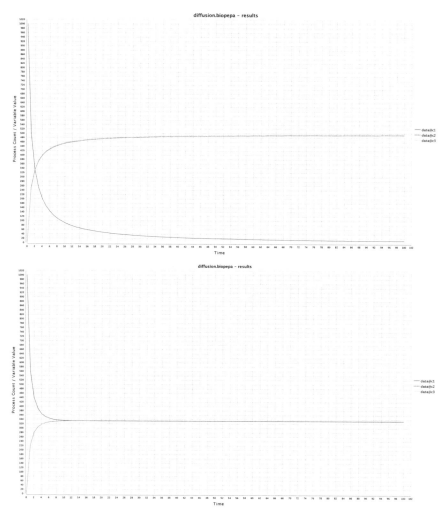

Fig. 3.11 At the *top*, usual fMA diffusion. At the *bottom*, equal-distribution driven by source compartment

concentration of *data* in its origin compartment, but asymptotically tends to balance the distribution of *data* items among the neighbouring compartments.

It should be noted that this emergent behaviour is driven by the source compartment in the sense that the process is faster the more *data* is concentrated in the origin compartment—in fact, it is fast-then-slow.

In Fig. 3.12, at the bottom, the same (almost) uniform distribution is achieved with the dual trend—that is, slow-then-fast—where what drives the emergent process is the concentration of *data* items in the destination compartment.

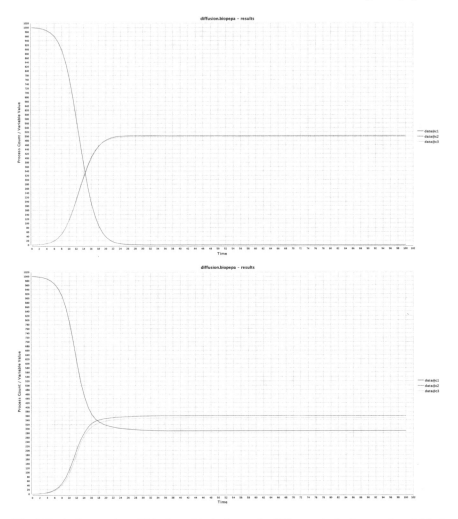

Fig. 3.12 At the *top*, the exhibited trend is dual w.r.t. the fMA one. At the *bottom*, the exhibited trend is dual w.r.t. the one with equal distribution, and driven by concentration of *data* in the source compartment concentration

Finally, Fig. 3.12, at the top, shows the dual trend w.r.t. to the fMA-only one (seen in Fig. 3.11, top), that is, a slow-then-fast global behaviour.

3.4   Uniform Primitives as Coordination Primitives

A foremost feature common to all the tuple-based coordination models mentioned in Chap. 2 is *non-determinism*, stemming from their roots in the LINDA model [25].

LINDA features *don't know* non-determinism in the access to tuples in tuple spaces, handled with a *don't care* approach: (i) a tuple space is a multiset of tuples where multiple tuples possibly match a given template; (ii) which tuple among the matching ones is actually retrieved by a getter operation (e.g. `in`, `rd`) can be neither specified nor predicted (*don't know*); (iii) nonetheless, the coordinated system is designed so as to keep on working safely whichever is the matching tuple returned (*don't care*). The latter assumption requires that when a process uses a template matching multiple tuples, which specific tuple is actually retrieved is not relevant for that process. This is not the case, however, in many of today adaptive and self-organising systems, where processes may need to implement *stochastic behaviours*—like "most of the time do this"—which obviously do not cope well with don't know non-determinism [43].

For instance, all the nature-inspired models and systems that emerged in the last decade—such as chemical, biochemical, stigmergic, and field-based—are examples of the broad class of self-organising systems that precisely require such a sort of behaviour [39], which by no means can be enabled by the canonical LINDA model and its direct derivatives.

To this end, in the following *uniform coordination primitives* (`uin`, `urd`)—first mentioned in [22]—are discussed, as the specialisation of LINDA getter primitives featuring *probabilistic non-determinism* instead of don't know non-determinism.

Roughly speaking, uniform primitives make it possible to both *specify* and (*statistically*) *predict* the probability to retrieve one specific tuple in a multiset of matching ones, thus making it possible to statistically control non-deterministic systems. This simple mechanism extends the reach of tuple-based coordination towards nature-inspired systems, allowing, e.g. coordination-based simulation of complex stochastic behaviours.

Uniform primitives are the basic mechanism upon which the $\mathcal{MoK}$ middleware prototype discussed in Part II of this book is designed, in particular, as regards artificial chemical reactions scheduling, and reactants consumption.

3.4.1 Related Approaches

In [46] simulation is supported by *biochemical tuple spaces* [49]. Technically, biochemical tuple spaces are built as ReSpecT *tuple centres* [42], distributed across the TuCSoN coordination infrastructure [44]. Tuples are logic-based tuples, while biochemical laws are implemented as ReSpecT *specification tuples*, so that they can be inserted, modified, and removed from the biochemical compartment (the tuple centre) via ReSpecT coordination primitives.

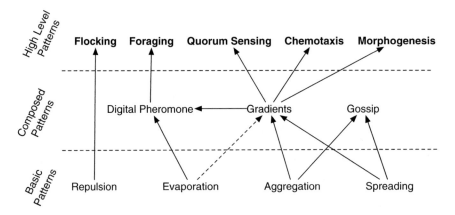

Fig. 3.13 Patterns layering and relationships (image taken from [20])

A *chemical solution simulator* is successfully built as a ReSpecT tuple centre, programmed to implement the Gillespie's algorithm for *exact* chemical solutions simulation [26]. Then, the Ras-mitogen-activated protein kinase (MAPK) signalling pathway is simulated, but uniform primitives are not exploited: thus, e.g. the peculiar feature of probabilistic, concentration-driven selection of reactants is lacking. In Sect. 3.4.3.3 such an implementation is redesigned on top of uniform primitives, to highlight their impact on system behaviour in spite of their simplicity—namely, real probabilistic selection of reactants based on an approximation of concentration values.

The idea of engineering nature-inspired self-organising systems attracted many researchers in the last decade: [13, 22, 29, 36] all proposed either bio-inspired coordination primitives or full-fledged design patterns aimed at easing the understanding and engineering of nature-inspired computational systems.

However, a step beyond primitives and patterns definition is taken in [20], by classifying patterns into *layers*, and by describing the *relationships* between patterns in different layers, so as to effectively outline a pattern composition schema suitable to be reused in different scenarios. Figure 3.13 depicts the aforementioned layers:

Basic patterns —*Repulsion, evaporation, aggregation*, and *spreading*, are interpreted as the most primitive nature-inspired patterns which all other patterns should be programmed upon, according to the composition represented by the arrows (dashed for optional composition, solid for mandatory)

Composite patterns —*Digital pheromone, gradients*, and *gossip*, are in the middle layer, because (i) being programmable as a composition of other patterns, they cannot be basic, and (ii) being exploitable to engineer other patterns by composition, they are not high level either

High-level patterns —*Flocking, foraging, quorum sensing, chemotaxis*, and *morphogenesis*, are all defined as high-level patterns: thus, as patterns directly usable at the application level, e.g. to implement self-organising coordination policies

In Sect. 3.4.3.2 uniform primitives are used to implement digital pheromones and foraging.

In [49] similar primitives are presented and formally defined to forge the *bio-chemical tuple space* notion. The main difference w.r.t. uniform primitives is that: (i) they rely on tuples multiplicity to model probability, leaving LINDA tuples' structure untouched, (ii) they are executed as LINDA getter primitives, whereas those in [49] are executed according to a *stochastic rate*.

3.4.1.1 Differentiation w.r.t. State of Art

Probabilistic extensions to LINDA found in state of art literature traditionally follow two main approaches [17]:

- *data-driven*, where the quantitative information required to model probability is associated with the data items (the tuples) in the form of weights, then the matching mechanism is extended so as to take into account *weights*—transforming them into probabilities by normalisation. This approach is adopted, e.g. in `ProbLinCa` [5], the probabilistic version of a LINDA-based process calculus
- *scheduler-driven*, where quantitative information is added to the processes using special probabilistic schedulers, ascribing different probabilities to different active processes—independently of the tuples involved. This is the approach taken by, e.g. [16], to define a probabilistic extension of the KLAIM model named pKLAIM

Instead, the approach adopted with uniform primitives belongs to a third, novel category, called *interaction-driven*, where probabilistic behaviour is (i) associated to communication primitives—thus, neither to processes (or schedulers), nor to tuples—and (ii) enacted during the interaction between a process and the coordination medium—that is, solely through primitives.

In fact, whereas `ProbLinCa` requires the change of tuple structure and matching mechanism so as to support probabilistic operations, and pKLAIM requires special, probabilistic schedulers for processes, uniform primitives extend LINDA by *specialising* standard LINDA primitives, without changing neither tuple structure nor scheduling policy. Accordingly, uniform coordination primitives could be used in place of LINDA standard ones without affecting the model, simply refining don't care non-determinism as probabilistic non-determinism: as a result, all the expressiveness results and all the applications based on the canonical LINDA model would still hold.

Furthermore, uniform primitives could be used to emulate both approaches: tuple weights could be reified by their multiplicity in the space, whereas probabilistic scheduling could be obtained by properly synchronising processes upon probabilistic consumption of shared tuples.

	uniform	Biochemical Tuple Spaces	ProbLinCa	pKLAIM	STOKLAIM	SAPERE
probabilistic approach	interaction driven	interaction driven	data driven	schedule driven	schedule driven	interaction driven
tuple structure w.r.t. LINDA	same	modified	modified	same	same	modified
primitives execution w.r.t. LINDA	same	timed	same	same	timed	timed

Fig. 3.14 Comparison of probabilistic coordination models [33]

More complex coordination models exist where uniform primitives could potentially play a key role in providing the probabilistic mechanisms required for the engineering of stochastic systems like adaptive and self-organising ones.

STOKLAIM [12] is an extension to KLAIM where process actions are equipped with *rates* affecting execution probability, and execution *delays* as well—that is, time needed to carry out an action. By reifying action rates as tuples in the space, with multiplicity proportional to rates, uniform-reading tuples would allow action execution to be probabilistically scheduled *à la* STOKLAIM. Furthermore, delays could be emulated, too, by uniform-reading a set of time tuples, where a higher value corresponds to a lower action rate.

In SAPERE [54], tuples are managed through *eco-laws*, which are a sort of chemical-like rules, scheduled according to their rates. Hence, uniform primitives could play in SAPERE the same role as in STOKLAIM—once eco-laws are reified as tuples with a multiplicity proportional to execution rate. Furthermore, from the pool of all the tuples which can participate in a eco-law, the ones actually consumed by the law—as *chemical reactants*—are selected probabilistically. Once again, this kind of behaviour could be enabled by uniform consumption of reactant tuples in eco-laws.

Figure 3.14 summarises the main differences between uniform primitives and the other aforementioned primitives.

3.4.2 Informal Definition

LINDA getter primitives, that is, data-retrieval primitives in and rd, are shared by all tuple-based coordination models, and provide them with *don't know non-determinism*: when one or more tuples in a tuple space match a given template, any of the matching tuples can be non-deterministically returned.

Therefore, in a single getter operation, only a *point-wise property* affects tuple retrieval: that is, the conformance of a tuple to the template, independently of the *spatial context*—namely, the other tuples in the same space. Furthermore, in a sequence of getter operations, don't know non-determinism makes any prediction of the overall behaviour impossible: e.g. reading one thousand times with the same template in a tuple space with ten matching tuples could possibly lead to retrieve the same tuple all times, or one hundred times each, or whatever admissible combination one could think of—no prediction possible, according to the model. Again, then, only a point-wise property can be ensured even in *time*: that is, only the mere compliance to the model of each individual operation in the sequence.

Uniform primitives instead, enrich tuple-based coordination models with the ability of performing operations that ensure *global system properties* instead of point-wise ones, in both space and time. More precisely, uniform primitives replace don't know non-determinism with *probabilistic non-determinism* to *situate* a primitive invocation in *space*—the tuple actually retrieved depends on the other tuples in the space—and to *predict* its behaviour in *time*—statistically, the distribution of the tuples retrieved will tend to be *uniform*.

The main motivation behind the formal definition and expressiveness study of uniform primitives, is that of introducing a *simple* yet *expressive* probabilistic mechanism in tuple-based coordination: simple enough to work as a specialisation of standard LINDA operations, expressive enough to allow modelling of the most relevant probabilistic behaviours exhibited by nature-inspired complex computational systems.

Whereas *expressiveness* is discussed informally in Sect. 3.2.2 and formally in Sect. 3.3, *simplicity* is achieved by defining uniform primitives as *specialised* versions of standard LINDA primitives: so, first of all, uin and urd are compliant with the standard semantics of in and rd.

In the same way as in and rd, uin and urd ask tuple spaces for one tuple matching a given template, possibly suspend when no matching tuple is available, and finally return a matching tuple chosen non-deterministically when one or more matching tuples are available in the tuple space. As a straightforward consequence, any tuple-based coordination system using in and rd would also work by exploiting instead uin and urd, respectively—and any process using in and rd could adopt uin and urd instead without any further change.

On the other hand, the nature of the specialisation lays precisely in the way in which a tuple is non-deterministically chosen among the (possibly) many tuples matching the template. While in standard LINDA the choice is performed based on don't know non-determinism, uniform primitives exploit instead *probabilistic non-determinism* with *uniform distribution*. So, if a standard getter primitive requires a tuple with template T, and m tuples $t_1, \ldots, t_m$ matching T are in the tuple space when the request is executed, any tuple $t_{i \in 1 \ldots m}$ could be retrieved, but nothing more could be said—no other assertion is possible about the result of the getter operation.

Instead, when a uniform getter primitive requires a tuple with a template T, and m tuples $t_1, \ldots, t_m$ matching T are available in the tuple space when the request is served, one assertion is possible about the result of the getter operation: each of the

m matching tuples $t_1, \ldots, t_m$ has exactly the *same probability* $\frac{1}{m}$ to be returned. So, for instance, if 2 `colour(blue)` and 3 `colour(red)` tuples occur in the tuple space when a `urd(colour(X))` is executed, the probability of the tuple retrieved to be `colour(blue)` or `colour(red)` is exactly 40 or 60 %, respectively.

Operationally, uniform primitives behave as follows. When executed, a uniform primitive takes a *snapshot* of the tuple space, freezing its state at a certain point in time—and space, being a single tuple space the target of basic LINDA primitives. The snapshot is then exploited to assign a probability value $p_i \in [0, 1]$ to any tuple $t_{i \in 1 \ldots n}$ in the space—where n is the number of tuples in the space. There, non-matching tuples have value $p = 0$, matching tuples have value $p = \frac{1}{m}$ (where $m \le n$ is the number of matching tuples), and the sum of probability values is $\sum_{i \in 1 \ldots n} p_i = 1$. The matching tuple returned is *statistically* chosen based on the probability values computed.

As a consequence, whereas standard getter primitives exhibit point-wise properties only, uniform primitives feature *global properties*, in both space and time.

In terms of spatial context, in fact, standard getter primitives return a matching tuple independently of the other tuples currently in the same space—so, they are *context unaware*. Instead, uniform getter primitives return matching tuples based on the overall state of the tuple space—so, their behaviour is *context aware*.

In terms of time, too, sequences of standard getter operations feature no meaningful properties. Instead, by definition, sequences of uniform getter operations tend to globally exhibit a *uniform distribution* over time. So, for instance, performing N `urd(colour(X))` operations over a tuple space containing 10 `colour(white)` and 100 `colour(black)` tuples, would lead to a sequence of returned tuples which, while growing, tends to contain 10 times more `colour(black)` tuples than `colour(white)` ones.

In principle, the snapshot behaviour above described may be computationally expensive, and potentially represent an implementation bottleneck: given the tuple space target of the uniform primitive, the set of matching tuples should be found, then each different matching tuple should be counted, finally one of those matching tuples chosen probabilistically. Furthermore, in the meanwhile no other primitive can be served by the tuple space, according to LINDA semantics.

Nevertheless, many techniques can be used to effectively deal with the issue: for instance, (i) using suitable data structures—e.g. an hashmap to conveniently store together identical copies of the same tuple; (ii) distributing tuples among several networked tuple spaces, so as to lower the load of tuples to snapshot for each one; (iii) tracking the number of tuples internally, so as to avoid counting.

Figure 3.15 compares execution semantics and expected usage of uniform primitives w.r.t. LINDA primitives—`out` is left out because its semantics is unchanged.

	in	rd	uin	urd
non-determinism semantics	don't know	don't know	probabilistic, uniform distribution	probabilistic, uniform distribution
usage	don't care approach	don't care approach	stochastic systems	stochastic systems

Fig. 3.15 Comparison of LINDA and ULINDA primitives [33]

3.4.3 Informal Expressiveness

In [5] the authors demonstrate that LINDA-based languages cannot implement probabilistic models: a LINDA process calculus, although Turing-complete, is not expressive enough to express probabilistic choice.

Since formally asserting a gap in expressiveness does not necessarily make it easy to fully appreciate how much this can make the difference when programming, e.g. adaptive and self-organising systems, in the remainder of this section a few examples are discussed, showing which kind of behaviours are straightforwardly enabled by uniform primitives.

3.4.3.1 Load Balancing

Two service providers are both offering the same service to clients through proper advertising tuples. The first is slower than the second, that is, it needs more time to process a request—modelling differences in, e.g. computational power.

Their working cycle is simple: a worker thread gets requests from a shared tuple space, then puts them in the bounded queue of the master thread (the actual service provider). The master thread continuously queries the queue looking for requests to serve: when one is found, it is served, then the master emits another advertising tuple; if none is found, the master does something else, then re-queries the queue—no advertising.

Decoupling enforced by the queue is useful to model the fact that service providers should not block on the space waiting for incoming requests, so as to be free of performing other jobs in the meanwhile—e.g. reporting, resource clean-up, etc. The queue is bounded to model, e.g. memory constraints.

It should be noted that this toy scenario is a simplified version of a multi-client/multi-server deployment that is quite common in web applications, distributed computing, service-oriented architectures, etc.

In this setting, clients (whose Java code is listed in Fig. 3.16) search for available services first via rd primitive (Fig. 3.17), then via urd (Fig. 3.18).

```
1    LogicTuple templ;
2    while(!die){
3      templ = LogicTuple.parse("ad(S)");
4      // Pick a server probabilistically
5      op = acc.urd(tid, templ, null);
6      // Plain Linda version
7      // op = acc.rd(tid, templ, null);
8      if (op.isResultSuccess()) {
9        service = op.getLogicTupleResult();
10       // Submit request
11       req = LogicTuple.parse(
12         "req("+service.getArg(0)+","+reqID+")"
13         );
14       acc.out(tid, req, null);
15     }
16   }
```

Fig. 3.16 Java code of clients looking for services [33]

All charts values are the average of several runs of the scenario—e.g. value plotted at time step 60 is the average of the number of requests observable at time step 60 in a number of runs (actually, 100).

By using the rd primitive, clients *blindly commit* to the actual implementation of the LINDA model currently at hand. For instance, Fig. 3.17 gives some hints about the implementation used in this scenario—the TuCSoN coordination middleware [44]: since provider 1 is almost unused, it may be inferred that rd is implemented as a FIFO queue, always matching the first tuple among many ones—provider 2 advertising tuple, in this case. The point here is that such a prediction is not possible before actually deploying the system, and with no information on the actual LINDA implementation used.

By using primitive urd instead (Fig. 3.18), it is known—and *predictable*—how much each service provider will be exploited by clients: since it is known by design that after successfully serving a request a provider emits an advertising tuple, and that tuples are those looked up by clients, it is known that the faster provider will produce more tuples, hence it will be more frequently found, than the slower one.

Figure 3.18, in fact, shows how competing service providers self-organise by sharing incoming requests. Furthermore, this behaviour is not statically designed or superimposed, but results by *emergence* from a number of run-time factors, such as clients interactions, service providers computational load, computational power, and memory.

It should also be noted that this form of *load balancing* is not the only benefit gained when using urd: actually, the urd scenario successfully serves ≈1600 requests—distributed among providers 1 and 2—losing ≈600, whereas the rd scenario serves successfully ≈1250—leaving provider 1 unused—losing over 2500.

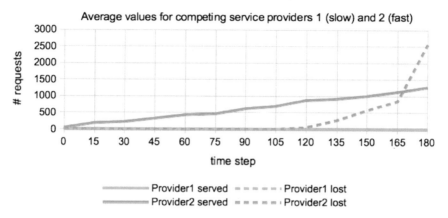

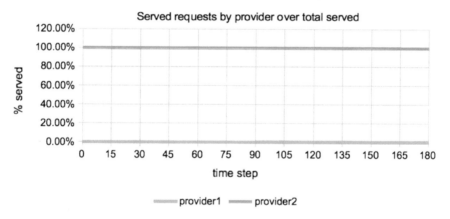

Fig. 3.17 Clients using rd primitive: service provider 1 is under-exploited [33]

Although quite simple, the load balancing scenario just described can be taken as an example of that kind of complex systems where probabilistic mechanisms and feedback loops altogether make self-organisation appear by emergence [39].

Furthermore, even more traditional real-world scenarios—such as the aforementioned service-oriented and distributed ones—could benefit from uniform primitives features to increase throughput, reliability, availability, and efficiency, as demonstrated by Figs. 3.17 and 3.18.

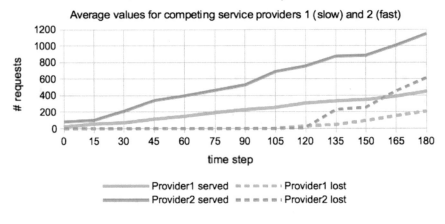

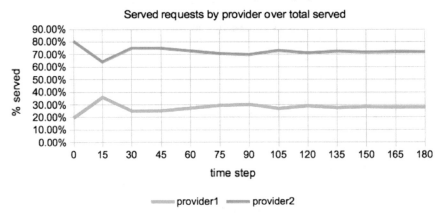

Fig. 3.18 Clients using `urd` primitive: a certain degree of fairness is guaranteed, based on self-organisation [33]

3.4.3.2 Pheromone-Based Coordination

In *pheromone-based coordination*, used by ants to find optimal paths—as well as by many ant-inspired computational systems, such as network routing algorithms [18] and autonomous unmanned vehicles [45]—each agent basically wanders *randomly* through a network of locations until it finds a pheromone trail, which the agent is *likely* to follow based on the trail strength.

Here, aspects such as pheromone release, scent, and evaporation are not relevant: instead, the above mentioned requirements of randomness and likelihood are, on the one hand, *essential* for pheromone-based coordination, while, on the other hand, to be designed using a tuple-based coordination model *require* uniform primitives.

In particular, consider a network of n nodes representing places p_i, with $i = 1 \ldots n$, through which ant agents walk. The default tuple space in node p_i contains at least one *neighbour* tuple $n(p_j)$ for each neighbour node p_j. The neighbourhood relation is symmetric—so, if node p_i and p_j are neighbours, tuple space p_i contains tuple $n(p_j)$ and tuple space p_j contains tuple $n(p_i)$. Pheromone deposit in nodes is modelled by the insertion of a new tuple $n(p_i)$ in every neighbour node p_j.

It should be noted that the described setting is common to a plethora of scenarios in computer science: essentially, any problem that can be represented by a graph-based structure. For instance, in the field of computer networks management, the following experiment could be taken as a reference for building much more complex applications, aimed at, e.g. routing of message packets, finding optimal paths from a source node to a destination one, reconfiguration of links between hubs, etc. Engineering solutions to this kind of problems using uniform primitives, instead of classical LINDA operations, would bring all the benefits of self-organisation highlighted in the following discussion.

In the scenario just depicted, ants wandering through places and ants following trails can be both easily modelled using uniform primitives: ant agents just need to look locally for neighbour tuples through a urd(n(P)). If no pheromone trail is detected nearby, every neighbour place is represented by a single tuple, so all neighbour places have the same probability to be chosen—leading to random wandering of ants. In case some of the neighbours contain a detectable trail, the corresponding neighbour tuple occurs more than once in the local tuple space: so, by using uniform primitives, the tuple corresponding to a neighbour place with a pheromone trail has a greater probability to be chosen than others.

The experiment was conducted in a toy scenario involving digital ants and pheromones programmed in ReSpecT [41] upon the TuCSoN coordination middleware [44]. The experiment involves ten digital ants starting from the anthill with the goal of finding food, and follows the canonical assumptions of ant systems [18]. So, at the beginning, any path has the same probability of being chosen, thus modelling random walking of ants in absence of pheromone. As ants begin to wander around, they eventually find food, and release pheromone on their path while coming back home. As a consequence, the shortest path finally gets the most pheromone since using it takes less time w.r.t. any other path.

Pheromones as well as connections between tuple centres are modelled as described above, with neighbour tuples: the more neighbour tuples of a certain type, the more likely ants will move to that neighbour tuple centre next.

Figure 3.19 depicts a few screenshots of the experiment: there, five distributed tuple centres (the large boxes) model a topology connecting the anthill to a food source: the leftmost path is longer—modelled as a 2-hop route—whereas the rightmost is shorter. The green spray-like effect on paths (black lines) models the strength of the pheromone scent: the greater and greener the path, the more pheromone on it.

By plotting pheromones strength evolution over time, Fig. 3.20 shows how expectations about digital ants behaviour are met: in fact, despite starting from the situation in which any path is equiprobable (the amount of pheromones on either path is the same), the system eventually detects the shortest path, which becomes the most

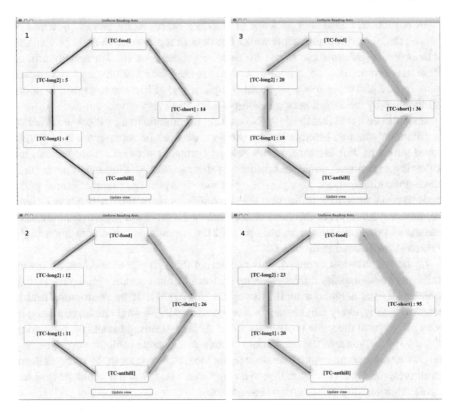

Fig. 3.19 Ants search food ("TC-food" box) wandering randomly from their anthill ("TC-anthill" box). By urd-ing digital pheromones left while carrying food, ants stochastically find the optimal path towards the food source [33]—numbers next to tuple centre names denote pheromone strength, that is, the number of n(NBR) tuples

exploited—and contains in fact more pheromone units. In the Java code describing the behaviour of ants (Fig. 3.21), in particular in method smellPheromone() (line 10), usage of the uniform primitive urd is visible on line 27, whereas line 29 shows the tuple template given as its argument, that is, n(NBR): at runtime, NBR unifies with a TuCSoN tuple centre identifier, making it possible for the ant to move there.

Quite obviously, the idea here is not just showing a new way to model ant-like systems. Instead, the example above is meant to point out how a non-trivial behaviour—that is, dynamically solving a shortest path problem—can be achieved by simply substituting uniform primitives to traditional LINDA getter primitives—which instead would not allow the system to work as required. Furthermore, the solution is adaptive, fully decentralised, based upon local information solely—thus, it appears by *emergence*—and robust against topology changes—a ReSpecT specification implementing pheromone evaporation was used.

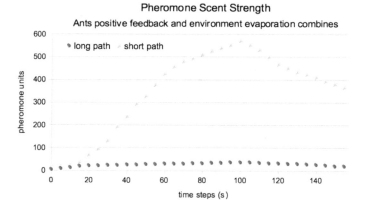

Fig. 3.20   Pheromone strength over time [33]. Descending phase corresponds to lack of pheromone deposit due to food depletion

These are the main reasons why similar algorithms inspired by ants behaviour are so popular in computer science, e.g. in the computer networks management field: a simple yet expressive probabilistic mechanism alone—here, uniform primitives— is able to impact the output of the algorithm, as well as to support new features. In other words, given a non-deterministic, distributed routing algorithm based on classical LINDA operations, a simple shift of calls from in and rd to uin and urd can dramatically impact both the output and the non-functional properties of the algorithm—e.g. robustness to topology change, adaptiveness to run-time bottlenecks formation, etc.

```
 1   while (!stopped) {
 2     if (!carryingFood) {
 3       // If not carrying food
 4       isFood = smellFood();
 5       if (isFood) {
 6         // pick up food if any
 7         pickFood();
 8       } else {
 9         // or stochastically follow pheromone
10         direction = smellPheromone();
11         move(direction);
12       }
13     } else {
14       // If carrying food
15       if (isAnthill()) {
16         // drop food if in anthill
17         dropFood();
18       } else {
19         // or move toward anthill
20         direction = smellAnthill();
21         move(direction);
22       }
23     }
24   }
25
26   private LogicTuple smellPheromone() {
27     ITucsonOperation op = acc.urd(
28       tcid,
29       LogicTuple.parse("n(NBR)"),
30       TIMEOUT
31     );
32     if (op.isResultSuccess()) {
33       return op.getLogicTupleResult();
34     }
35   }
```

Fig. 3.21 Java code for ants [33]

It should be noted that, w.r.t. the classification represented by Fig. 3.13 in Sect. 3.4.1, coordination between ants and the environment, especially, the feedback loop created by ants depositing pheromone and evaporation depleting it, actually implements some of the patterns therein defined [20]. In particular: (i) the digital pheromone composite pattern and the foraging high-level pattern, but also, to some extent, (ii) the gradient pattern, by interpreting pheromone trails as ant-steering gradients, and the chemotaxis, by interpreting pheromone trails as carriers of ants, driving them from the anthill to the food source and back.

3.4.3.3 Gillespie's Chemical Solution Simulation Algorithm

A number of extensions to tuple-based coordination models exploit programmability of tuple spaces [14]: there, while the tuple space interface is left unchanged (coordination primitives are the usual LINDA ones), the tuple space behaviour in response to coordination events can be programmed so as to embed coordination laws. The approach is adopted by LGI [35], MARS [7], TuCSoN [44] among the many. For instance, the TuCSoN coordination model provides ReSpecT [38] as a Turing-complete language for programming TuCSoN tuple centres, therefore allowing tuple spaces to embed any computable coordination law. In particular, ReSpecT coordination is obtained by means of reactions, that is, logic-based computational activities—triggered in response to coordination events—which include, among the operations available, the basic LINDA primitives.

However, Turing equivalence within a coordination medium is still not enough to embed probabilistic behaviours in tuple centres: uniform primitives are required. This can be seen by building a chemical solution dynamics simulator based on Gillespie's well-known stochastic algorithm [26] upon a TuCSoN tuple centre programmed in ReSpecT. The simulator depends on the availability of uniform primitives in ReSpecT—that is, available for use *within* ReSpecT reactions.

Given: (i) a multiset of chemical laws of the form `law(RTs,Rate,RTs')`, where $RTs, RTs' ::= \bot \mid RT \mid RT, RTs$ and `RT` is a template for chemical reactants and products; and (ii) a multiset of reactants of the form `reactant(R,C)`, representing concentration `C` for reactant `R`; then, Gillespie's chemical solution simulation algorithm could be summarised by the following steps—to be executed in loop:

1. collect only the *triggerable laws*, that is, those for which at least one `R` for each `RT` exists, then, for each of them, consider any possible combination of $\mu(\texttt{R}, \texttt{RT})$—where μ is a given matching function—and define *actual laws*
2. for each actual law, compute its *effective rate* `ERate` as the product between the given `Rate` and each $\texttt{R}_i$'s concentration $c_i = \frac{|R_i|}{\sum_j |R_j|}$ (using ReSpecT, the value could be automatically kept up-to-date)
3. compute the corresponding law *execution probability* as $p_i = \frac{\texttt{ERate}_i}{\sum_j \texttt{ERate}_j}$, according to which one law is selected for execution with a probabilistic choice

All steps but the third are easily computed using standard ReSpecT—namely, no uniform primitives are needed. In particular, actual laws can be represented as logic tuples of the form `actual(IL,OL)`—where `IL,OL` represent reactants and products, respectively—whose multiplicity in the space should be kept as desired to represent its execution probability. What cannot be done without uniform primitives is last part of step 3: there, in fact, a `urd(actual(IL,OL))` is to be used so as to probabilistically select the chemical law to be executed.

As shown by the ReSpecT code snippet listed in Fig. 3.22, using a uniform primitive (line 17) to probabilistically *sample* the space of chemical laws allows step 3 of the Gillespie simulation algorithm to be faithfully implemented. In particular, given that step 2 inserts in the tuple centre a number of actual law tuples proportional

```
1    % Invoked by timed ReSpecT reaction.
2    gillespie():-
3      % Steps 1-2
4      collectTriggerable(-Trig),
5      buildActual(+Trig, -Actual),
6      % Step 2: higher rates => higher multiplicity
7      computeRates(+Actual),
8      % Step 3
9      choose(-ALaw, -DeltaT),
10     % Law execution & scheduling of simulator.
11     execute(+ALaw, +DeltaT),
12     schedule(+DeltaT).
13   [...]
14   % Probabilistically, pick a law.
15   choose(AL, D):-
16     % higher multiplicity => higher probability
17     urd(actual(IL, OL)),
18     AL = actual(IL, OL),
19     rd_all(AL, L),
20     length(L, D).
21   [...]
```

Fig. 3.22 Snippet of ReSpecT code implementing Gillespie's algorithm [33]

to the effective rate determined in steps 1–2—so that higher rates correspond to higher multiplicity of tuples—then predicate choose/2 effectively selects for execution the most probable law, since, according to uniform primitives semantics, the higher the multiplicity of a tuple, the higher the probability it will be selected for matching.

Enhancing the ReSpecT language with uniform primitives makes it possible for a TuCSoN tuple centre to work as a *biochemical tuple space* [49], thus, to play a key role in the design of complex computational systems, such as adaptive and self-organising ones. In particular, by replacing the implementation of Gillespie's chemical solution simulation algorithm of [46] with the uniform primitive-based one sketched in Fig. 3.22, the probabilistic, concentration-driven mechanism for selection of reactants to be consumed in reactions can be effectively and easily implemented—leading to a more accurate simulation, more faithfully following Gillespie's algorithm.

It should be noted that building accurate chemical-like mechanisms in a distributed setting—like the tuple-based one here proposed—is interesting not just for the obvious benefits it can bring to the computational chemistry community—which is focussed, e.g. on reliable simulation of biochemical networks and intracellular pathways—but also for its impact on the engineering of nature-inspired self-organising systems.

A chemical-like middleware, in fact, is well suited for supporting self-* features, e.g. self-configuration, self-management, self-healing, self-optimisation, etc., and to inject these features in many different computational scenarios, such as pervasive systems [54], service-oriented architectures [49], and distributed algorithms [10].

3.4.4 Formalisation

A core issue for computer science since the early days, expressiveness of computational languages is still essential nowadays, in particular for coordination languages, which, by focussing on interaction, deal with the most relevant source of complexity in computational systems [52].

Unsurprisingly, the area of coordination models and languages has produced a long stream of ideas and results on the subject, both adopting/adapting traditional approaches—such as Turing equivalence for coordination languages [6, 15]—and inventing its own original techniques [53].

Comparing languages based on either their structural properties or the observable behaviour of the systems built upon them is seemingly a good way to classify their expressiveness. Among the many available approaches, the notion of *modular embedding* [3], refinement of Shapiro's *embedding* [47], is particularly effective in capturing the expressiveness of concurrent and coordination languages.

However, the emergence of classes of systems featuring new sorts of behaviours—pervasive, adaptive, self-organising systems [40, 43]—is pushing computational languages beyond their previous limits, and asks for new models and techniques to observe, model and, measure their expressiveness. In particular, modular embedding fails in telling probabilistic languages apart from non-probabilistic ones, thus, the notion of *probabilistic modular embedding* (PME) sketched in [31] and later refined in [32] is needed as a formal framework to capture the expressiveness of probabilistic languages and stochastic systems.

To enable these kind of formal analysis, in the following uniform primitives are defined formally.

> For the interested reader, in [31] PME is used on uniform primitives, whereas in [32] it is slightly refined and applied to other probabilistic languages.

3.4.4.1 Formal Framework

To define the semantics of (getter) uniform primitives, a simplified version of the process-algebraic framework in [4] is exploited, dropping multi-level priority probabilities. Therein, the proposed formalism aims at dealing with the issue of open transition systems specification, requiring *quantitative information* to be attached to synchronisation actions at run-time—that is, based on the *environment* state during the computation.

The idea is that of *partially closing* labelled transition systems via a process-algebraic *closure* operator ($\uparrow$), which associates quantitative values—e.g. probabilities—to admissible transition actions based upon a set of *handles* defined in an application-specific manner, dictating which quantity should be attached to which action. More precisely:

1. actions labelling open transitions are equipped with handles
2. the operator $\uparrow$ is exploited to compose a system to a specification G, associating at run-time each handle to a given value—e.g. a value $\in \mathbb{N}$
3. quantitative information with which to equip actions—e.g. probabilities $\in [0, 1]$ summing up to 1—are computed from handle values for each enabled action, possibly based on the action context (environment)
4. quantitatively-labelled actions turn an open transition into a reduction, which then executes according to the quantitative information

Here, closure operator $\uparrow$, handles h, and closure term G, are exploited as follows:

- handles coupled to actions (open transition labels) represent tuple templates associated to corresponding primitives
- handles listed in restriction term G represent tuples offered (as synchronisation items) by the tuple space
- restriction term G associates handles (tuples) to their weight in the tuple space
- restriction operator $\uparrow$ *(i)* matches admissible synchronisations between processes and the tuple space, cutting out unavailable actions, and *(ii)* computes their associated probability distribution based upon handle-associated values

It is worth to note that closure operator $\uparrow$ could be seen as following the operational interpretation of a uniform primitive: it takes a snapshot of the tuple space state—*matching*, step *(i)*—then samples it probabilistically—*sampling*, step *(ii)*.

3.4.4.2   Semantics of `uin` (Uniform Consumption)

Three transition rules define the operational semantics of the `uin` primitive for *uniform consumption*:

SYNCH- C   open transition representing the request for process-space synchronisation upon template T, which leads to the snapshot:

$$\texttt{uin}(T).P \mid \langle t_1, \ldots, t_n \rangle \xrightarrow{T} \texttt{uin}(T).P \mid \langle t_1, \ldots, t_n \rangle \uparrow \{(t_1, v_1), \ldots, (t_n, v_n)\}$$

where $v_{i=1\ldots n} = \mu(T, t_i)$, and $\mu(\cdot, \cdot)$ is the standard matching function of LINDA, hence $\forall i, v_i :: = 1 \mid 0$

CLOSE- C   closed unlabelled transition (reduction) representing the internal computation assigning probabilities to synchronisation items (uniform distribution computation):

$$\texttt{uin}(T).P \mid \langle t_1, \ldots, t_n \rangle \uparrow \{(t_1, v_1), \ldots, (t_n, v_n)\} \hookrightarrow \texttt{uin}(T).P \mid \langle t_1, \ldots, t_n \rangle \uparrow \{(t_1, p_1), \ldots, (t_n, p_n)\}$$

where $p_j = \frac{v_j}{\sum_{i=1}^{n} v_i}$ is the absolute probability of retrieving tuple t_j, with $j = 1 \ldots n$

EXEC- C open transition representing the probabilistic response to the requested synchronisation (the sampling):

$$\texttt{uin}(T).P \mid \langle t_1, \ldots, t_n \rangle \uparrow \{\ldots, (t_j, p_j), \ldots\} \xrightarrow{t_j}_{p_j} P[t_j/T] \mid \langle t_1, \ldots, t_n \rangle \setminus t_j$$

where $[\cdot/\cdot]$ represents term substitution in process P continuation, and $\setminus$ is multiset difference, expressing removal of tuple t_j from the tuple space

3.4.4.3 Semantics of `urd` (uniform reading)

As for standard LINDA getter primitives, the only difference between *uniform reading* (`urd`) and uniform consumption (`uin`) is the non-destructive semantics of the reading primitive `urd`. This is reflected by EXEC- R open transition:

EXEC- R the same as EXEC- C, except for the fact that it does not remove matching tuple

$$\texttt{urd}(T).P \mid \langle t_1, \ldots, t_n \rangle \uparrow \{\ldots, (t_j, p_j), \ldots\} \xrightarrow{t_j}_{p_j} P[t_j/T] \mid \langle t_1, \ldots, t_n \rangle$$

whereas other transitions are left unchanged.

Reduction Example

As an example, in the following system state

$$\texttt{uin}(T).P \mid \langle ta, ta, tb, tc \rangle$$

where $\mu(T, tx)$ holds for $x = a, b, c$, the following synchronisation transitions are enabled:

(a) $\texttt{uin}(T).P \mid \langle ta, ta, tb, tc \rangle \xrightarrow{ta}_{0.5} P[ta/T] \mid \langle ta, tb, tc \rangle$

(b) $\texttt{uin}(T).P \mid \langle ta, ta, tb, tc \rangle \xrightarrow{tb}_{0.25} P[tb/T] \mid \langle ta, ta, tc \rangle$

(c) $\texttt{uin}(T).P \mid \langle ta, ta, tb, tc \rangle \xrightarrow{tc}_{0.25} P[tc/T] \mid \langle ta, ta, tb \rangle$

For instance, if transition *(a)* wins the probabilistic selection, then the system evolves according to the following trace—simplified by summing up cardinalities and probabilities in order to enhance readability:

$$\text{uin}(T).P \mid \langle ta, ta, tb, tc \rangle$$
$$\xrightarrow{T}$$
$$\text{uin}(T).P \mid \langle ta, ta, tb, tc \rangle \uparrow \{(ta, 2), (tb, 1), (tc, 1)\}$$
$$\hookrightarrow$$
$$\text{uin}(T).P \mid \langle ta, ta, tb, tc \rangle \uparrow \{(ta, \tfrac{1}{2}), (tb, \tfrac{1}{4}), (tc, \tfrac{1}{4})\}$$
$$\xrightarrow[\frac{1}{2}]{ta}$$
$$P[ta/T] \mid \langle ta, tb, tc \rangle$$

References

1. Alves, R., Antunes, F., Salvador, A.: Tools for kinetic modeling of biochemical networks. Nat. Biotechnol. **24**(6), 667–672 (2006). doi:10.1038/nbt0606-667
2. Beal, J., Bachrach, J.: Infrastructure for engineered emergence on sensor/actuator networks. Int. Syst. IEEE **21**(2), 10–19 (2006)
3. de Boer, F.S., Palamidessi, C.: Embedding as a tool for language comparison. Inf. Comput. **108**(1), 128–157 (1994). doi:10.1006/inco.1994.1004
4. Bravetti, M.: Expressing priorities and external probabilities in process algebra via mixed open/closed systems. Electron. Notes Theor. Comput. Sci. **194**(2), 31–57 (2008). doi:10.1016/j.entcs.2007.11.003
5. Bravetti, M., Gorrieri, R., Lucchi, R., Zavattaro, G.: Quantitative information in the tuple space coordination model. Theoret. Comput. Sci. **346**(1), 28–57 (2005). doi:10.1016/j.tcs.2005.08.004
6. Busi, N., Gorrieri, R., Zavattaro, G.: On the expressiveness of linda coordination primitives. Inf. Comput. **156**(1), 90–121 (2000)
7. Cabri, G., Leonardi, L., Zambonelli, F.: MARS: A programmable coordination architecture for mobile agents. IEEE Int. Comput. **4**(4), 26–35 (2000). doi:10.1109/4236.865084
8. Cardelli, L.: On process rate semantics. Theor. Comput. Sci. **391**(3), 190–215 (2008)
9. Casadei, M., Viroli, M.: Toward approximate stochastic model checking of computational fields for pervasive computing systems. In: Pitt, J. (ed.) Self-Adaptive and Self-Organizing Systems Workshops (SASOW), pp. 199–204. IEEE CS (2013). doi:10.1109/SASOW.2012.42. 2012 IEEE Sixth International Conference (SASOW 2012), Lyon, France, 10-14 Sep. 2012. Proceedings
10. Casadei, M., Viroli, M., Gardelli, L.: On the collective sort problem for distributed tuple spaces. Sci. Comput. Program. **74**(9), 702–722 (2009). doi:10.1016/j.scico.2008.09.018
11. Ciocchetta, F., Hillston, J.: Bio-PEPA: A framework for the modelling and analysis of biological systems. Theor. Comput. Sci. **410**(33–34), 3065–3084 (2009). doi:10.1016/j.tcs.2009.02.037. Concurrent Systems Biology: To Nadia Busi (1968–2007)
12. De Nicola, R., Latella, D., Katoen, J.P., Massink, M.: StoKlaim: A stochastic extension of Klaim. Tech. Rep. 2006-TR-01, Istituto di Scienza e Tecnologie dell'Informazione "Alessandro Faedo" (ISTI) (2006). http://www1.isti.cnr.it/~Latella/StoKlaim.pdf
13. De Wolf, T., Holvoet, T.: Design patterns for decentralised coordination in self-organising emergent systems. In: Engineering Self-organising Systems, pp. 28–49. Springer (2007)
14. Denti, E., Natali, A., Omicini, A.: Programmable coordination media. In: Garlan, D., Le Métayer, D. (eds.) Coordination Languages and Models, LNCS, vol. 1282, pp. 274–288. Springer (1997). doi:10.1007/3-540-63383-9
15. Denti, E., Natali, A., Omicini, A.: On the expressive power of a language for programming coordination media. In: 1998 ACM Symposium on Applied Computing (SAC'98), pp. 169–177. ACM, Atlanta, GA, USA (1998)

16. Di Pierro, A., Hankin, C., Wiklicky, H.: Probabilistic KLAIM. In: De Nicola, R., Ferrari, G.L., Meredith, G. (eds.) Coordination Models and Languages, *LNCS*, vol. 2949, pp. 119–134. Springer Berlin/Heidelberg (2004). doi:10.1007/978-3-540-24634-3
17. Di Pierro, A., Hankin, C., Wiklicky, H.: Probabilistic Linda-based coordination languages. In: de Boer, F.S., Bonsangue, M.M., Graf, S., de Roever, W.P. (eds.) 3rd International Conference on Formal Methods for Components and Objects (FMCO'04), LNCS, vol. 3657, pp. 120–140. Springer, Berlin, Heidelberg (2005). doi:10.1007/11561163
18. Dorigo, M., Birattari, M.: Ant colony optimization. In: Sammut, C., Webb, G. (eds.) Encyclopedia of Machine Learning, pp. 36–39. Springer US (2010). doi:10.1007/978-0-387-30164-8
19. Fernandez-Marquez, J.L., Di Marzo Serugendo, G., Arcos, J.L.: Infrastructureless spatial storage algorithms. ACM Trans. Auton. Adapt. Syst. (TAAS) **6**(2), 15 (2011)
20. Fernandez-Marquez, J.L., Di Marzo Serugendo, G., Montagna, S., Viroli, M., Arcos, J.L.: Description and composition of bio-inspired design patterns: a complete overview. Nat. Comput. **12**(1), 43–67 (2013). doi:10.1007/s11047-012-9324-y
21. Fernandez-Marquez, J.L., Serugendo, G.D.M., Montagna, S.: Bio-core: Bio-inspired self-organising mechanisms core. Bio-Inspired Models of Networks. Information, and Computing Systems, Lecture Notes of the Institute for Computer Sciences, Social Informatics and Telecommunications Engineering, vol. 103, pp. 59–72. Springer, Berlin, Heidelberg (2012)
22. Gardelli, L., Viroli, M., Casadei, M., Omicini, A.: Designing self-organising MAS environments: The collective sort case. In: D. Weyns, H.V.D. Parunak, F. Michel (eds.) Environments for MultiAgent Systems III, LNAI, vol. 4389, pp. 254–271. Springer (2007). doi:10.1007/978-3-540-71103-2
23. Gardelli, L., Viroli, M., Omicini, A.: On the role of simulations in engineering self-organising MAS: The case of an intrusion detection system in TuCSoN. In: Brueckner, S.A., Di Marzo Serugendo, G., Hales, D., Zambonelli, F. (eds.) Engineering Self-Organising Systems, LNAI, vol. 3910, pp. 153–168. Springer, Berlin, Heidelberg (2006). doi:10.1007/11734697. 3rd International Workshop (ESOA 2005), Utrecht, The Netherlands, 26 July 2005. Revised Selected Papers
24. Gardelli, L., Viroli, M., Omicini, A.: Combining simulation and formal tools for developing self-organizing MAS. In: Uhrmacher, A.M., Weyns, D. (eds.) Multi-Agent Systems: Simulation and Applications, Computational Analysis, Synthesis, and Design of Dynamic Systems, Chap. 5, pp. 133–165. CRC Press (2009). http://crcpress.com/product/isbn/9781420070231
25. Gelernter, D.: Generative communication in Linda. ACM Trans. Program. Lang. Syst. **7**(1), 80–112 (1985). doi:10.1145/2363.2433
26. Gillespie, D.T.: Exact stochastic simulation of coupled chemical reactions. J. Phys. Chem. **81**(25), 2340–2361 (1977). doi:10.1021/j100540a008
27. Gilmore, S., Hillston, J.: The PEPA workbench: A tool to support a process algebra-based approach to performance modelling. In: Haring, G., Kotsis, G. (eds.) Computer Performance Evaluation Modelling Techniques and Tools, Lecture Notes in Computer Science, vol. 794, pp. 353–368. Springer, Berlin, Heidelberg (1994). doi:10.1007/3-540-58021-2
28. Hermanns, H.: Interactive Markov Chains: And the Quest for Quantified Quality. Springer (2002)
29. Mamei, M., Menezes, R., Tolksdorf, R., Zambonelli, F.: Case studies for self-organization in computer science. J. Syst. Architect. **52**(8), 443–460 (2006)
30. Mariani, S.: On the "local-to-global" issue in self-organisation: Chemical reactions with custom kinetic rates. In: Eighth IEEE International Conference on Self-adaptive and Self-organizing Systems Workshops, SASOW 2014, Eighth IEEE International Conference on Self-Adaptive and Self-organizing Systems Workshops, SASOW 2014, pp. 61–67. IEEE, London, UK (2014). doi:10.1109/SASOW.2014.14. Best student paper award
31. Mariani, S., Omicini, A.: Probabilistic embedding: Experiments with tuple-based probabilistic languages. In: 28th ACM Symposium on Applied Computing (SAC 2013), pp. 1380–1382. Coimbra, Portugal (2013). doi:10.1145/2480362.2480621. Poster Paper

32. Mariani, S., Omicini, A.: Probabilistic modular embedding for stochastic coordinated systems. In: Julien, C., De Nicola, R. (eds.) Coordination Models and Languages, LNCS, vol. 7890, pp. 151–165. Springer (2013). doi:10.1007/978-3-642-38493-6. 15th International Conference (COORDINATION 2013), Florence, Italy, 3–6 June 2013. Proceedings

33. Mariani, S., Omicini, A.: Coordination mechanisms for the modelling and simulation of stochastic systems: The case of uniform primitives. SCS M&S Magazine **IV**, 6–25 (2014). Special Issue on "Agents and Multi-Agent Systems: From Objects to Agents"

34. Merelli, E., Armano, G., Cannata, N., Corradini, F., d'Inverno, M., Doms, A., Lord, P., Martin, A., Milanesi, L., Möller, S., Schroeder, M., Luck, M.: Agents in bioinformatics, computational and systems biology. Briefings Bioinf. **8**(1), 45–59 (2007). doi:10.1093/bib/bbl014

35. Minsky, N.H., Ungureanu, V.: Law-Governed interaction: A coordination and control mechanism for heterogeneous distributed systems. ACM Trans. Soft. Eng. Methodol. (TOSEM) **9**(3), 273–305 (2000). doi:10.1145/352591.352592

36. Nagpal, R.: A catalog of biologically-inspired primitives for engineering self-organization. In: Engineering Self-organising Systems, pp. 53–62. Springer (2004)

37. Nardini, E., Omicini, A., Viroli, M.: Description spaces with fuzziness. In: Palakal, M.J., Hung, C.C., Chu, W., Wong, W.E. (eds.) 26th Annual ACM Symposium on Applied Computing (SAC 2011), vol. II: Artificial Intelligence & Agents, Information Systems, and Software Development, pp. 869–876. ACM, Tunghai University, TaiChung, Taiwan (2011). doi:10.1145/1982185.1982375

38. Omicini, A.: Formal ReSpecT in the A&A perspective. Electron. Notes Theor. Comput. Sci. **175**(2), 97–117 (2007). doi:10.1016/j.entcs.2007.03.006

39. Omicini, A.: Nature-inspired coordination for complex distributed systems. In: Intelligent Distributed Computing VI, pp. 1–6. Springer (2013)

40. Omicini, A.: Nature-inspired coordination models: Current status, future trends. ISRN Softw. Eng. **2013** (2013). doi:10.1155/2013/384903

41. Omicini, A., Denti, E.: Formal ReSpecT. Electron. Notes Theor. Comput. Sci. **48**, 179–196 (2001). doi:10.1016/S1571-0661(04)00156-2

42. Omicini, A., Denti, E.: From tuple spaces to tuple centres. Sci. Comput. Program. **41**(3), 277–294 (2001). doi:10.1016/S0167-6423(01)00011-9

43. Omicini, A., Viroli, M.: Coordination models and languages: From parallel computing to self-organisation. Knowl. Eng. Rev. **26**(1), 53–59 (2011). doi:10.1017/S026988891000041X

44. Omicini, A., Zambonelli, F.: Coordination for Internet application development. Auton. Agent. Multi-Agent Syst. **2**(3), 251–269 (1999). doi:10.1023/A:1010060322135

45. Parunak, H.V.D., Brueckner, S., Sauter, J.: Digital pheromone mechanisms for coordination of unmanned vehicles. In: Castelfranchi, C., Johnson, W.L. (eds.) 1st International Joint Conference on Autonomous Agents and Multiagent systems, vol. 1, pp. 449–450. ACM, New York, NY, USA (2002). http://dx.doi.org/10.1145/544741.544843

46. Pérez, P.G., Omicini, A., Sbaraglia, M.: A biochemically inspired coordination-based model for simulating intracellular signalling pathways. J. Simul. **7**(3), 216–226 (2013)

47. Shapiro, E.: Separating concurrent languages with categories of language embeddings. In: 23rd Annual ACM Symposium on Theory of Computing (STOC'91), pp. 198–208. ACM, New York, NY, USA (1991). doi:10.1145/103418.103423

48. Tchao, A.E., Risoldi, M., Di Marzo Serugendo, G.: Modeling self-* systems using chemically-inspired composable patterns. In: Self-Adaptive and Self-organizing Systems (SASO), 2011 Fifth IEEE International Conference on, pp. 109–118 (2011). doi:10.1109/SASO.2011.22

49. Viroli, M., Casadei, M.: Biochemical tuple spaces for self-organising coordination. In: Field, J., Vasconcelos, V.T. (eds.) Coordination Languages and Models, LNCS, vol. 5521, pp. 143–162. Springer, Lisbon, Portugal (2009). doi:10.1007/978-3-642-02053-7

50. Viroli, M., Casadei, M., Montagna, S., Zambonelli, F.: Spatial coordination of pervasive services through chemical-inspired tuple spaces. ACM Trans. Auton. Adapt. Syst. **6**(2), 14:1–14:24 (2011). doi:10.1145/1968513.1968517

51. Viroli, M., Casadei, M., Omicini, A.: A framework for modelling and implementing self-organising coordination. In: Shin, S.Y., Ossowski, S., Menezes, R., Viroli, M. (eds.) 24th

Annual ACM Symposium on Applied Computing (SAC 2009), vol. III, pp. 1353–1360. ACM, Honolulu, Hawai'i, USA (2009). doi:10.1145/1529282.1529585

52. Wegner, P.: Why interaction is more powerful than algorithms. Commun. ACM **40**(5), 80–91 (1997). doi:10.1145/253769.253801

53. Wegner, P., Goldin, D.: Computation beyond Turing machines. Commun. ACM **46**(4), 100–102 (2003). doi:10.1145/641205.641235

54. Zambonelli, F., Omicini, A., Anzengruber, B., Castelli, G., DeAngelis, F.L., Di Marzo Serugendo, G., Dobson, S., Fernandez-Marquez, J.L., Ferscha, A., Mamei, M., Mariani, S., Ye, J.: Developing pervasive multi-agent systems with nature-inspired coordination. Pervasive Mob. Comput. **17**, 236–252 (2015). doi:10.1016/j.pmcj.2014.12.002. Special Issue "10 years of Pervasive Computing" In Honor of Chatschik Bisdikian

55. Zambonelli, F., Viroli, M.: Architecture and metaphors for eternally adaptive service ecosystems. In: Intelligent Distributed Computing, Systems and Applications, Studies in Computational Intelligence, vol. 162/2008, pp. 23–32. Springer (2008). doi:10.1007/978-3-540-85257-5. 2nd International Symposium on Intelligent Distributed Computing (IDC 2008), Catania, Italy, 18–19 Sep. 2008. Proceedings

Chapter 4
Coordination of Pervasive Systems

Abstract In this chapter a novel approach to coordination in situated Multi-Agent Systems (MAS) is described, by presenting a meta-model for situated MAS engineering, an architecture for the design of tuplespace-based middleware for situated coordination, and a language dealing with situatedness-related issues. Accordingly, a review of meta-models and architectures from an historical perspective discusses their evolution, up to a reference meta-model and abstract architecture (Sect. 4.1); then, instantiation of the reference architecture on the TuCSoN middleware is described, focussing on the issue of environmental situatedness (Sect. 4.2); finally, spatial situatedness is analysed, by describing how the ReSpecT language deals with it (Sect. 4.3).

4.1 The Quest Towards Situatedness in MAS

Nowadays, *activities* in computational systems are typically modelled by means of *agents* in MAS. Modelling activities through agents basically means representing *actions* along with their motivations—namely, the *goals* that determine and explain the agent's course of actions [10]. Handling *dependencies* among activities in MAS is in essence a *coordination* problem [21].

Accordingly, *coordination models* are the most suitable conceptual tools to harness complexity in MAS [13]. Through the notion of *social action* [9], dependencies are modelled in MAS in terms of agent *societies*, in turn represented computationally by means of *coordination artefacts* [41], also called *coordination media* [12].

However, agents and societies are not the only main bricks for MAS: *environment* is an essential abstraction for MAS modelling and engineering [56], which needs to be suitably represented, and related to agents. This is the core of the notion of *situated action*, as the realisation that coordinated, social, intelligent action arises from strict interaction with the environment, rather than from rational practical reasoning [51].

The need for *situatedness* of agents and MAS is often translated into the requirement of being sensitive to *environment change* [18]. This basically means dependency, again: so, agent activity should be affected by environment change.

In all, this means that *(i)* things happen in a MAS because of either agent activities or environment change—the only two sources of *events* in MAS—*(ii)* complexity

© Springer International Publishing AG 2016
S. Mariani, *Coordination of Complex Sociotechnical Systems*,
Artificial Intelligence: Foundations, Theory, and Algorithms,
DOI 10.1007/978-3-319-47109-9_4

arises from both agent–agent and agent–environment dependencies—roughly speaking, from both *social* and *situated* interaction. Also, this suggests that coordination—in charge of *managing dependencies* [21]—could be used to deal with both forms of dependencies in a uniform way; so, also, that coordination artefacts could be exploited to handle both social and situated interaction [35].

Accordingly, an agent-oriented, *event-driven architecture* for situated pervasive systems is described, that exploits coordination to handle both social and situated interaction. By focussing on situatedness, it is first observed the evolution of the notion of environment in MAS meta-models (Sect. 4.1.1), then the approach to situatedness of some well-known agent frameworks is analysed (Sect. 4.1.2). The reference architecture is presented and detailed (Sect. 4.1.3), then its implementation within the TuCSoN middleware for MAS coordination [42] is discussed (Sect. 4.2).

4.1.1 Review of Meta-Models

A linear account of the evolution of the concepts and ideas within any field of human knowledge is likely to be at the same time artificial and essential. Artificial, in that evolution of concepts is actually never linear, so that for instance several contrasting ideas typically coexist altogether at the same time on the same subject in the same field. Essential, in that understanding history of ideas typically requires some linearisation, for instance when trying to explain the emergence of new concepts, or, to foresee the next steps of their evolution.

In this section a short linear account of the evolution of agent-oriented *meta-models* along the years is provided, by focussing on the abstractions adopted to address the issues of *situatedness* and *coordination* in MAS engineering.

4.1.1.1 Activities by Agents

While the essential role of the environment was made clear since the early days of research on MAS [18]—mostly based on the work on reactive agents [6, 14]—all the focus then was on activities, with no abstractions devoted to model either environment change or dependencies. Figure 4.1 roughly depicts the corresponding (implicit) meta-model. There, first of all, agents' only means of interaction is by messages exchange. This means that inter-agent dependencies are basically dealt with via inter-agent communication, handling all coordination issues at the individual level—using the so-called *subjective* approach to coordination [36, 50]. Furthermore, no specific abstraction is devoted to *environment engineering* [56]: every agent is basically supposed to directly deal with environment resources, thus providing no specific support to agent-environment interaction.

So, on the one hand, the only thing that makes things happen in a MAS are activities, modelled through agents. On the other hand, any sort of situatedness requires

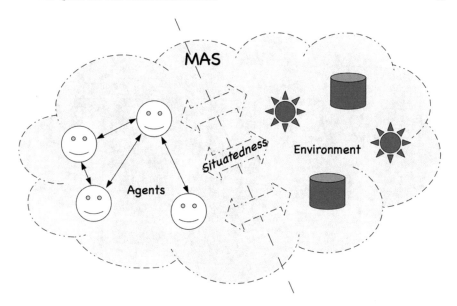

Fig. 4.1 MAS meta-model in the early days of MAS history: only activities are explicitly accounted for, modelled as agents, and the only way to handle their mutual dependencies is essentially by *plain communication* [28]

ad-hoc solutions—such as bridges to lower level languages—with no general-purpose abstraction to directly support environment engineering.

4.1.1.2   Environment Change by Agents

When the notion of environment was not yet recognised as a first-class MAS abstraction—as the one of agent—but as a sort of technical missing link between agent technology and real-world applications, the easiest approach to environment modelling in MAS was quite obvious: environment resources and properties are represented and manipulated by *environment agents*, acting as wrappers—as in [11], for instance.

Thus, no novel, specific abstraction is provided for capturing environment change: simply, the agent abstraction is somehow abused, exploiting autonomy just to reproduce unpredictable behaviour. Correspondingly, situatedness is (poorly) handled merely as inter-agent communication.

Figure 4.2 depicts the corresponding MAS scenario: a software layer of environmental agents is built upon the lower level of environmental resources—the one of low-level languages and legacy API. In this way, situatedness of proper agents (those on the left side of Fig. 4.2) is just a consequence of their communication with their reactive siblings (those within the "*Layer 1*" frame). As far as dependencies are concerned, nothing new happens: agents in a MAS are still a bunch of threads

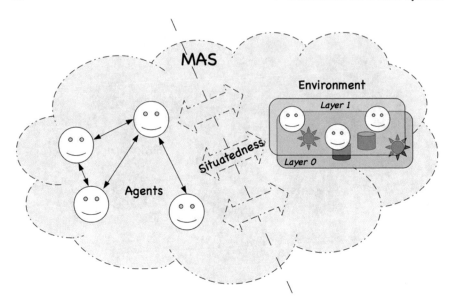

Fig. 4.2 MAS environment recognised as a technical issue in MAS design: environment activities are delegated to wrapper environment agents; both coordination and situatedness are correspondingly reduced to message passing issues [28]

exchanging messages, and the reach of subjective coordination is extended to cover all dependencies among activities, including agent–environment interactions.

4.1.1.3 Coordination for Social Dependencies

Since MAS became the reference paradigm for complex computational systems [43], direct inter-agent communication turned out to be a feeble solution for handling non-trivial dependencies. The recognition that an *interaction space* exists in MAS, and is a primary source of complexity, made the need of specific abstractions emerge, devoted to the management of social interaction.

Along this line—as depicted in Fig. 4.3—the importance of governing the interaction space *outside* the agents was recognised, and the shift towards *objective coordination* began [36, 50], that is, coordination provided to agents *as a service* [53], rather than cooperatively built by agent themselves through communication protocols. Starting from the simplest attempts, such as inter-agent communication protocols and individual agent mailboxes, a number of general-purpose *coordination models* were defined [44]—such as TuCSoN [42], Lime [46], and MARS [7]—allowing MAS engineers to manage MAS interaction space via coordination artefacts—handling social dependencies by ruling agent–agent interaction [13].

However, no specific attention is still devoted here to the interaction with MAS environment, since environment representation lacks suitable abstractions supporting

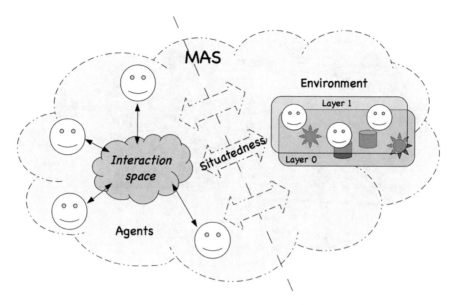

Fig. 4.3 The existence of an *interaction space* outside the agents is recognised, requiring suitable abstractions to be modelled and governed; agent–environment interactions are not considered as part of the space [28]

agent–environment dependencies. Thus, even though clearly a coordination issue, situatedness here is still conceived as a separated problem independent of coordination, and consequently managed just at the technology level—that is, according to the custom solutions provided by the MAS development framework at hand.

4.1.1.4   Coordination for All Dependencies

As soon as situatedness is considered as a proper coordination issue, since it deals with agent–environment interaction, the chance of a uniform meta-model emerges, which could handle both social and situated dependencies in a coherent way. This is for instance the view promoted by the TuCSoN architecture [26], where ReSpecT tuple centres work as coordination artefacts handling both agent–agent and agent–environment interaction [23].

The corresponding meta-model is depicted in Fig. 4.4, where also interaction with MAS environment is considered to be part of the MAS interaction space—now, a *situated coordination space*—promoting a view of MAS in which all dependencies are uniformly handled by coordination abstractions [26]. In this scenario, the property of being situated can be interpreted at both the individual *agent level* and at the overall *system level*, as a property belonging to the whole coordinated MAS—since agent–environment interaction can be handled at both the individual and at the social level by coordination artefacts [41].

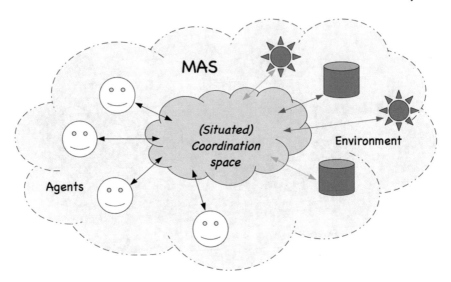

Fig. 4.4 The fundamental role of *situated coordination* in supporting situatedness in MAS is recognised: thus, a uniform, coherent, and comprehensive *situated coordination service* is provided to promote a system-level view of MAS coordination [28]

4.1.2 Review of Architectures

Agent-oriented programming frameworks bring agent abstractions to life, by reifying agent (meta-)models, and making them available to MAS engineers. It is then easy to understand how the conceptual evolution devised in Sect. 4.1 led to different frameworks for MAS development over the years.

Accordingly, in this section agent-oriented *architectures* are focussed, as they are adopted by some well-known agent-oriented programming frameworks, and a discussion about how they address the issues of situatedness and coordination in the engineering of MAS is provided. In particular, three MAS development frameworks are analysed, that is, JADE, Jason, and CArtAgO, chosen for their relevance and widespread adoption, as well as for their belonging to different periods of MAS research.

4.1.2.1 Activities, Dependencies, Environment Change in JADE

JADE (Java Agent DEvelopment framework)[1] [4] is a Java-based framework providing an API and a run-time middleware to develop and deploy agent-based applications in compliance with FIPA[2] standards for MAS. Generally speaking, JADE most

---

[1]http://jade.tilab.com/.

[2]http://www.fipa.org/.

notable features are: transparent message passing based on FIPA ACL (agent communication language), white and yellow pages services, support for strong mobility, and built-in FIPA protocols.

The most relevant architectural components of the JADE middleware are:

Agents—JADE agents are Java objects executed by a single thread of control. The ability to pursue different goals at the same time is provided by JADE *behaviour model*: each agent has a set of behaviours (again, Java objects) representing task-achieving jobs, which are executed by a non-preemptive round-robin scheduler internal to the agent (thus hidden to JADE programmers). The only means agents have to communicate (and coordinate) is by exchanging FIPA ACL messages

ACC—The Agent Communication Channel is the run-time facility in charge of *asynchronous* delivery of messages: each agent has its own mailbox, and is notified upon reception of any message, whereas if and when to process the message is left to the agent's own deliberation—for the sake of preserving its autonomy

FIPA protocols—JADE supports FIPA standard *communication protocols* (built on top of ACC services) by providing built-in behaviours that the programmer extends by specifying what to do in each step of the protocol: upon reception of the expected message according to the protocol state, the proper callback method is automatically called by JADE run-time

In relation to the pictures in Sect. 4.1.1 it can be stated that: *(i)* agents are the abstractions to handle activities in JADE; *(ii)* JADE provides no specific environment abstraction, so that JADE agents have to be used to capture environment change, too; and *(iii)* the only JADE abstraction to handle dependencies is the FIPA protocol, governing agent–agent communication. Accordingly, Fig. 4.5 relates JADE architectural model with the meta-model of Fig. 4.3, emphasising how JADE agents are abused to represent environment properties and resources.

As a result, the implicit JADE coordination model is somehow a hybrid one, borrowing from both subjective and objective coordination: on the one hand, most is charged upon subjective coordination, since coordination is based on protocols, and protocols are implemented as agent behaviours; on the other hand, the fact that protocols are behaviours—hence, Java objects different from agents—makes it possible to separate to some extent the coordination (social) logic (indeed, inside the protocols) from the agent (individual) logic (inside non-protocol agents' behaviours). Also, as depicted in Fig. 4.5, situatedness in JADE is merely handled as an inter-agent communication issue.

4.1.2.2   Activities, Dependencies, Environment Change in Jason

Jason[3] [5] is both a programming language, an agent development framework, and a runtime system. As a language, it implements a dialect of AgentSpeak [47]; as a development framework, it comes with an API to design agents and MAS; as a

---

[3]http://jason.sourceforge.net/.

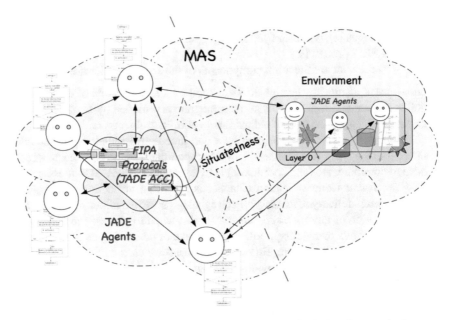

Fig. 4.5 In JADE, the only abstraction given to handle dependencies is that of *protocol*, whereas no specific abstraction exists for the environment; agent–agent interaction can be governed by FIPA communication protocols, and situatedness is achieved through *environment agents* [28]—that is, agents deployed ad-hoc to model the environment and represent its change

runtime system, it provides the infrastructure needed to execute a MAS—in a non-distributed setting; to enable distribution, an integration with JASON exists.

Although Jason is entirely programmed in Java, it features BDI agents, so that a higher level language (the Jason language) is used to program Jason agents using BDI architectural abstractions. Jason natively supports the notion of MAS environment and situatedness: in particular, Jason agents are said to be *situated* in an environment since they can *sense* it through sensors, and *act* upon it through actuators. Jason sensors and actuators have to be implemented directly using Java—along with all the environment resources needed to model the MAS environment.

As a result, Jason architectural components that are worth to be mentioned here are:

Agents—Jason agents are BDI architectures whose reasoning cycle encompasses environment perception, beliefs update, message exchange, plan selection/execution, action. Different plans can be executed concurrently as expected by a goal-directed agent architecture. Jason agents can also interact *(i)* directly by sharing goals/plans/beliefs (via messages) as well as *(ii)* indirectly by acting upon the environment—knowing that other agents will perceive any environment change

Messages—By exploiting message passing, Jason agents can exchange data structures belonging to the BDI architecture, such as goals, plans, and beliefs. Neither

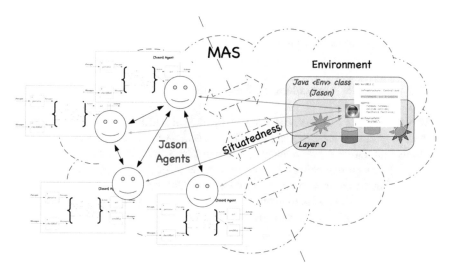

Fig. 4.6 In Jason, there is no abstraction for the interaction space whereas a (limited) layer of abstraction for the environment is given through Java objects. Social dependencies are mostly governed by *goal/plan/beliefs sharing*, whereas situatedness is achieved through a *Java-programmed environment layer* featuring individual agents' sensors and actuators [28]

explicit protocols nor specific abstractions to objectively govern the interaction space are provided by Jason

Environment—Unlike JADE, Jason supports the environment as a first-class abstraction in MAS modelling, by automatically updating agent beliefs based upon *perception*, and by providing an environment layer offering an *acting API*. Nevertheless, the environment layer has to be programmed in Java, since no high-level, specific architectural component is provided by Jason

Events—Somehow hidden inside Jason agent architecture, the notion of *event* is what drives agent internal reasoner: almost everything is an event in Jason, from beliefs addition/removal to plan triggering. However, events are *internal to agents*— Sect. 4.1.3 describes a more general notion of event

Figure 4.6 depicts how the Jason architectural model can be mapped upon the architecture in Fig. 4.2: the environment layer is simply based on Java, with no higher level abstraction provided, furthermore no explicit abstraction to govern the interaction space is given neither—other than message passing and goal/plan/beliefs sharing.

Thus, Jason coordination model is in principle a *subjective* one, since agents themselves are in charge of properly coordinate: however, coordination may occur either directly, by means of message passing, or indirectly, that is, mediated by environment perception and action, as in stigmergy-coordinated MAS [32].

Situatedness is still a feature belonging to individual agents, but, unlike JADE, it is achieved through the environment abstractions of sensors ($\rightarrow$ *perception*) and actuators ($\rightarrow$ *action*)—although no specialised architectural component is given except for an abstract Java class.

4.1.2.3 Activities, Dependencies, Environment Change in CArtAgO

CArtAgO[4] [48] is a Java-based framework and infrastructure based on the A&A (agents & artefacts) meta-model [40]. The A&A meta-model introduces *artefacts* as the tools that agents use to enhance their own capabilities, for achieving their own goals [37]—as human beings do with their tools [29]. So, artefacts can be used to (computationally) represent any kind of environmental resource within a MAS in a uniform way: from sensors to actuators, from databases to legacy OO applications, from real-world objects to virtual blackboards.

Given its focus on artefact design, implementation, and run-time support, rather than on agent development, CArtAgO is designed so as to be as much orthogonal as possible w.r.t. the agent platform. Nevertheless, Java bridges exist, e.g. towards both JADE and Jason. Correspondingly, CArtAgO main architectural components are:

Artefacts—Artefacts are the basic bricks in the A&A meta-model, then the basic bricks in the CArtAgO framework, too. Technically, CArtAgO artefacts are Java objects equipped with Java annotations, exploited by CArtAgO runtime infrastructure to recognise available operations (aka *effectors*) and generate observable events (aka *perceptions*). Thus, artefacts are the tools for MAS designers to properly model and implement the portion of the environment agents can control/should deal with

Workspaces—Workspaces play the role of the topological containers for agents and artefacts, representing the agent working environments. In particular, since every agent and every artefact are always associated to a workspace in CArtAgO, workspaces can be used to define the scope of event generation/perception for agents and artefacts

Agent bodies—By exposing *effectors* API and enabling *perception* of environment (artefact-generated) events (through sensors), CArtAgO agent bodies are the architectural components enabling agent interaction with artefacts—thus, in the very end, situatedness, at least from the individual agent viewpoint. Technically, agent bodies work as Java bridges towards existing agent platforms, such as JADE and Jason

Observable events—While implementing artefacts, CArtAgO programmers can define events to be generated in response to specific operation invocations as well as observable states to monitor for changes—generating events as soon as the state changes. Events can then be captured by sensors linked to agent bodies, either proactively got by agent minds, or automatically dispatched to the agents explicitly focussing on the artefact source of the event

---

[4]http://cartago.apice.unibo.it.

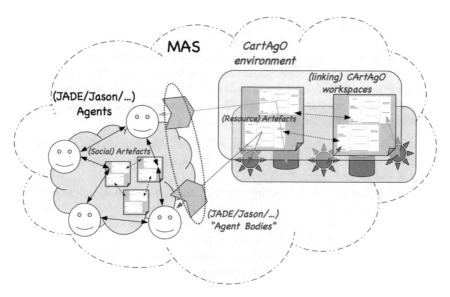

Fig. 4.7 In CArtAgO, MAS environment is modelled through artefacts. Thus, situatedness is the consequence of artefacts use/observation by agent bodies. As regards interactions, artefacts can be used as well, even though they are not explicitly devoted to coordination [28]

Figure 4.7 depicts the aforementioned architectural components along with their mutual relationships. In summary, CArtAgO handles situated interaction by providing artefacts as a means to mediate agents interaction with their environment—via agent bodies. As far as coordination is concerned, neither built-in services nor abstractions are given specifically for that purpose: coordination could be then achieved only by means of ad-hoc-designed social artefacts—e.g. by implementing a channel, a mailbox, a shared blackboard as a coordination artefact.

4.1.3 A Reference Architecture

A well-founded software architecture relies on a well-defined meta-model, that is, the set of concepts and abstractions the architecture is grounded on. Besides setting the architecture within a sound conceptual framework, this makes it possible to place the proposed architecture within the historical perspective taken in Sect. 4.1.1, in particular, by mapping the architecture onto the meta-model depicted in Fig. 4.4.

4.1.3.1   Meta-Model

In the widespread acceptation of MAS nowadays, *agents*, *environment* and *societies* are the three fundamental abstractions around which MAS should be modelled and engineered [41]. While the upcoming meta-model still adopts those three abstractions as its reference conceptual framework, there are three core concepts that motivate the architecture, which the meta-model should account for:

Activities—*Goal-directed/oriented* proceedings resulting into *actions* of any sort, which make things happen within a MAS; through actions, activities in a MAS are *social* [9] and *situated* [51]

Environment change—The (possibly unpredictable) variations in the properties or structure of the world surrounding a MAS that affect it in any way; variations do not express any specific goal, either because this does not exist, or because it has/can not being/be modelled in the MAS

Dependencies—In any non-trivial MAS, activities *depend* on other activities (*social dependencies*), and on environment change (*situated dependencies*); thus, dependencies both motivate and cause *interaction*—both social and situated interaction

The core notion that links the architecture to the meta-model is the one of *event*:

Events—Despite their intrinsic diversity, actions and environment change constitute altogether the only sources of dynamics in a MAS—what makes everything happen; in order to provide a uniform view of MAS dynamics, and a simpler modelling of social and situated dependencies, both actions and environment changes are represented here as *events*

4.1.3.2   Architecture

The reference event-driven architecture for MAS is depicted in Fig. 4.8, and is made of the following components:

Agents—Agents are the autonomous entities in charge of the (goal-directed/oriented, social, and situated) activities, that is, undertaking the course of actions aimed at achieving their own goal. Agents are characterised by their own goals, and articulate their activities in terms of actions. Actions affect either other agents or the environment, leading to social (agent–agent) and situated (agent–environment) interactions. Agents in a MAS are in principle *heterogeneous* and *unpredictable*: either by design or by necessity—as in the case of open MAS

Environment resources—While the notion of environment is quite a hazy one, dealing with MAS makes it possible here to model it as populated by many items, here called *resources*, capable of interacting in some way with a computational system. Resources encapsulate the properties of the environment that are of interest for the agents in a MAS; as such, they are the instruments by which agent actions affect environment properties, and the sources of (possibly unpredictable) changes in

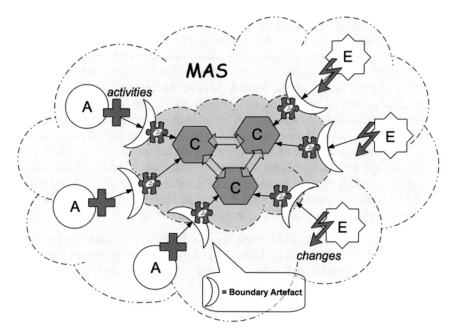

Fig. 4.8 *Boundary artefacts* take care of *events* in the proposed event-driven architecture [28]: they are in charge of mapping activities as well as changes onto events, to be uniformly handled by the *coordination artefacts* within the MAS—responsible for handling dependencies of any sort

    the environment surrounding the MAS. Also environment resources in a MAS are heterogeneous and unpredictable: the variety and dynamics of resources accounts for the diversity and dynamics of MAS environment

Boundary artefacts—Heterogeneity of agents and resources, along with their dissimilar nature, might lead to theoretical and practical problems when dealing with social and situated dependencies. In order to represent all the sources of change in a MAS in a uniform way, without neglecting specificity, a mediating architectural abstraction is first of all required. This is the role of *boundary artefacts*, as the architectural components representing agents as well as environmental resources within the MAS. As such, they work as an interface between the agent (or, the environmental resource) and the MAS interaction space, mapping agents' activities and environment change into events, dispatching them to the *coordination artefacts*, collecting the outcomes of dependency resolution (coordination), then dispatching them back to agents and environmental resources

Coordination artefacts—Coordination artefacts are the components in charge of dealing with *dependencies* in MAS—both social and situated dependencies. As both agents and resources are represented by boundary artefacts within a MAS, coordination artefacts actually work by handling dependencies between events representing agent activities and environment change in a *uniform* way. Thus, dependencies are handled by managing interaction among agents (*social coordination*) and between agents and environmental resources (*situated coordination*)

Events—First of all, boundary artefacts generate *external* events, as the data structures reifying agent activities and environment change. Then, coordination artefacts generate *internal* events, which represent MAS internal activity, related to the management of both social and situated interaction. As coordination artefacts handle events in order to manage dependencies, boundary artefacts translate events coming from coordination artefacts that target either agents or environment resources, thus taking care of heterogeneity of agents and resources. Correspondingly, every event records all the information potentially relevant to coordination, such as its cause (either the agent action or the environment change), spatiotemporal data (when it happened and where), the source and the target entities involved (agents, environment, coordination artefacts), and so on

Summing up, in the abstract architecture depicted by Fig. 4.8 *(i) agents* and *environmental resources* interact through *boundary artefacts*, *(ii)* mapping agent activities and environment changes into *events*, *(iii)* which are then handled by *coordination artefacts*.

4.2   On Situated Coordination

The need for *situatedness* in multi-agent systems (MAS) deployed within pervasive computing scenarios is often translated into the requirement of being sensitive to *environment change* [18], possibly affecting the environment in turn. This requirement lays at the core of the notion of *situated action*—complementing that of *social action* [9]—as those actions arising from strict interaction with the environment [51].

This leads to recognise *dependencies* among agents and the environment as a fundamental source of complexity within a MAS—the other being dependencies between agents' activities [21]. Therefore, *coordination*—as the discipline of managing dependencies [21]—could be used to deal with both *social* and *situated interaction*, by exploiting *coordination artefacts* for handling both social and situated dependencies [35].

As far as situated interaction is concerned, coordination artefacts are required to deal with every facet of situatedness, that is:

- *environmental* situatedness, as the property of a MAS of being immersed in a either computational, physical, or hybrid environment, composed by heterogeneous environmental *resources* (modelled, e.g. through environment artefacts), which may spontaneously generate events in the form of, e.g. environmental properties change, and execute commands dispatched by agents—namely, they can be *sensors*, *actuators*, or both
- *temporal* situatedness, as the property of a MAS of being immersed in a virtual or physical world where a notion of time is, on the one hand, available thus usable for

designing *time-dependant* computations, on the other hand, capable of affecting the MAS dynamics—e.g. introducing *latencies*
- *spatial* situatedness, as the property of a MAS of being immersed in a either virtual or physical space, whose properties—e.g. topology—may, on the one hand, be exploited by software engineers to design *space-dependant* computations, on the other hand, affect the MAS dynamics—e.g. moving devices beyond communication range, moving objects within a robot pathway

The issues above may be dealt with in a number of ways, at different levels. They may be completely delegated to the application, or tackled within the middleware from either the architectural/infrastructural viewpoint, or from a linguistic perspective.

Providing a comprehensive discussion of the viable alternatives and of the approaches existing in the literature would require a book on its own, thus, in the following three examples are described: an architectural approach to situatedness w.r.t. a general computational/physical environment in Sect. 4.3, a linguistic approach to situatedness w.r.t. the temporal dimension of computation in Sect. 4.4, and another linguistic approach to situatedness w.r.t. the spatial dimension of computation in Sect. 4.5. For each approach, also the infrastructural level is considered and the corresponding middleware is provided with application-level API to exploit built-in situatedness-related services. Also, practical usage examples on concrete readily available technologies are discussed.

4.3 Environmental Situatedness in TuCSoN

In this section TuCSoN implementation of the reference architecture is discussed, to provide an example of how to deal with situatedness-related issues from the architectural standpoint, and focussing on situatedness w.r.t. the MAS environment. In particular, Sect. 4.3.1 describes the architectural components devoted to enable situatedness in TuCSoN, then Sect. 4.3.2 overviews the interaction flow supporting situated coordination among the aforementioned components, finally Sect. 4.3.3 describes how to implement situated coordination in TuCSoN and ReSpecT on a demonstrative use case.

4.3.1 Architectural Overview

TuCSoN implements the event-driven architecture just described. In fact, TuCSoN main architectural abstractions (as well as runtime components) are—as depicted in Fig. 4.9:

Agents—Any computational entity relying on TuCSoN coordination services [53] to interact with a TuCSoN-coordinated MAS is a TuCSoN *agent*. This choice,

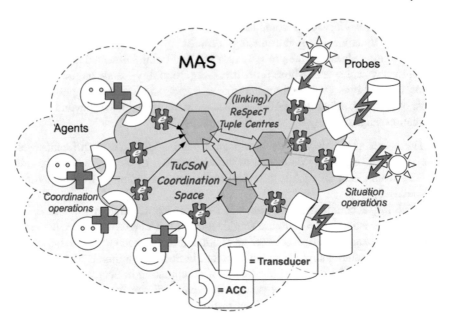

Fig. 4.9 In TuCSoN, both social (agent–agent) and situated (agent–environment) interaction is *mediated* by ReSpecT tuple centres [28]. The unifying abstractions in TuCSoN are ACC and transducers (as *boundary artefacts*), the TuCSoN *event model*, and the ReSpecT tuple centres (as *coordination artefacts*)

when admissible, is modelled by assigning an ACC (see below) to the agent, which mediates its interaction with the MAS. Agents actions result into *coordination operations*, in principle targeting the coordination media (tuple centres), actually handled by the associated ACC

Probes—Environmental resources in TuCSoN are called *probes*. They are uniformly dealt with either as sources of perceptions (like *sensors*) or targets of actions (like *actuators*)—or even both. Actions over probes are called *situated operations*, and are executed by *transducers* (see below): in fact, as for agents, probes do not directly interact with the MAS, but through transducer mediation

ACC—*Agent Coordination Contexts* [30] are TuCSoN boundary artefacts devoted to agents. ACCs both enable and constrain agents interaction capabilities by exposing an API including only the *admissible coordination operations*—according, e.g. to the agent role in the MAS [54]. In particular, ACCs map coordination operations into events, dispatch them to the coordination medium, wait for the outcome of dependency resolution (that is, coordination), then send back to the agent the operation results. ACCs are also fundamental to guarantee and preserve agent autonomy [30]: while the agent is free to choose its course of actions, its associated ACC translates the corresponding events into the MAS interaction space only in case they comply with the agent role, and the state of its interaction [54]

Transducers—Analogously to ACC for agents, **TuCSoN** *transducers* [8] are the boundary artefacts geared towards probes. Each probe is assigned a transducer, which is specialised to handle events from that probe, and to act on probes through situated operations. So, in particular, transducers translate probes property changes into events, which are modelled through the same general event model used for agents' operations—thus leading to a uniform MAS interaction/coordination space

Events—**TuCSoN** adopts and generalises the **ReSpecT** event model, depicted in Table 4.1, representing in a uniform way both events stemming from agents actions and those stemming from changes in the environment—as further explained by Table 4.2. Events are the connectors of the architecture, the run-time data structure reifying any relevant information about the activity or change that generated the events themselves. In particular, **TuCSoN** events record: the *immediate* and *primary* cause of the event [49], its outcome, who is the source of the event, who is its target, when and where the event was generated. Thus, the spatiotemporal fabric is always accounted for by any **TuCSoN** event. Being based on the **ReSpecT** event model, **TuCSoN** events are fully inspectable by **ReSpecT** reactions, hence seamlessly integrated with the tuple centre programmable machinery: this means that the coordination medium—in the case of **TuCSoN**, **ReSpecT** tuple centres—is able to perform computations over MAS events

Tuple centres—**ReSpecT** tuple centres [34] are the **TuCSoN** architectural component working as the coordination artefacts. They are run by the **TuCSoN** middleware to rule and decouple (in *control, reference, space* and *time*) dependencies between agents' activities as well as environment change—in other words, both

Table 4.1 **ReSpecT** situated *event model* [28]

$$\langle Event \rangle ::= \langle StartCause \rangle , \langle Cause \rangle , \langle Evaluation \rangle$$
$$\langle StartCause \rangle , \langle Cause \rangle ::= (\langle Activity \rangle \mid \langle Change \rangle) , \langle Source \rangle , \langle Target \rangle , \langle Time \rangle , \langle Space:Place \rangle$$
$$\langle Source \rangle , \langle Target \rangle ::= \langle AgentId \rangle \mid \langle CoordArtefactId \rangle \mid \langle EnvResId \rangle \mid \bot$$
$$\langle Evaluation \rangle ::= \bot \mid \{\langle Result \rangle\}$$

Table 4.2 **ReSpecT** *triggering events* [28]

$$\langle Activity \rangle ::= \langle Operation \rangle \mid \langle Situation \rangle$$
$$\langle Operation \rangle ::= \texttt{out} (\langle Tuple \rangle) \mid (\texttt{in} \mid \texttt{rd} \mid \texttt{no} \mid \texttt{inp} \mid \texttt{rdp} \mid \texttt{nop} \mid \ldots) (\langle Template \rangle [, \langle Term \rangle])$$
$$\langle Situation \rangle ::= \texttt{env} (\langle Key \rangle , \langle Value \rangle)$$
$$\langle Change \rangle ::= \texttt{env} (\langle Key \rangle , \langle Value \rangle) \mid \texttt{time} (\langle Time \rangle) \mid \texttt{from} (\langle Space \rangle , \langle Place \rangle) \mid$$
$$\texttt{to} (\langle Space \rangle , \langle Place \rangle)$$

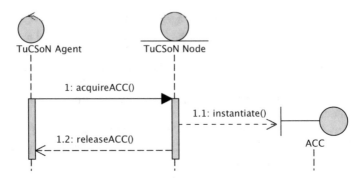

Fig. 4.10 ACC acquisition by TuCSoN agents [27]. Nothing can be done by an agent with the TuCSoN middleware prior to ACC acquisition

social as well as situated interactions [35]. By adopting ReSpecT tuple centres, TuCSoN relies on *(i)* the ReSpecT language to program coordination laws, and *(ii)* the ReSpecT situated event model to reify events

Summing up, TuCSoN tackles the issues of coordination and situatedness in open MAS with a *uniform and coherent* set of abstractions and architectural components: ACC and transducers represent coordinated entities (agents as well as the environment) in the MAS, and translate activities and changes coming from them in a common event model (ReSpecT situated event model), while tuple centres coordinate both social dependencies as well as situated dependencies by allowing the management of events to be programmed using a situatedness-aware coordination language.

The situated architecture just described is necessary to provide *MoK* with the context awareness needed by sociotechnical systems, as discussed in Sect. 5.2 of Chap. 5. Once social and situated interactions generate events according to a situated event model, coordination services, as well as the application at hand, have access to all the relevant information, either for the purpose of coordination, or for users to improve their collaboration towards reaching their business goals.

Within *MoK*, e.g. through situated events reifying social and situated interaction, users may become aware of each other activities, and take advantage of this awareness. Furthermore, being all the interactions mediated by the environment, stigmergic and observation-based coordination are enabled and promoted by default, providing thus all the necessary ingredients for supporting the kind of user behaviour driven coordination envisioned in *MoK*.

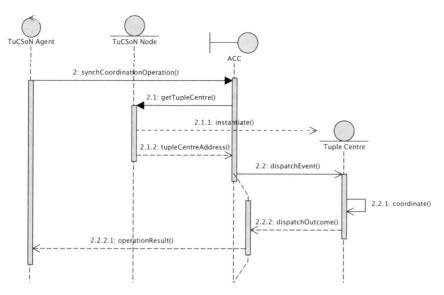

Fig. 4.11 Synchronous operation invocation [27]. The control flow is released back to the agent only when the operation result is available—thus, only when the coordination process ends

4.3.2 Flow of Interactions

4.3.2.1 Agent Side

The *agent side* of a TuCSoN-coordinated MAS is basically represented by the run-time relationships between agents, ACC, and tuple centres. First of all, as depicted in Fig. 4.10, TuCSoN agents have to acquire an ACC before issuing any sort of coordination operation towards the TuCSoN infrastructure. They do so by asking the TuCSoN middleware to release an ACC. Whether an ACC is actually released, and which one among those available,[5] is dynamically determined by the TuCSoN middleware itself, based upon the agent request and its *role* inside the MAS [54].

Once a TuCSoN agent obtains an ACC, all its interactions are mediated by the ACC itself. In particular, as depicted in Fig. 4.11, in case a coordination operation is requested through a *synchronous invocation*:

1. first of all (messages 2 − 2.1.2), the target tuple centre associated to the ACC is dynamically instantiated by the TuCSoN runtime infrastructure, and its network address given to the ACC for further reference
2. then (message 2.2), the ACC takes charge of building the corresponding event and of dispatching it to the tuple centre target of the interaction

---

[5]See the TuCSoN official guide at http://www.slideshare.net/andreaomicini/the-tucson-coordination-model-technology-a-guide.

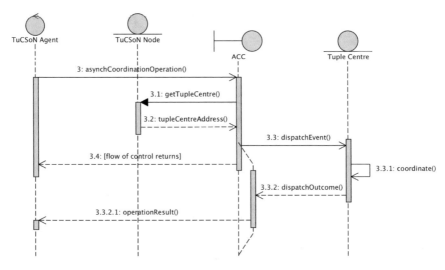

Fig. 4.12 Asynchronous operation invocation [27]. The control flow is released back to the agent as soon as the event related to the request is generated and dispatched by the ACC

3. finally (messages 2.2.1−2.2.2.1), the ACC is notified when the outcome of the coordination operation requested is available—after a proper coordination stage, possibly involving other events from other entities—so that it can send the operation result back to the agent

Only the coordination operation request from the agent to its ACC is a *synchronous method call*: any other interaction is *asynchronous* as well as *event-driven*. This is necessary in every open and distributed scenario, and enables uncoupling in control, reference, space, and time. Nevertheless, in this scenario—synchronous operation invocation—the control flow of the caller agent is retained by the ACC as long as the operation result is not available (message 2.2.2.1).

Conversely, Fig. 4.12 depicts the *asynchronous invocation* scenario: the only difference w.r.t. the synchronous one lays in the fact that the control flow is given back to the caller agent as soon as the corresponding event is dispatched to the target tuple centre (messages 3.3−3.4). The actual result of the requested coordination operation is dispatched to the agent as soon as it becomes available, asynchronously (message 3.3.2.1). TuCSoN lets client agents choose which semantics to use for their coordination operations invocation, either synchronous or asynchronous, so as to preserve their autonomy.

The scenario depicted in Fig. 4.12 assumes that the target tuple centre is already up and running—e.g. as a consequence of a previous operation invocation—thus, the TuCSoN node simply retrieves its reference, and passes it to the ACC.

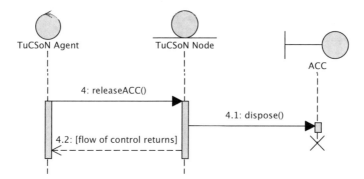

Fig. 4.13 ACC release by TuCSoN agents [27]. Nothing can be done by an agent with the TuCSoN middleware after ACC release

Whenever an agent no longer needs TuCSoN coordination services, it should release its ACC back to TuCSoN middleware, which promptly destroys it in order to prevent resources leakage—as depicted in Fig. 4.13.

Summing up, designers of agents exploiting TuCSoN should make their agents: *(i)* acquire an ACC; *(ii)* choose the invocation semantics for each coordination operation they perform, and *(iii)* expect operations result to be available accordingly; *(iv)* release their ACC when TuCSoN services are no longer needed—at agents shutdown TuCSoN automatically releases orphan ACCs.

4.3.2.2 Environment Side

On the *environment side* of the TuCSoN architecture, agents and ACCs are replaced by probes and transducers, respectively. Thus, first of all, probes should register to the TuCSoN middleware in order to get their transducer and interact—as depicted by Fig. 4.14. After probe registration, any interaction resulting from environmental property change affecting the MAS is mediated by the transducer.

Figure 4.15 depicts interaction among TuCSoN runtime entities in case of a sensor probe, thus a sensor transducer, whereas Fig. 4.16 shows the case of an actuator probe. By comparing the two pictures, the flow of interactions is almost the same, except for the first invocation, which depends on the nature of the probe—either sensor (Fig. 4.15) or actuator (Fig. 4.16).

In particular, perception by a sensor probe works as follows:

1. first of all (messages 2−2.1.2), the target tuple centre associated to the transducer is dynamically instantiated by the TuCSoN runtime infrastructure, and its network address passed to the transducer for further reference
2. then (message 2.2), the transducer builds the event corresponding to the perception operation, and dispatches it to the tuple centre target of the interaction

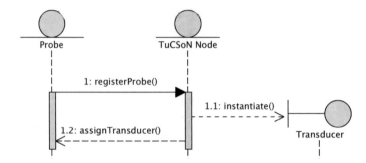

Fig. 4.14 Probes registration and transducers association. No events can be perceived nor actions undertaken on a probe prior to transducer association [27]

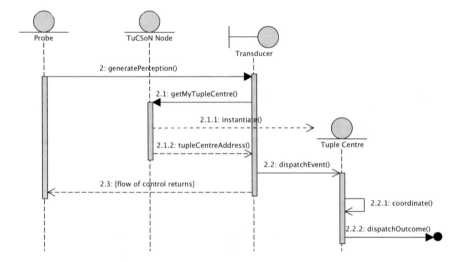

Fig. 4.15 Sensor probe interaction [27]. The control flow returns to the probe as soon as the environmental event is generated and dispatched by the transducer, thus, everything happens asynchronously

3. finally (messages 2.2.1−2.2.2), the tuple centre enacts the coordination process triggered by the event (if any), properly dispatching its outcome

As far as probe interaction is concerned, there is no distinction between synchronous or asynchronous semantics. In fact, being representations of environmental resources, probes are not supposed to expect any feedback from the MAS: they simply cause/undergo changes that are relevant to the MAS. For this reason, the semantics of situation operations invocation on probes is always asynchronous. As depicted in Figs. 4.15 and 4.16 in fact, the control flow is always returned to the probe as soon as the corresponding event is generated.

When a probe is no longer needed, it should be deregistered from TuCSoN, which subsequently destroys the associated transducer—as depicted in Fig. 4.17. Wrapping

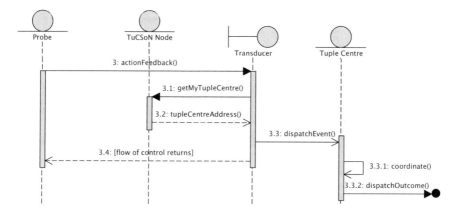

Fig. 4.16 Actuator probe interaction [27]. Again, everything happens asynchronously

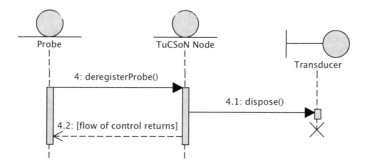

Fig. 4.17 Probe deregistration [27]. Nothing can be either sensed or effected by the MAS upon the deregistered probe, since the mediating transducer is no longer running

up, TuCSoN situatedness services require MAS designers to: *(i)* always register probes causing their transducer instantiation; *(ii)* be aware that environmental events are always generated asynchronously; *(iii)* deregister probes when they are no longer needed—no automatic deregistration is performed by the TuCSoN middleware.

4.3.2.3 Between Agents and Environment: Situated Coordination

Putting together the agent and the environment side of TuCSoN event-driven architecture, Figs. 4.18 and 4.19 depict the synchronous interaction of an agent with a sensor, and the asynchronous interaction of an agent with an actuator, respectively.

By inspecting the whole interaction sequence, one could see how *(i)* TuCSoN ACC and transducers play a central role in supporting distribution and uncoupling of agents and probes within the MAS, and *(ii)* how TuCSoN tuple centres and the ReSpecT language are fundamental to support *situated objective coordination* [36, 50].

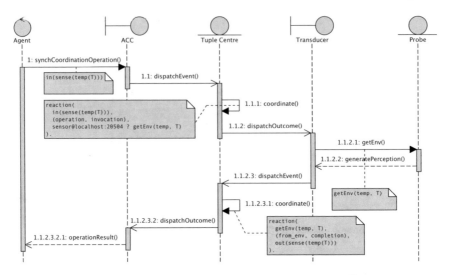

Fig. 4.18 Synchronous situation operation querying a sensor [27]. ReSpecT plays a fundamental role in binding both the agent coordination operation to its corresponding situation operation (annotation in step 1.1.1) and the probe response back to the agent original request (annotation in step 1.1.2.3.1)

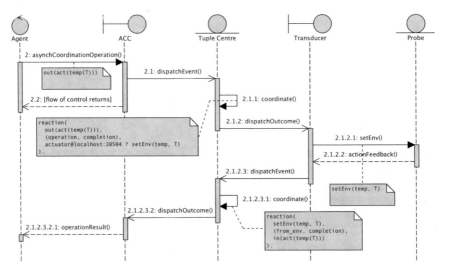

Fig. 4.19 Asynchronous situation operation commanding an actuator [27]. As in Fig. 4.18, ReSpecT role in enabling situatedness is visible in annotations 2.1.1 and 2.1.2.3.1

In particular, in Fig. 4.18 the agent is issuing a synchronous coordination operation request involving a given tuple (sense(temp(T)))—message 1.

After event dispatching (all the dynamic instantiation interactions have been left out for the sake of clarity), the tuple centre target of the operation reacts to invocation by triggering the ReSpecT reaction in annotation 1.1.1, which generates a situated event (step 1.1.2) aimed at executing a situation operation (getEnv(temp, T)) on the probe (sensor).[6] The transducer associated to the tuple centre and responsible for the target probe intercepts the event and takes care of actually executing the operation on the probe (message 1.1.2.1). Reply of the sensor probe (message 1.1.2.2) generates a sequence of events propagation terminating in the response to the original coordination operation issued by the agent (message 1.1.2.3.2.1).

It is worth noticing the role of the tuple centre in supporting situatedness: in fact, step 1.1.2.3.1 properly reacts to the completion of situation operation getEnv(temp, T) by the sensor probe, emitting exactly the tuple originally requested by the agent (sense(temp(T))).

In Fig. 4.19 the sequence of interactions as well as annotations are very similar to those in Fig. 4.18. In particular, annotation 2.1.1 shows how the ReSpecT reaction triggering event matches the event raised as a consequence of agent coordination operation request (act(temp(T))), while annotation 2.1.2.3.1 highlights how the tuple centre maps the situation operation outcome (setEnv(temp, T))[7] in the original tuple (act(temp(T))) through a proper ReSpecT reaction. The only differences w.r.t. Fig. 4.18 are the asynchronous invocation semantics used by the agent and the actuator nature of the interacting probe—thus, messages 2.1.2.1 and 2.1.2.2.

In summary, ReSpecT is fundamental to program TuCSoN tuple centres so as to correctly bind coordination operations with situation operations—while preserving interacting entities' autonomy—, ultimately supporting agent–environment interactions, thus, situatedness, in distributed open MAS.

4.3.3 Methodology: Example Scenario

Imagine many different smart appliances (e.g. smart fridge, smart thermostat, smart lights, smart A/C, etc.) scattered in an indoor environment (e.g. a flat). Either inhabitants have an Android smartphone or a desktop PC is available in the environment (or even both): this ensures the TuCSoN middleware can be running, being the JVM its only requirement. Some kind of connection is available at least between each appliance and the smartphone/desktop—appliances may also be connected together to improve decentralisation and resilience, although not strictly necessary.

Inhabitants want the smart home system to self-manage towards a given goal (e.g. always optimise power consumption) according to their preferences (e.g. prefer turning on fans rather than switching A/C on), while keeping the capability to control

---

[6]Primitive getEnv(temp, T) is an alias for env(temp, T), making explicit that the operation is meant to perceive something from the environment.

[7]Primitive setEnv(temp, T) is an alias for env(temp, T), making explicit that the operation is meant to affect something in the environment.

it despite self-management, when desired (e.g. "I want frozen beers now, forget about power consumption!").

Starting from requirement analysis, the core desiderata of the proposed scenario is, essentially, that environmental resources (e.g. the A/C, the fridge, etc.) should be able to adapt to environment change (e.g. temperature drops, food depletion, etc.) as well as users' actions (e.g."I'm coming home late, order pizza"), striving to achieve a system goal (e.g. optimise inhabitants comfort) while accounting for each user's desires.

According to the TuCSoN meta-model as described in Sect. 4.1.3.1, this can be interpreted as follows:

- users continuously and unpredictably perform their daily *activities*…
- …which may *depend* on the environment being in a certain enabler state (e.g. food must be available to enable cooking dinner), as well as may both impact and be affected by the environment…
- …causing some *change* to happen (e.g. "since I'll be late, delay lights turning on", "there is no food, thus I must go to the grocery shop")

Once recognised that activities and environment change both make *events* happen, thus managing dependencies between activities and change ultimately resort to managing events, a perfect and complete match with TuCSoN reference meta-model is achieved.

As far as the design phase of the software engineering methodology is concerned, once the problem at hand (smart home appliances coordination) has being reinterpreted in light of the TuCSoN meta-model, TuCSoN architecture provides all the necessary components to design a solution. Thus:

- users activities are generated by *agents*, making it possible to also ascribe goals to actions, and mediated by *ACCs*, enabling and constraining interactions according to the system goals
- changes in the environment are generated by *probes* and mediated by *transducers*, enabling uniform representation of properties despite appliances heterogeneity
- activities and change (thus ACCs and transducers) generate *events* as their own representation within the situated MAS coordinated by TuCSoN, which are then managed by *tuple centres* suitably programmed with adaptable coordination laws

Consequently: agents are deployed to users' personal devices (smartphone/desktop pc), probes are deployed to home appliances, ACCs and transducers are deployed either on-board along with agents and probes, respectively (e.g. on the smartphone), or remotely (e.g. on the desktop), tuple centres are deployed again either on-board or remotely, all performing activities and enacting/undergoing changes generating events, automatically handled by TuCSoN according to the designed coordination laws.

It should be noted that a similar scenario has been depicted in [15], although much more thoroughly. There, TuCSoN is taken as the underlying infrastructure on top of which the Butlers Architecture for smart home management is deployed. In particular, agents are used therein to model environmental resources as well (e.g. home appliances), whereas the proposed approach would have modelled them as probes, thus handled (coordinated) within the MAS by transducers.

Benefits of doing so are not limited to a cleaner architecture and separation of concerns, but also include smaller computational load (transducers are simpler than full-fledged agents), better run-time adaptiveness (replacing a transducer is much simpler than replacing an agent), improved management of heterogeneity (despite probes API differences, transducers map any event to a common event model).

Accordingly, an ongoing effort of the authors of [15] is devoted to redesign the Home Manager middleware and application so as to exploit TuCSoN transducers and ReSpecT situatedness-related language features.

4.3.4 Related Work

By considering the technologies described in Sect. 4.1.2, one can easily see how they could be read as progressively improving the way in which MAS deals with environment modelling and situatedness.

The first one, JADE, provides more or less nothing on the environment side, being focussed on supporting agents with a set of services, mostly dedicated to communication, mobility and interoperability. On the coordination side, JADE adopts ACL messages as the data structure to exchange and FIPA protocols as the only means to manage (social) dependencies—thus, in a subjective way. Thus, situated dependencies should be managed without a specific abstraction, by falling back to agents and message passing reuse (or abuse). This can be seen also by considering the (implicit) meta-model behind JADE, that of Fig. 4.3, which somehow recognises the existence of an interaction space between agents, but fails short in taking also MAS environment into account.

When considering Jason, environment modelling improves thanks to an explicit Java environment layer, which enables agents to sense perceptions (mapped into beliefs) and to act on effectors (mapped into Jason internal actions). Furthermore, the notion of event as the central abstraction around which the whole agent inner reasoning cycle as well as its perception–action loop should revolve around is recognised in Jason. Nevertheless, something is still missing on the coordination side: Jason features nothing more than message passing and plans/goals sharing, thus leaving coordination issues to agents themselves. For these reasons, Jason (implicit) meta-model corresponds to the one depicted in Fig. 4.2, although Jason support to situatedness is better w.r.t. JADE.

Finally, CArtAgO is the technology whose architecture is closest to the one described in Sect. 4.1.3—hence, to the TuCSoN architecture, too. To some extent, in fact, the following mapping could be attempted: CArtAgO artefacts are explicitly conceived to model and implement environmental resources (in some sense, the union of probes and transducers, in TuCSoN); agent bodies could be classified as (sorts of) boundary artefacts (they may also resemble TuCSoN ACCs and transducers) although the latter concept is much more generally applicable; CArtAgO observable events are one of the possible implementations of the event abstraction (as TuCSoN events are based on ReSpecT event model). Also, CArtAgO artefacts could as well be used to implement coordination artefacts, e.g. TuCSoN tuple centres.

Nevertheless, the mapping is actually quite imprecise as well as somewhat unnatural. Focussing, for instance, on CArtAgO implementation of the event abstraction, the difference is quite evident: CArtAgO observable events are bound to the artefact they come from, as a means to check the outcome of agents situated actions and to reactively respond to environment stimuli—hence they reify only situated dependencies; whereas events in TuCSoN are the reification of whatever happens within the MAS—hence social dependencies, too.

A much more general difference lies in the artefact abstraction itself: whereas CArtAgO allows MAS designers to program any kind of artefact they need according to any sort of interaction model they decide to ascribe to the artefact (e.g. depending on whether it is a social or situated artefact), TuCSoN provides a fixed set of artefacts—that is, ACCs, transducers and tuple centres—which are both *(i)* each responsible for a general aspect of MAS situated coordination—ACCs for activities, transducers for environment changes, tuple centres for social and situated coordination—and *(ii)* actually specialisable depending on the MAS at hand—e.g. although exposing the same API, transducers behaviour can be specialised according to the nature of the resource they model.

This leads to a fundamental difference w.r.t. *uniformity*: in a CArtAgO-coordinated MAS, artefacts can be *heterogeneous* in both exposed APIs and in semantics, whereas in a TuCSoN-coordinated MAS, ACCs, transducers, and tuple centres have a well-defined semantics which remains coherent regardless of the actual specialisation required. Furthermore, CArtAgO observable events are created by the artefact they belong to in a custom way, that is, by storing the information MAS designers believe to be useful at design time. In TuCSoN instead, the event model used by, e.g. transducers is always the same—actually, ReSpecT event model—regardless of the environmental resource nature or the MAS deployment scenario.

Among the works not considered in Sect. 4.1.2, at least the following two are worth to be mentioned here: the SADE [17] and ELDA [19] development frameworks.

SADE is a development environment for the engineering of self-adaptive MAS. Acknowledging the role played by the environment in MAS, authors adopt the *event* abstraction to design a self-adaptation mechanism based on the *organisation* metaphor—similar to the concept of society. In particular, environmental events are notified to agents according to a publish/subscribe architecture, possibly triggering a change of role—leading to a change of behaviour.

Nevertheless, the environment abstraction is not realised to its full extent. In fact, environmental events are generated by other agents, playing the role of wrappers of that part of the environment which should be observable to the MAS. Furthermore, situatedness support is limited, since the only fields describing an event in [17] are: *(i)* its *type*, which can refer to a change in agents' state, behaviour, role, or offered services; *(ii)* its *source* (the agent who generated it); and *(iii)* a set of *constraints* whose function is not clearly explained—at least in [17].

In ELDA [19] the event abstraction is adopted to design a lightweight agent model—indeed, ELDA. In particular, any ELDA agent is a single-threaded autonomous entity interacting through asynchronous events, whose behaviour is expressed reactively in response to incoming events. Although ELDA does not natively support any environment abstraction, it has been extended to support the PACO model abstractions [20], splitting MAS into four parts: agents, environment, interactions, and organisation.

Nevertheless, the extension seemingly accounts for agents' position only, and the only agent–environment interaction is due to a *monitor agent*—again, a wrapper—which continuously monitor the environment and the agents' state, triggering events when some preconditions are met.

4.4 Temporal Situatedness in ReSpecT

Most of those application scenarios characterised by a high degree of *openness* and *dynamism*, such as pervasive ones, often demand coordination tasks sensible to *timing* aspects. On the one side, temporal *awareness* is necessary to specify and enforce properties on interacting agents such as liveness and quality of service; on the other side, temporal *situatedness* is fundamental for interacting agents willing to provide services in compliance with such properties [39]. In other words, it is needed a coordination-based approach supporting definition of *timed coordination laws* through suitable coordination abstractions.

From the A&A meta-model perspective [49], *coordination artefacts* [40] are the general-purpose run-time abstraction meant to provide agents with coordination as a service [53]. Thus, in following sections, the notion of time-aware coordination media is defined, then tailored to tuple centres coordination media [34], finally implemented in the ReSpecT coordination language [31].

4.4.1 Time-Aware Coordination Media

Timed coordination requires temporal *situatedness* and *awareness* of the coordination media, which translates in a number of technical requirements [39].

4.4.1.1 Situatedness

First of all, a *time-aware coordination abstraction* should at any time be associated to any one notion of time [39].

Local and *relative* time is the most natural choice for *distributed* systems, since it can always be made available without conceptual nor implementation difficulties. Global and absolute time could be reconstructed from there by, e.g. relying on a specific artefact working as a time server (global) and properly labelling time 0 of the artefact so as to exploit relative time as a delta. Finally, *discrete* time is the most natural choice for *computational* systems, enabling any coordination-related event to be labelled by the artefact currently handling it with its own (local, relative and discrete) time.

4.4.1.2 Awareness

Time has to be included in the *ontology* of any time-aware coordination artefact [39], be it *local*, thus referring to the artefact local time flow, or *global*, when, e.g. referring to a shared time server; *relative*, if time starts at artefact boot, or *absolute*, if some convention regarding "time 0" is adopted; *continuous* or *discrete*.

A coordination artefact should allow coordination laws to *talk about time* [39]. An expressive enough set of predicates/functions should be provided to *(i)* manipulate temporal information labelling coordination events and *(ii)* perform computations over time.

Time has to be embedded into the *working cycle* of the coordination artefact [39]. Any one notion of *temporal event* is needed to trigger time-related computations within the artefact, so as to enable expression of time-related coordination laws such as "if servicing of requests takes more than *t* seconds, assign a penalty to the server". So, temporal events should be *spontaneously* generated[8] by the coordination artefact so as to trigger time-related laws as part of the normal working cycle of the artefact.

Coordination artefacts should also be able to *capture* time events and to react appropriately [39], by enforcing the programmed time-aware coordination laws which express behaviours depending on time.

Finally, coordination artefacts should allow coordination policies to be *changed* over time [39], by enabling modifications to the set of coordination laws during time. Accordingly, it should be possible to add/remove coordination laws at run-time, so as to *adapt* the artefact behaviour (thus the coordination process) to the flow of time.

4.4.1.3 Timed Tuple Centres

Timed tuple centres extend tuple centres with the temporal framework just described [39].

---

[8]Care should be taken not to overload the artefact while not being too coarse in time intervals.

As the notion of current time for a tuple centre is chosen a local, relative, and discrete time, thus, no relations can be established between time of two different tuple centres.

Timed reactions—that is, reactions triggered by temporal events—follow the same semantics of other reactions [34]: once triggered, they are placed in the triggered reaction set, and executed, atomically and transactionally, in a non-deterministic order. It is worth noting that at any given time *only one* time event can happen, thus each timed reaction is executed *only once*.

4.4.2 Time-Aware Extension to ReSpecT

Following the timed tuple centre model above, the ReSpecT language [31] can be extended accordingly by *(i)* introducing *temporal predicates* to query tuple centre and event time, and *(ii)* enabling specification of *timed reactions*.

4.4.2.1 Temporal Observation Predicates

Three *temporal observation predicates* are introduced [39]:

`current_time(?T)`—Succeeds if `T` unifies with the current tuple centre time.
`event_time(?T)`—Succeeds if `T` unifies with the tuple centre time when the event triggering current reaction happened.
`start_time(?T)`—Succeeds if `T` unifies with the tuple centre time when the original event triggering the cascade of events causing current reaction happened.

4.4.2.2 Temporal Guard Predicates

Three *temporal guard predicates* are introduced [39]:

`before(@T)`—Succeeds if the current tuple centre time is less than `T`.
`after(@T)`—Succeeds if the current tuple centre time is greater than `T`.
`between(@T1,T2)`—Succeeds if the current tuple centre time is between `T1` and `T2`.

4.4.2.3 Temporal Event Descriptors

Reactions to time events are specified analogously to ordinary reactions [39]:

$$reaction(time(\mathit{Time}),\ \mathit{Guards},\ \mathit{Body}).$$

The intended semantics is that as soon as the tuple centre time reaches the value *Time*, temporal event `time(Time)` is generated, then all timed reactions whose triggering event matches *event descriptor* `time(Time)` are triggered, their *Guards* are evaluated, and (if guards hold) their *Body* is inserted in the triggered reaction set, waiting to be executed.

4.4.2.4   Semantics

With respect to the formal model of [31], a *time transition* is added to tuple centres working cycle, having *priority* over all other transitions—the reacting one there included. *Conceptually*, a time transition is executed at *each* tick of the tuple centre clock, but, in practice, a time transition needs to be executed only when the tuple centre specification actually contains triggerable timed reactions.[9]

4.4.3   Expressiveness Showcase

In order to give the reader a flavour of Timed-ReSpecT expressiveness, here follows some simple yet effective example of time-aware coordination patterns.

4.4.3.1   Expiring Requests

Agents requesting information and/or services may need to receive a reply within a given deadline. If it expires some form of notification of failure should be dispatched to the requesting agent. Furthermore, it is reasonable to track such a failure, e.g. for starting recovery reactions.

This interaction pattern can be easily realised in Timed-ReSpecT by programming tuple centres to react to requests of the kind

```
rd(expiring(Req,DeltaT,Result))
```

meaning that the agent needs to know whether a tuple matching template *Req* is available within *DeltaT* time units. Variable *Result* is unified with a success/failure flag, e.g. yes/no.

Such a behaviour is easily implemented through ReSpecT code in Fig. 4.20. The first reaction intercepts incoming requests causing a pendReq tuple to be reified tracking all the relevant information about the request. The second reaction (triggered by the previous one) checks if tuple Req already occurs, so as to remove tuple pendReq and reply with a positive result tuple. Otherwise, tuple pendReq is consumed and a timed reaction is scheduled for expiring time, to cause both the agent to be provided with a negative reply, and a fault to be reified (tuple failReq).

---

[9] A simple mechanism implemented on top of Java java.util.TimerTask does the job.

```
 1  reaction(
 2      rd(expiring(Req,DeltaT,_)),
 3      (operation,invocation),
 4      (
 5          event_source(Ag),
 6          current_time(CurrT),
 7          ExpT is DeltaT + CurrT,
 8          out(pendReq(Req,Ag,StartT,DeltaT,ExpT))
 9      )).
10  reaction(
11      out(pendReq(Req,Ag,StartT,DeltaT,ExpT)),
12      internal,
13      (
14          rd(Req),
15          in(pendReq(Req,Ag,StartT,DeltaT,ExpT)),
16          out(expiring(Req,_,yes))
17          ;
18          out_s(
19              time(ExpT),
20              internal,
21              (
22                  in(pendReq(Req,Ag,StartT,DeltaT,ExpT)),
23                  out(expiring(Req,_,no)),
24                  out(failReq(Req,Ag,StartT,ExpT))
25              )
26          )
27      )).
28  reaction(
29      out(Tuple),
30      success,
31      (
32          in(pendReq(Tuple,_,_,_,_)),
33          out(expiring(Tuple,_,yes)),
34          out(Tuple),
35          in(Tuple)
36      )).
```

Fig. 4.20 ReSpecT code snippet for the expiring requests pattern (adapted from [39])

4.4.3.2   Leasing

Dually w.r.t. previous example, coordinating agents may want to put tuples in the tuple centre with availability limited in time, to realise some sort of *leasing* concept. Accordingly, tuples may be inserted in the tuple centre with a *lease time*, indicating the maximum time for which they will remain available in the tuple centre before automatic removal.

   Agents insert tuples of the form

```
out(leased(@Time,@Tuple))
```

then ReSpecT code in Fig. 4.21 carries out the desired behaviour. When a tuple with lease time LeaseTime is put in the tuple centre, a timed reaction is scheduled

```
 1  reaction(
 2      out(leased(Tuple,LeaseTime)),
 3      (operation,success),
 4      (
 5          out(Tuple),
 6          current_time(Time),
 7          ExpireTime is Time + LeaseTime,
 8          out_s(
 9              time(ExpireTime),
10              internal,
11              in(Tuple)
12          )
13      )).
```

Fig. 4.21 ReSpecT code snippet for the leasing tuples pattern (adapted from [38])

to be triggered when it expires, so as to remove the tuple in leasing. If the tuple is not found anymore, the timed reaction execution has no effect, for it simply fails.

4.4.3.3   Action Commitment

Agents may want to commit to execute an action within a deadline. One way to do so amounts to allowing an agent to put a tuple signalling future insertion of a tuple matching a given template, within a specified period of time. If this does not occur, a fault is raised.

Such an interaction pattern can be easily realised in Timed-ReSpecT by programming tuple centres to react to requests of the kind

$$out(interval(Templ,T1,T2))$$

causing commitment of the agent to insert a tuple matching $Templ$ in the period $\in [T1, T2]$. In this example, commitment is only relative to first insertion of a tuple matching the template.

Such a behaviour is easily implemented through ReSpecT code in Fig. 4.22. The first reaction intercepts insertion of the commitment tuple: two tuples tracking commitment violations ($notBefore$ and $notAfter$) are added along with two timed reactions for the start and end time of the interval. When the former is triggered, tuple $notBefore$ is removed. When the latter is triggered and tuple $notAfter$ is still available, a fault is raised. The second reaction captures insertion of a matching tuple when not expected: both tuples are removed and a fault is raised. The third reaction captures insertion of a matching tuple when expected: tuple $notAfter$ is removed and tuple $onTime$ is put to reify that the commitment has been respected.

```
1  reaction(
2      out(interval(Templ,T1,T2)),
3      (operation,invocation),
4      (
5          event_source(Ag),
6          in(interval(Templ,T1,T2)),
7          current_time(CurrT),
8          BeginT is CurrT + T1,
9          EndT is CurrT + T2,
10         out(notBefore(Ag,Templ,BeginT)),
11         out(notAfter(Ag,Templ,EndT)),
12         out_s(
13             time(BeginT),
14             internal,
15             in(notBefore(Ag,Templ,BeginT))
16         ),
17         out_s(
18             time(EndT),
19             internal,
20             (
21                 in(notAfter(Ag,Templ,EndT)),
22                 out(outOfTimeFailure(Ag,Tuple,EndT))
23             )
24         )
25     )).
26 reaction(
27     out(Tuple),
28     success,
29     (
30         in(notBefore(Ag,Tuple,BeginT)),
31         in(notAfter(Ag,Tuple,EndT)),
32         event_source(Ag),
33         current_time(CurrT),
34         BeginT > CurrT,
35         out(beforeTimeFailure(Ag,Tuple,CurrT,BeginT))
36     )
37 ).
38 reaction(
39     out(Tuple),
40     success,
41     (
42         event_source(Ag),
43         current_time(CurrT),
44         no(notBefore(Ag,Tuple,BeginT)),
45         in(notAfter(Ag,Tuple,EndT)),
46         out(onTime(Ag,Tuple,BeginT,CurrT,EndT))
47     )).
```

Fig. 4.22 ReSpecT code snippet for the action commitment pattern (adapted from [39])

4.5 Spatial Situatedness in ReSpecT

MAS deployed in pervasive computing scenarios are stressing more and more the requirements for coordination middleware [57]. In particular, the availability of a plethora of mobile devices, with motion sensors and motion coprocessors, is pushing forward the need for *space-awareness* of computations and systems: awareness of the spatial context is often essential to establish which tasks to perform, which goals to achieve, and how.

More generally, spatial issues are fundamental in many sorts of complex software systems, including intelligent, multi-agent, adaptive, and self-organising ones [3]. In most of the application scenarios where *situatedness* plays an essential role, coordination is required to be *space aware*.

This is implicitly recognised by a number of proposals in the coordination field trying to embody spatial mechanisms and constructs into coordination languages—such as TOTA [22], $\sigma\tau$-LINDA [55], GEOLINDA [45], and SAPERE [57]—which, however, are mostly tailored around specific application scenarios. On the contrary, in what follows generality is the main goal, thus a few *basic* mechanisms and constructs required to *generally* enable and promote *space-aware coordination* are discussed.

Along this line, the general notion of *space-aware coordination medium* is described (Sect. 4.3.1), then it is shown how the ReSpecT coordination media and language can be extended so as to support space-aware coordination (Sect. 4.3.2). Finally, after sketching the semantics of the spatial extension, Sect. 4.5.3 showcases space-aware ReSpecT expressiveness reach by dealing with a benchmark problem in the field of *spatial computing*: implement the "T-program" [2].

The space-aware extension of ReSpecT is fully supported by the porting of the TuCSoN infrastructure over the Android platform (codebase available at http://bitbucket.org/smariani/tucsonandroid), where it can benefit from therein provided location services. Through its Android-hosted distribution, the extended ReSpecT promoted rethinking the actual architecture of the Home Manager (http://apice.unibo.it/xwiki/bin/view/Products/HomeManager) middleware for smart home appliances [16], so as to delegate geolocation-related issues to the underlying TuCSoN infrastructure, instead of relying on ad-hoc software agents.

4.5.1 Space-Aware Coordination Media

Spatial coordination requires spatial *situatedness* and *awareness* of the coordination media, which translates in a number of technical requirements.

4.5.1.1 Situatedness

First of all, *situatedness* requires that a *space-aware coordination abstraction* should at any time be associated to an absolute positioning, both physical (i.e. the position in space of the computational device where the medium is being executed on) and virtual (i.e. the network node on which the coordination medium is executed). If not a must-have, geographical positioning is also desirable, and quite a cheap requirement, too, given the widespread availability of mapping services nowadays.

More generally, this concerns both *position* and *motion*—every sort of motion— which in principle includes speed, acceleration, and all variations in the space-time fabric, also depending on the nature of space. In fact, software abstractions may move along a *virtual* space—typically, the network—which is usually *discrete*, whereas physical devices (robots, mobile devices) move through a *physical* space, which is mostly *continuous*—software abstractions, however, may also be hosted by mobile physical devices, and share their motion. As a result, a coordination abstraction may move through either a physical, continuous space, (e.g. "I am in a given position of a tridimensional physical space") or a virtual, discrete space (e.g. "I am on a given network node").

Physical positioning could be either *absolute* (e.g. "I am currently at latitude X, longitude Y, altitude Z"), *geographical* ("I am in via Sacchi 3, Cesena, Italy"), or *organisational* ("I am in Room 5 of the DISI, site of Cesena"). Absolute positioning is often available in the days of mobile devices, usually through GPS services— which, coupled with mapping services, typically provides geographical positioning, too.

Virtual positioning is available as a network service, and might be also labelled as either absolute (in terms of IP address, for instance) or relative (as a domain/ subdomain localisation via DNS). Organisational location should be instead defined application- or middleware-level, and related to either physical or virtual positioning.

4.5.1.2 Awareness

The main requirement of *spatial awareness* is that the ontology of a space-aware coordination medium should include some notion of space. This means, first of all, that the position of the coordination medium should be available to the coordination laws it contains in order to make them capable of *reasoning about space*, that is, to implement *space-aware coordination laws*. So, generally speaking, a range of predicates/functions should be provided to access spatial information associated to any event occurring in the coordination medium (e.g. where the action causing the event took place, where the coordination medium is currently executing), and to perform simple computations over spatial information.

Also, space has to be embedded into the working cycle of the coordination medium: the event model should include *spatial events*, which affect coordination by triggering some space-related computation within the coordination abstraction. In fact, associating spatial information to events is not enough: space-related laws like "when at home, switch on the lights" cannot be expressed only by referring to actions performed, but require instead a specialised notion of spatial event (such as "I am at home") to be triggered.

So, a spatial event should be generated within a coordination medium, conceptually corresponding to changes in space—so, related to *motion*, such as starting from/arriving to a place. Spatial events should then be captured by the coordination medium, and used to activate space-aware coordination laws, within the normal working cycle of the coordination abstraction.

4.5.1.3 Spatial Tuple Centres

Tuple centres are coordination media meant at encapsulating any computable coordination policy within the coordination abstraction [34]. Technically, a tuple centre is a *programmable* tuple space, i.e. a tuple space whose behaviour in response to events can be programmed so as to specify and enact any coordination policy [31]. Tuple centres can then be thought of as general-purpose coordination abstractions, which can be suitably forged to provide specific coordination services. In the same way as timed tuple centres empower tuple centres with the ability of embodying timed coordination laws [38], *spatial tuple centres* extend tuple centres so as to address the spatial issues outlined in previous subsection.

First of all, the location of a tuple centre is obtained through the notion of *current place*, which could be, for instance, the absolute position in space of the computational device where the coordination medium is being executed on, or the domain name of the TuCSoN node hosting the tuple centre, or its location on a map. Then, motion is conceptually represented by two sorts of spatial events: moving from a starting place, and stopping at an arrival place—in any sort of space/place.

> With respect to the formal model defined in [8], this is achieved by extending the input queue of environmental events to become the multiset *SitE* of time, environmental, and spatial events, handled as input events by the *situation* transition ($\longrightarrow_s$)—as shortly discussed at the end of Sect. 4.3.2.

Whenever some motion of any sort occurs (such as the physical device starting/stopping, or the node identifier changing), a spatial event is generated. Then, analogously to operation, situation, and time events, it is possible to specify reactions triggered by spatial events: the so-called *spatial reactions*.

Spatial reactions follow the same semantics of other reactions: once triggered, they are placed in the triggered reaction set and then executed, atomically, in a non-deterministic order. As a result, a spatial tuple centre can be programmed to react to the motion either in physical or in virtual space, so as to enforce space-aware coordination policies.

4.5.2 Space-Aware Extension to ReSpecT

ReSpecT tuple centres are based on first-order logic (FOL). FOL is adopted for both the communication language (logic tuples), and for the behaviour specification language (ReSpecT) [33]. Basically, reactions in ReSpecT are defined as Prolog-like facts, called reaction *specification* tuples, of the form

<code>reaction(Activity, Guards, Goals)</code>

A reaction specification tuple specifies the list of the operations (`Goals`) to be executed when a given event occurs (called *triggering event*, caused by an `Activity`) and some conditions on the event hold (`Guards` evaluate to true). These operations make it possible to insert/read/remove tuples from the tuple space and the specification space of the tuple centre, but also to observe the properties of the triggering event, as well as to invoke operations over other coordination media. The core syntax of ReSpecT is shown in Table 4.3.

According to the abstract model described in Sect. 4.5.1.3, the ReSpecT language is extended to address spatial issues *(i)* by introducing some spatial predicates to get information about the spatial properties of both the tuple centre and the triggering event, and *(ii)* by making it possible to specify reactions to the occurrence of spatial events. The extension to the ReSpecT language is shown in Table 4.4.

Table 4.3 ReSpecT Syntax: Core [25]—no forgeability, bulk, uniform predicates

⟨*Program*⟩ ::= {⟨*Specification*⟩ . }
⟨*Specification*⟩ ::= reaction (⟨*Activity*⟩ [, ⟨*Guards*⟩] , ⟨*Reactions*⟩)
⟨*Activity*⟩ ::= ⟨*Operation*⟩	⟨*Situation*⟩
⟨*Operation*⟩ ::= out (⟨*Tuple*⟩)	(in	rd	no	inp	rdp	nop) (⟨*Template*⟩ [, ⟨*Term*⟩])
⟨*Situation*⟩ ::= time (⟨*Time*⟩)	env (⟨*Key*⟩ , ⟨*Value*⟩)
⟨*Guards*⟩ ::= ⟨*Guard*⟩	(⟨*Guard*⟩ { , ⟨*Guard*⟩})
⟨*Guard*⟩ ::= request	response	success	failure	endo	exo	intra	inter	from_agent	to_agent	from_tc	to_tc	before (⟨*Time*⟩)	after (⟨*Time*⟩)	from_env	to_env
⟨*Reactions*⟩ ::= ⟨*Reaction*⟩	(⟨*Reaction*⟩ { , ⟨*Reaction*⟩})
⟨*Reaction*⟩ ::= [⟨*TupleCentre*⟩	⟨*EnvRes*⟩ ?] ⟨*Operation*⟩	env (⟨*Key*⟩ , ⟨*Value*⟩)	⟨*Observation*⟩	⟨*Computation*⟩	(⟨*Reaction*⟩ ; ⟨*Reaction*⟩)
⟨*Observation*⟩ ::= ⟨*Selector*⟩_⟨*Focus*⟩
⟨*Selector*⟩ ::= current	event	start
⟨*Focus*⟩ ::= (activity	source	target) (⟨*Term*⟩)	time (⟨*Term*⟩)

Table 4.4 Spatial extension to ReSpecT [25]—only the definitions introduced/affected by the spatial extension are shown

⟨*Specification*⟩ ::= reaction(⟨*Activity*⟩ | ⟨*Change*⟩ [, ⟨*Guards*⟩] , ⟨*Reactions*⟩)
⟨*Situation*⟩ ::= env(⟨*Key*⟩ , ⟨*Value*⟩) |
⟨*Change*⟩ ::= env(⟨*Key*⟩ , ⟨*Value*⟩) | time(⟨*Time*⟩)
from(⟨*Space*⟩ , ⟨*Place*⟩) | to(⟨*Space*⟩ , ⟨*Place*⟩)
⟨*Guard*⟩ ::= request | response | success | failure | endo | exo |
intra | inter | from_agent | to_agent | from_tc | to_tc |
before(⟨*Time*⟩) | after(⟨*Time*⟩) | from_env | to_env |
at(⟨*Space*⟩ , ⟨*Place*⟩) | near(⟨*Space*⟩ , ⟨*Place*⟩ , ⟨*Radius*⟩)
⟨*Focus*⟩ ::= (activity | source | target) (⟨*Term*⟩) | time(⟨*Term*⟩) |
place(⟨*Space*⟩ , ⟨*Term*⟩)
⟨*Space*⟩ ::= ph | ip | dns | map | org

4.5.2.1 Spatial Observation Predicates

In particular, the following *observation predicates* are introduced for getting spatial properties of triggering events within ReSpecT reactions[10]:

- current_place(@S, ?P) succeeds if P unifies with the position of the node which the tuple centre belongs to
- event_place(@S, ?P) succeeds if P unifies with the position of the node where the triggering event was originated
- start_place(@S, ?P) succeeds if P unifies with the position of the node where the event chain that led to the triggering event was originated

where the node position can be specified either as its absolute physical position (S=ph), its IP number (S=ip), its domain name (S=dns), its geographical location (S=map)—as typically defined by mapping services like Google Maps—, or its organisational position (S=org)—that is, a location within an organisation-defined virtual topology.

As an example, execution of the reaction specification tuple

```
reaction(
    in(q(X)),
    ( operation, completion ),
    (
        current_place(ph,DevPos),
        event_place(ph,AgentPos),
        out(in_log(AgentPos,DevPos,q(X)))
```

---

[10] A Prolog-like notation is adopted for describing the modality of arguments: + is used for specifying input argument, – output argument, ? input/output argument, @ input argument which must be fully instantiated (ground).

```
  )
  ).
```

inserts a tuple (`in_log/3`) with spatial information each time a TuCSoN agent
retrieves a tuple of the form `q(_)` from the tuple centre, actually implementing a
spatial log, tracking absolute positions of both the querying agent and the device
hosting the tuple centre.

4.5.2.2   Spatial Guard Predicates

Also, the following *guard predicates* are introduced to select reactions to be triggered
based on spatial event properties:

- `at(@S,@P)` succeeds when the tuple centre is currently executing at the position
  P, specified according to S[11]
- `near(@S,@P,@R)` succeeds when the tuple centre is executing at the position
  included in the spatial region with centre P and radius R, specified according to S

So, for instance, `near(dns,'apice.unibo.it',2)` succeeds when the tuple centre
is currently executing on a device whose second-level domain is `.unibo.it`.

4.5.2.3   Spatial Event Descriptors

Reactions to spatial events are specified similarly to ordinary reactions, by introducing the following new event descriptors:

- `from(?S, ?P)` matches a spatial event raised when the device hosting the tuple
  centre starts moving from position P, specified according to S
- `to(?S, ?P)` matches a spatial event raised when the device hosting the tuple centre
  stops moving and reaches position P, specified according to S

As a result, the following are admissible reaction specification tuples dealing with
spatial events:

```
reaction(from(?Space,?Place), Guards, Goals).
reaction(to(?Space,?Place), Guards, Goals).
```

As a simple example, consider the following specification tuples (wherever *Guards*
is omitted, it is by default `true`):

```
reaction( from(ph,StartP),
  ( current_time(StartT)
    out(start_log(StartP,StartT)) )).
reaction( to(ph,ArrP),
  ( current_time(ArrT)
    out(stop_log(ArrP,ArrT)) )).
reaction( out(stop_log(ArrP,ArrT)),
```

---

[11]Precision of the GPS service available applies.

```
( internal, completion ),
( in(start_log(StartP,StartT))
  in(stop_log(ArrP,ArrT))
  out(m_log(StartP,ArrP,StartT,ArrT)) )).
```

which altogether record a simple *physical motion log*, including start/arrival time
and position. In fact, the first reaction stores information about the beginning of a
physical motion in a `start_log/2` tuple, the second the end of the motion in a
`stop_log/2` tuple, whereas the latter removes both sort of tuples and records their
data altogether in a `m_log/4` tuple, representing the essential information about the
whole trajectory of the mobile device hosting the tuple centre.

4.5.2.4 Semantics

The basic **ReSpecT** semantics was first introduced in [33], then extended towards
time-aware coordination in [38], reshaped to support the notion of coordination
artefact in [31], finally enhanced with situatedness in [8]—which represents the
reference semantics for **ReSpecT** until now.

In order to formalise the semantics for the space-aware extension of **ReSpecT**,
two are the main changes with respect to [8]. First of all, a new, generalised event
model should be defined to include both spatial events, and spatial information for
any sort of event. Then, the *environment* transition, already handling both time and
general environment events, should be extended to include spatial events—so as to
handle the full spectrum of situatedness-related events. All other required extensions
(such as the formalisation of each spatial construct semantics) are technically simple,
and trivially extend tables in [8].

The first fundamental extension to the event model is depicted in Table 4.4: a
new sort of *spatial* ⟨*Activity*⟩ is introduced. In particular, the notion of ⟨*Situation*⟩
is extended with the two spatial activities from(⟨*Space*⟩ ⟨*Place*⟩) , to (⟨*Space*⟩
⟨*Place*⟩), reflecting the initial and final stages of a motion trajectory, respectively—
in whatever sort of space.

However, spatial extension of the event model cannot be limited to introducing
spatial activities: another issue is represented by *spatial qualification* of events, that
is, in short, making *all* **ReSpecT** events featuring spatial properties—in the same
way as temporal properties were introduced for all **ReSpecT** events in [38]. This is
represented by the ⟨*Place*⟩ property featured by ⟨*Cause*⟩ and ⟨*StartCause*⟩, as shown
in Table 4.5, where the extended **ReSpecT** event model is depicted.

Essentially, all **ReSpecT** events are in principle qualified with both time and
space properties—the latter one defined as the position (in whichever sort of space)
where the (initial) cause of the event takes place. Of course, properties may be
actually defined or not at execution time, depending on the capabilities available
when the event is generated. For instance, if absolute physical positioning is made
available by the hosting device, and the device is currently in location *P* when an event
is generated, the coordination middleware associates *P* to the event as its physical
location—which otherwise would be undefined.

Table 4.5 Extending ReSpecT events with space [25]

$$\langle Event\rangle ::= \langle StartCause\rangle\,,\,\langle Cause\rangle\,,\,\langle Evaluation\rangle$$
$$\langle StartCause\rangle\,,\,\langle Cause\rangle ::= \langle Activity\rangle\,,\,\langle Source\rangle\,,\,\langle Target\rangle\,,\,\langle Time\rangle\,,$$
$$\langle Space:Place\rangle$$
$$\langle Source\rangle\,,\,\langle Target\rangle ::= \langle AgentId\rangle \mid \langle TCId\rangle \mid \langle EnvResId\rangle \mid \bot$$
$$\langle Evaluation\rangle ::= \bot \mid \{\langle Result\rangle\}$$
$$\langle Place\rangle ::= \langle GPSCoordinates\rangle\,,\,\langle IPAddress\rangle\,,\,\langle DomainName\rangle\,,$$
$$\langle MapLocation\rangle\,,\,\langle VirtualPosition\rangle$$

According to [8], the operational semantics of a ReSpecT tuple centre is expressed by a transition system over a state represented by a labelled triple $^{OpE,SitE}\langle Tu, Re, Op\rangle_n^{OutE}$ (abstracting away from the specification tuples Σ, which are not of interest here). In particular, Tu is the multiset of the ordinary tuples in the tuple centre; Re is the multiset of the triggered reactions waiting to be executed; Op is the multiset of the requests waiting for a response; OpE is the multiset of incoming $\langle Operation\rangle$ events; $SitE$ is the multiset of incoming $\langle Situation\rangle$ events, including time, spatial, and general environment events; $OutE$ is the outgoing event multiset; n is the local tuple centre time.

$OutE$ is automatically emptied by emitting the outgoing events, with no need for special transitions. In the same way, OpE and $SitE$ are automatically extended whenever a new incoming (either operation or situation) event enters a tuple centre—again, no special transitions are needed for incoming events. In particular, $SitE$ is added new environment events by transducers [8], new time events by the passing of time [38], and—in the spatial extension of ReSpecT discussed here—also new spatial events whenever some sort of motion takes place.

So, as described in [8], the behaviour of a ReSpecT tuple centre is modelled by a transition system composed of four different transitions: *reaction* ($\longrightarrow_r$), *situation* ($\longrightarrow_s$), *operation* ($\longrightarrow_o$), *log* ($\longrightarrow_l$). Quite intuitively, spatial events are handled—in the same way as time and environment events—by the *situation* transition, which triggers ReSpecT reactions in response to spatial events. As a result, the *situation* transition is the fundamental ReSpecT machinery supporting situatedness in the full acceptation of the term—that is, suitably handling reactiveness of the coordination abstraction to time, space, and general environment events.

4.5.3 Expressiveness Showcase

In [2], a layered architecture for devices running *spatial computing* programs is described, which helps bridging the gap between the hardware and *Spatial Computing Languages* (SCL):

Physical platform—The lowest level in the hierarchy, identifying the medium upon which the computation actually executes—e.g. a smartphone, a drone with a whole set of sensors and actuators, even a virtual device in the case of a simulation

System management—Typically the OS layer, abstracting away from physical details, (hopefully) providing all the low-level drivers needed by spatial applications—e.g. for a GPS module, or a motion engine

Abstract device—The top abstraction level exposing the basic API for SCL—e.g. a clock service, GPS coordinates tracking, and the like

Independently of the layer of abstraction at which a given SCL can be placed, as well as of the kind of Abstract Device Model (ADM) it implements, three classes of operators are required to reach maximal expressiveness and computational power—the sort of "spatial Turing equivalence" discussed in [1]:

Measure space—Transforming spatial properties into computable information—e.g. distances, angles, areas

Manipulate space—Translating information into some modification of the spatial properties of the device—e.g. turning wheels to face a given direction, slowing down the motion engine

Compute—Besides usual computation, any kind of spatial-pointwise operation, e.g. an interaction, or a non-spatial sensor or actuator operation—e.g. turning on a light sensor

A fourth class (*physical evolution*) looks more like a sort of assumption over the (possibly autonomous) dynamics a given program/device can rely upon—e.g. the existence of actuators responding to the program/device commands, or the independent motion of a colony of cells.

As a reference benchmark to test the expressive power and the computational completeness of SCL, the "T-Program" is proposed in [2], consisting of the following three stages, depicted in Fig. 4.23 in the case of the Proto language [52]: *(i)* cooperatively creating a local coordinate system; *(ii)* moving devices to create a "T-shaped" structure; *(iii)* computing the centre of gravity of the structure and draw a ring around it. Stage *(i)* requires the capability to measure the spatial context where the program/device lives; stage *(ii)* requires the ability to manipulate the spatial properties of each device (thus relying also on the fourth category); stage *(iii)* requires both computational capabilities and, again, measuring capabilities.

The spatial extension to **ReSpecT** meets all the requirements to successfully implement the above benchmark at the level of the ADM. In fact:

- a combination of three *Observation Predicates* is given to measure spatial properties:

  - `current_place` measuring where the tuple centre executing the current **ReSpecT** reaction is
  - `event_place`, `start_place` measuring respectively where the *direct cause* and *start cause* [31] of the event triggering the current **ReSpecT** computation took place

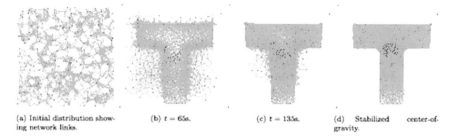

(a) Initial distribution showing network links.   (b) $t = 6.5s$.   (c) $t = 13.5s$.   (d) Stabilized center-of-gravity.

Fig. 4.23 T-Program run from [2], implemented using the Proto language [52]

- given that the modification of spatial properties is necessarily bound to the facilities provided by the host device, the manipulation requirement can be addressed by situatedness-related constructs of ReSpecT:

  - ⟨*EnvResId*⟩ ? env(⟨*Key*⟩, ⟨*Value*⟩) precisely meant to be used as an interface to device actuators, allowing an agent to dispatch commands to a device ⟨*EnvResId*⟩ at the most appropriate level of abstraction—that is, as a part of the environment managed through the coordination medium

- while the computing requirement is orthogonal w.r.t. the spatial dimension, some predicates may be considered here as they ease the process of computing over spatial information—in particular, guards:

  - at(⟨*Space*⟩, ⟨*Place*⟩) triggers a reaction when the reacting tuple centre is at a given location
  - near(⟨*Space*⟩, ⟨*Place*⟩, ⟨*Radius*⟩) triggers a reaction when the reacting tuple centre is near a given location

Finally, it should be noted that some constructs are left out, in particular those in ⟨*TCEvent*⟩. They belong to the aforementioned fourth class (physical evolution), since they allow the Abstract Device—that is, the ReSpecT VM—to *perceive motion events* generated either autonomously or on demand by the physical device hosting the VM.

Respectively, from(⟨*Space*⟩, ⟨*Place*⟩) is the spatial event generated by the ReSpecT VM when the host tuple centre *starts moving* (leaving a location), whereas to(⟨*Space*⟩, ⟨*Place*⟩) is the spatial event generated when it *stops moving* (approaching a location). These events are meant to reify a *change of state* in the spatial dimension of computation: therefore, no events have to be generated while the VM is staying still, since there is no state change to reify.

Now follows description of how space-aware ReSpecT can successfully implement the T-program benchmark.

4.5.3.1 Coordinate System

Setting a local coordinate system basically amounts at *(i)* choosing an origin node, *(ii)* making it spread a vector tuple to neighbours, then (recursively) *(iii)* making them increment the vector, and *(iv)* forwarding it to neighbours. Thus, the basic mechanism needed by the VM at the application level is *neighbourhood spreading*. Assuming a *physical* neighbourhood relation is used, the following reactions—installed on every node—achieve the goal [24]:

```
1   // Check range then forward.
2   reaction(    out(nbr_spread(msg(Msg),nbr(Dist),req(ID))),
3     ( completion, success ),
4     ( no(req(ID)), out(req(ID)), // Avoid flooding
5       current_place(Me), event_place(Sender),
6       within(Me,Sender,Dist), // Prolog computation
7       out(msg(Msg)),
8       rd(nbrs(Nbrs)), // Neighbours list
9       out(forward(Msg,Dist,req(ID),Nbrs))
10    )
11  ).
12  // Delete multicast request.
13  reaction( out(nbr_spread(msg(Msg),nbr(Dist),req(ID))),
14    ( completion, success ),
15    in(spread(msg(Msg),nbr(Dist),req(ID)))
16  ).
17  // Forward to every neighbour.
18  reaction( out(forward(Msg,Dist,req(ID),[H|T])), // Some Nbrs
19    ( intra, completion ),
20    ( H ? out(spread(msg(Msg),nbr(Dist),req(ID))), // Forward
21      out(forward(Msg,Dist,req(ID),T)) // Iterate
22    )
23  ).
24  // Delete iteration tuple.
25  reaction( out(forward(Msg,Dist,req(ID),Nbrs)),
26    ( intra, completion ),
27    in(forward(Msg,Dist,req(ID),Nbrs)) // Delete it anyway
28  ).
```

Reactions 2–10 and 12–15 manage spreading requests: the former checks if the incoming request has been already served, gets reacting node position and sender node's one, checks if it's in the desired range, and if so stores the tuple (Msg) then starts forwarding it; the latter simply removes the request. Reactions 17–21 and 23–26 manage the forwarding process, that is, iterate neighbours forwarding the spreading command. Neighbourhood is set here at the VM level through a tuple nbrs([nbr_1,...,nbr_N]), but could also be set at the middleware level by using a coordination middleware such as TuCSoN [42].

4.5.3.2 "T-Shape"

To arrange nodes (tuple centres) so as to form a T-shaped structure, it is needed to *(i)* define spatial constraints representing the T (how much tall, fat, etc.), then *(ii)* make every node move so as to satisfy them. Thus, the basic mechanism needed at the VM level is *motion monitoring and control* [24]:

```
1  // Compute motion vector then start moving.
2  reaction( out(move(Constraints)),
3    ( completion, success ),
4    ( current_place(Here),current_time(Now),Check is Now+1000,
5      direction(Constraints,Here,Vec), // Prolog computation
6      out_s(
7        // Reaction 13-26
8      ),
9      engine ? env(mode,'on'), engine ? env(dir,Vec) // Start actuators
10   )
11 ).
12 // Motion constraints monitoring.
13 reaction( time(Check),
14   internal,
15   ( current_place(Here),
16     rd(move(Constraints)),
17     ( check(Here,Constraints), // Prolog computation
18       engine ? env(mode,'off')
19     ;
20       current_time(Now), Check is Now+1000,
21       out_s(
22         // Reaction 13-26
23       )
24     )
25   )
26 ).
27 // Arrival clean-up.
28 reaction( to(Dest),
29   internal,
30   in(move(Constraints))
31 ).
```

An interesting feature of **ReSpecT** is exploited in the code above. Besides reacting to a motion request by properly controlling actuators, Reaction 2–11 performs a *meta-coordination operation*, by inserting a new coordination law in the tuple centre (Reaction 13–26), which is responsible for arrival check.

4.5.3.3   Focal Point

To first compute the focal point (FC) of the T-shape, then draw a sphere around it, two basic mechanisms are needed, both very similar to the *neighbourhood spreading* previously shown—thus whose code is not reported to avoid redundancy: *(i)* a *bidi-rectional* neighbourhood spreading to collect replies to sent messages—enabling to aggregate all the node's coordinates and counting them—and *(ii)* a *spherical multi-cast* to draw the ring pattern.

The code for spherical multicast is almost identical to neighbourhood spreading, but with a fundamental difference (besides the `req(ID)` test to avoid flooding), that is the use of observation predicate `start_place` instead of `event_place`. This replacement alone stops the spreading process and completely changes the *spatial properties* of communication. This is a notable example of **ReSpecT** expressiveness.

The language extension just showcased is necessary w.r.t. $\mathcal{MoK}$ for two reasons at least. The first one, most obvious, is to enable the coordination laws to get advantage of the situatedness of coordination-related events generated by the underlying infrastructure. The second, possibly less apparent, is that of allowing adaptiveness of the coordination laws to the ever-changing computational context within which social and situated activities happen.

Thanks to ReSpecT programs capability to change themselves at run-time, any aspect of the coordination laws installed within TuCSoN tuple centres may be re-programmed anytime. In the case of the $\mathcal{MoK}$ prototype described in Sect. 7.1 of Chap. 7, this means any facet of artificial chemical reactions, such as their rate, as well as of the chemical engine resembling chemical compartments, may be changed by the middleware itself, in face of, e.g. users' interactions.

References

1. Beal, J.: A basis set of operators for space-time computations. In: Proceedings of the 2010 Fourth IEEE International Conference on Self-Adaptive and Self-Organizing Systems Workshop (SASOW 2010), pp. 91–97. IEEE Computer Society, Washington, DC, USA (2010). doi:10.1109/SASOW.2010.21
2. Beal, J., Dulman, S., Usbeck, K., Viroli, M., Correll, N.: Organizing the aggregate: Languages for spatial computing. CoRR **abs/1202.5509** (2012)
3. Beal, J., Michel, O., Schultz, U.P.: Spatial computing: Distributed systems that take advantage of our geometric world. ACM Trans. Auton. Adapt. Syst. **6**(2), 11:1–11:3 (2011). doi:10.1145/1968513.1968514
4. Bellifemine, F.L., Poggi, A., Rimassa, G.: JADE–a FIPA-compliant agent framework. In: 4th International Conference and Exhibition on the Practical Application of Intelligent Agents and Multi-Agent Technology (PAAM-99), pp. 97–108. The Practical Application Company Ltd., London, UK (1999)
5. Bordini, R.H., Hübner, J.F., Wooldridge, M.J.: Programming Multi-Agent Systems in AgentSpeak using Jason. John Wiley & Sons, Ltd (2007)
6. Brooks, R.A.: Achieving artificial intelligence through building robots. Tech. Rep. AIM-899, Massachussets Institute of Technology (MIT) (1986)
7. Cabri, G., Leonardi, L., Zambonelli, F.: MARS: A programmable coordination architecture for mobile agents. IEEE Int. Comput. **4**(4), 26–35 (2000). doi:10.1109/4236.865084
8. Casadei, M., Omicini, A.: Situated tuple centres in ReSpecT. In: Shin, S.Y., Ossowski, S., Menezes, R., Viroli, M. (eds.) 24th Annual ACM Symposium on Applied Computing (SAC 2009), vol. III, pp. 1361–1368. ACM, Honolulu, Hawai'i, USA (2009). doi:10.1145/1529282.1529586
9. Castelfranchi, C.: Modelling social action for AI agents. Artif. Intell. **103**(1–2), 157–182 (1998). doi:10.1016/S0004-3702(98)00056-3
10. Castelfranchi, C.: Goals, the true center of cognition. In: Paglieri, F., Tummolini, L., Falcone, R., Miceli M. (eds.) The Goals of Cognition. Essays in Honor of Cristiano Castelfranchi, *Tributes*, vol. 20, Chap. 41, pp. 837–882. College Publications, London (2012)
11. Cheyer, A., Martin, D.: The open agent architecture. Auton. Agent. Multi-Agent Syst. **4**(1–2), 143–148 (2001). doi:10.1023/A:1010091302035

12. Ciancarini, P.: Coordination models and languages as software integrators. ACM Comput. Surv. **28**(2), 300–302 (1996). doi:10.1145/234528.234732
13. Ciancarini, P., Omicini, A., Zambonelli, F.: Multiagent system engineering: The coordination viewpoint. In: Jennings, N.R., Lespérance, Y. (eds.) Intelligent Agents VI. Agent Theories, Architectures, and Languages, LNAI, vol. 1757, pp. 250–259. Springer (2000). doi:10.1007/10719619
14. Demazeau, Y., Müller, J.P.: From reactive to intentional agents. Decentralized A.I. **2**, 3–10 (1991)
15. Denti, E.: Novel pervasive scenarios for home management: the butlers architecture. SpringerPlus **3**(52), 1–30 (2014). doi:10.1186/2193-1801-3-52
16. Denti, E., Calegari, R.: Butler-ising HomeManager: A pervasive multi-agent system for home intelligence. In: Loiseau, S., Filipe, J., Duval, B., Van Den Herik, J. (eds.) 7th International Conference on Agents and Artificial Intelligence 2015 (ICAART 2015), pp. 249–256. SCITEPRESS—Science and Technology Publications, Lisbon, Portugal (2015). doi:10.5220/0005284002490256
17. Dong, M., Mao, X., Yin, J., Chang, Z., Qi, Z.: Sade: A development environment for adaptive multi-agent systems. In: Yang, J.J., Yokoo, M., Ito, T., Jin, Z., Scerri, P. (eds.) Principles of Practice in Multi-Agent Systems, Lecture Notes in Computer Science, vol. 5925, pp. 516–524. Springer Berlin Heidelberg (2009). doi:10.1007/978-3-642-11161-7
18. Ferber, J., Müller, J.P.: Influences and reaction: A model of situated multiagent systems. In: Tokoro, M. (ed.) 2nd International Conference on Multi-Agent Systems (ICMAS-96), pp. 72–79. AAAI Press, Tokio, Japan (1996)
19. Fortino, G., Garro, A., Mascillaro, S., Russo, W.: Using event-driven lightweight DSC-based agents for MAS modelling. Int. J. Agent-Oriented Softw. Eng. **4**(2), 113–140 (2010). doi:10.1504/IJAOSE.2010.032798
20. Hallenborg, K., Jensen, A.J., Demazeau, Y.: Reactive agent mechanisms for manufacturing process control. In: 2007 IEEE/WIC/ACM International Conferences on Web Intelligence and Intelligent Agent Technology Workshops (WI-IATW '07), pp. 399–403. IEEE Computer Society, Washington, DC, USA (2007)
21. Malone, T.W., Crowston, K.: The interdisciplinary study of coordination. ACM Comput. Surv. **26**(1), 87–119 (1994). doi:10.1145/174666.174668
22. Mamei, M., Zambonelli, F.: Programming pervasive and mobile computing applications: The TOTA approach. ACM Trans. Softw. Eng. Methodol. (TOSEM) **18**(4), 15:1–15:56 (2009). doi:10.1145/1538942.1538945
23. Mariani, S., Omicini, A.: Event-driven programming for situated MAS with ReSpecT tuple centres. In: M. Klusch, M. Thimm, M. Paprzycki (eds.) Multiagent System Technologies, LNAI, vol. 8076, pp. 306–319. Springer (2013). doi:10.1007/978-3-642-40776-5_26. 11th German Conference (MATES 2013), Koblenz, Germany, 16-20 Sep. 2013. Proceedings
24. Mariani, S., Omicini, A.: Promoting space-aware coordination: ReSpecT as a spatial-computing virtual machine. In: Spatial Computing Workshop (SCW 2013). AAMAS 2013, Saint Paul, Minnesota, USA (2013)
25. Mariani, S., Omicini, A.: Space-aware coordination in ReSpecT. In: Baldoni, M., Baroglio, C., Bergenti, F., Garro, A. (eds.) From Objects to Agents, CEUR Workshop Proceedings, vol. 1099, pp. 1–7. Sun SITE Central Europe, RWTH Aachen University, Turin, Italy (2013). XIV Workshop (WOA 2013). Workshop Notes
26. Mariani, S., Omicini, A.: TuCSoN on cloud: An event-driven architecture for embodied / disembodied coordination. In: Aversa, R., Kolodzej, J., Zhang, J., Amato, F., Fortino, G. (eds.) Algorithms and Architectures for Parallel Processing, *LNCS*, vol. 8286, pp. 285–294. Springer International Publishing Switzerland (2013). doi:10.1007/978-3-319-03889-6. 13th International Conference (ICA3PP-2013), Vietri sul Mare, Italy, 18-20 Dec. 2013. Proceedings, Part II
27. Mariani, S., Omicini, A.: TuCSoN coordination for MAS situatedness: Towards a methodology. In: Santoro, C., Bergenti, F. (eds.) WOA 2014—XV Workshop Nazionale "Dagli Oggetti agli Agenti", CEUR Workshop Proceedings, vol. 1260, pp. 62–71. RWTH Aachen University, Catania, Italy, Sun SITE Central Europe (2014)

28. Mariani, S., Omicini, A.: Coordinating activities and change: An event-driven architecture for situated MAS. Engineering Applications of Artificial Intelligence **41**, 298–309 (2015). doi:10.1016/j.engappai.2014.10.006. Special Section on Agent-oriented Methods for Engineering Complex Distributed Systems

29. Nardi, B.: Context and Consciousness: Activity Theory and Human-computer Interaction. MIT Press (1996)

30. Omicini, A.: Towards a notion of agent coordination context. In: Marinescu, D.C., Lee, C. (eds.) Process Coordination and Ubiquitous Computing, Chap. 12, pp. 187–200. CRC Press, Boca Raton, FL, USA (2002)

31. Omicini, A.: Formal ReSpecT in the A&A perspective. Electron. Notes Theor. Comput. Sci. **175**(2), 97–117 (2007). doi:10.1016/j.entcs.2007.03.006

32. Omicini, A.: Agents writing on walls: Cognitive stigmergy and beyond. In: Paglieri, F., Tummolini, L., Falcone, R., Miceli, M. (eds.) The Goals of Cognition. Essays in Honor of Cristiano Castelfranchi, *Tributes*, vol. 20, Chap. 29, pp. 543–556. College Publications, London (2012)

33. Omicini, A., Denti, E.: Formal ReSpecT. Electron. Notes Theor. Comput. Sci. **48**, 179–196 (2001). doi:10.1016/S1571-0661(04)00156-2

34. Omicini, A., Denti, E.: From tuple spaces to tuple centres. Sci. Comput. Program. **41**(3), 277–294 (2001). doi:10.1016/S0167-6423(01)00011-9

35. Omicini, A., Mariani, S.: Coordination for situated MAS: Towards an event-driven architecture. In: Moldt, D., Rölke, H. (eds.) International Workshop on Petri Nets and Software Engineering (PNSE'13), CEUR Workshop Proceedings, vol. 989, pp. 17–22. RWTH Aachen University, Sun SITE Central Europe (2013)

36. Omicini, A., Ossowski, S.: Objective versus subjective coordination in the engineering of agent systems. In: Klusch, M., Bergamaschi, S., Edwards, P., Petta, P. (eds.) Intelligent Information Agents: An AgentLink Perspective, LNAI: State-of-the-Art Survey, vol. 2586, pp. 179–202. Springer (2003). doi:10.1007/3-540-36561-3

37. Omicini, A., Piunti, M., Ricci, A., Viroli, M.: Agents, intelligence, and tools. In: Bramer, M. (ed.) Artificial Intelligence: An International Perspective, LNAI: State-of-the-Art Survey, vol. 5640, chap. 9, pp. 157–173. Springer (2009). doi:10.1007/978-3-642-03226-4

38. Omicini, A., Ricci, A., Viroli, M.: Time-aware coordination in ReSpecT. In: Jacquet, J.M., Picco, G.P. (eds.) Coordination Models and Languages, LNCS, vol. 3454, pp. 268–282. Springer (2005). doi:10.1007/11417019

39. Omicini, A., Ricci, A., Viroli, M.: Timed environment for Web agents. Web Intell. Agent Syst. **5**(2), 161–175 (2007)

40. Omicini, A., Ricci, A., Viroli, M.: Artifacts in the A&A meta-model for multi-agent systems. Auton. Agent. Multi-Agent Syst. **17**(3), 432–456 (2008). doi:10.1007/s10458-008-9053-x

41. Omicini, A., Ricci, A., Viroli, M., Castelfranchi, C., Tummolini, L.: Coordination artifacts: Environment-based coordination for intelligent agents. In: Jennings, N.R., Sierra, C., Sonenberg, L., Tambe, M. (eds.) 3rd international Joint Conference on Autonomous Agents and Multiagent Systems (AAMAS 2004), vol. 1, pp. 286–293. ACM, New York, USA (2004). doi:10.1109/AAMAS.2004.10070

42. Omicini, A., Zambonelli, F.: Coordination for Internet application development. Auton. Agent. Multi-Agent Syst. **2**(3), 251–269 (1999). doi:10.1023/A:1010060322135

43. Omicini, A., Zambonelli, F.: MAS as complex systems: A view on the role of declarative approaches. In: Leite, J.A., Omicini, A., Sterling, L., Torroni, P. (eds.) Declarative Agent Languages and Technologies, LNAI, vol. 2990, pp. 1–17. Springer (2004). doi:10.1007/b97923. 1st International Workshop (DALT 2003), Melbourne, Australia, 15 July 2003. Revised Selected and Invited Papers

44. Omicini, A., Zambonelli, F., Klusch, M., Tolksdorf, R. (eds.): Coordination of Internet Agents: Models, Technologies, and Applications. Springer (2001)

45. Pauty, J., Couderc, P., Banatre, M., Berbers, Y.: Geo-Linda: a geometry aware distributed tuple space. In: Advanced Information Networking and Applications, pp. 370–377 (2007). doi:10.1109/AINA.2007.74. 21st International Conference (AINA '07), 21–23 May 2007, Niagara Falls, ON, CA. Proceedings

46. Picco, G.P., Murphy, A.L., Roman, G.C.: LIME: Linda meets mobility. In: 21st International Conference on Software Engineering (ICSE'99), pp. 368–377. ACM Press, New York, NY, USA (1999). doi:10.1145/302405.302659

47. Rao, A.S.: AgentSpeak(L): BDI agents speak out in a logical computable language. In: Van de Velde, W., Perram, J.W. (eds.) Agents Breaking Away, LNCS, vol. 1038, pp. 42–55. Springer (1996). doi:10.1007/BFb0031845. 7th European Workshop on Modelling Autonomous Agents in a Multi-Agent World (MAAMAW'96), Eindhoven, The Netherlands, 22-25 Jan. 1996, Proceedings

48. Ricci, A., Viroli, M., Omicini, A.: CArtAgO: A framework for prototyping artifact-based environments in MAS. In: Weyns, D., Parunak, H.V.D., Michel, F. (eds.) Environments for MultiAgent Systems III, LNAI, vol. 4389, pp. 67–86. Springer (2007). doi:10.1007/978-3-540-71103-2

49. Ricci, A., Viroli, M., Omicini, A.: The A&A programming model and technology for developing agent environments in MAS. In: Dastani, M., El Fallah Seghrouchni,, A. Ricci, A., Winikoff, M. (eds.) Programming Multi-Agent Systems, LNCS, vol. 4908, pp. 89–106. Springer (2008). doi:10.1007/978-3-540-79043-3

50. Schumacher, M.: Objective Coordination in Multi-Agent System Engineering. Design and Implementation, LNCS, vol. 2039. Springer (2001). doi:10.1007/3-540-44933-7

51. Suchman, L.A.: Situated actions. Plans and Situated Actions: The Problem of Human-Machine Communication, Chap. 4, pp. 49–67. Cambridge University Press, New York, NYU, USA (1987)

52. Viroli, M., Beal, J., Casadei, M.: Core operational semantics of Proto. In: Palakal, M.J., Hung, C.C., Chu, W., Wong, W.E. (eds.) 26th Annual ACM Symposium on Applied Computing (SAC 2011), vol. II: Artificial Intelligence & Agents, Information Systems, and Software Development, pp. 1325–1332. ACM, Tunghai University, TaiChung, Taiwan (2011)

53. Viroli, M., Omicini, A.: Coordination as a service. Fundamenta Informaticae **73**(4), 507–534 (2006). Special Issue: Best papers of FOCLASA 2002

54. Viroli, M., Omicini, A., Ricci, A.: Infrastructure for RBAC-MAS: An approach based on Agent Coordination Contexts. Applied Artificial Intelligence: An International Journal **21**(4–5), 443–467 (2007). doi:10.1080/08839510701253674. Special Issue: State of Applications in AI Research from AI*IA 2005

55. Viroli, M., Pianini, D., Beal, J.: Linda in space-time: an adaptive coordination model for mobile ad-hoc environments. In: M. Sirjani (ed.) Coordination Languages and Models, LNCS, vol. 7274, pp. 212–229. Springer (2012)

56. Weyns, D., Omicini, A., Odell, J.J.: Environment as a first-class abstraction in multi-agent systems. Auton. Agent. Multi-Agent Syst. **14**(1), 5–30 (2007). doi:10.1007/s10458-006-0012-0

57. Zambonelli, F., Omicini, A., Anzengruber, B., Castelli, G., DeAngelis, F.L., Di Marzo Serugendo, G., Dobson, S., Fernandez-Marquez, J.L., Ferscha, A., Mamei, M., Mariani, S., Molesini, A., Montagna, S., Nieminen, J., Pianini, D., Risoldi, M., Rosi, A., Stevenson, G., Viroli, M., Ye, J.: Developing pervasive multi-agent systems with nature-inspired coordination. Pervasive Mob. Comput. **17**, 236–252 (2015). doi:10.1016/j.pmcj.2014.12.002 Chatschik Bisdikian

Chapter 5
Coordination of Sociotechnical Systems

Abstract In this chapter socio-cognitive theories of action and interaction are discussed w.r.t. to their (potential) application to software systems, multi-agent systems in particular, for the sake of improving the quality of the coordination processes as perceived by users. Accordingly, firstly those challenges peculiar to either Knowledge-Intensive Environments (KIE) or STS, which mostly impact the issue of coordination, are discussed (Sect. 5.1); then, some research works applying to computer-based Multi-Agent Systems (MAS) principles borrowed from Activity Theory (AT), (cognitive) stigmergy, and BIC are reviewed (Sect. 5.2); finally, the notion of perturbation action is described and related to BIC notion of tacit message (Sect. 5.3), so as to sketch the basic ideas underlying the approach to self-organising coordination in STS thoroughly detailed in Part II of this book.

5.1 Sociotechnical Systems and Knowledge-Intensive Environments

In this section some of the peculiar traits of sociotechnical (Sect. 5.1.1) knowledge-intensive environments (Sect. 5.1.2) are described, with particular emphasis on the corresponding software engineering issues they bring along. This enables outlining a research roadmap for exploiting socio-cognitive theories of action and interaction within computational systems (Sect. 5.1.3), which is further discussed in Sect. 5.2.

5.1.1 Challenges of Sociotechnical Systems

Sociotechnical systems (STS) arise when *cognitive* and *social interaction* is mediated by information technology rather than by the natural world (alone) [36]. As such, STS include non-technical elements such as people, processes, regulations, etc., which are inherent parts of the system. Since social activity is fluid and nuanced, STS are technically difficult to design properly—especially from a coordination

© Springer International Publishing AG 2016   129
S. Mariani, *Coordination of Complex Sociotechnical Systems*,
Artificial Intelligence: Foundations, Theory, and Algorithms,
DOI 10.1007/978-3-319-47109-9_5

perspective—and often awkward to use [1]. Also, a number of peculiarities, with related engineering challenges, have been highlighted by various research works [1]. Among the many

- STS have *emergent* properties, which cannot be attributed to individual parts of the system, depending on the relationships and *dependencies* between system components. Given this complexity, the aforementioned properties can only be evaluated once the system has been assembled and deployed, not at design time
- STS are often *non-deterministic*, that is, when presented with a specific input, they may not always produce the same output. This happens because system behaviour depends on human operators, and people do not always react in the same way to the same situation
- people may use the STS in ways completely *unpredictable* from the designers standpoint. In large-scale open networks like the Internet, users behaviour is uncontrolled, so that very few assumptions can be made about it. In particular, it is almost impossible to globally foresee and influence the space of potential interactions. Most probably, users, as well as software components, will behave in a self-interested fashion, which may help to *anticipate* some of their actions, and may provide some clues on how to design coordination strategies at the micro level [22]
- *awareness*, that is, knowing who is present, and *peripheral awareness*, namely monitoring of others' activity, are fundamental in STS [10], because visibility of information flow—thus *observability* of dependencies—enables learning and greater efficiency [11]—as well as *observation-based coordination* [25]
- people not only *adapt* to their systems, they adapt their systems to their needs (*co-evolution*) [16, 21]

Failing to recognise one of the above facets of STS, thus neglecting to address the corresponding issue, inevitably leads to a *sociotechnical gap* in the STS, that is, a gap between what the computational platform strives to provide, and what the users participating the STS are expecting to have [1].

All the mentioned peculiarities imply challenges which is possible to approach from a *coordination perspective*, in particular, exploiting coordination techniques supporting *programmable* (to deal with unpredictability and adaptation, mostly), *self-organising* (to account for emergence and non-determinism), *situated* (supporting awareness) coordination. Not by chance, this is exactly the approach to coordination discussed in Chaps. 2 and 3 (programmability & self-organisation), and 4 (situatedness).

5.1.2 Challenges of Knowledge-Intensive Environments

In general, data are considered as raw facts, information is regarded as an *organised* set of data, and knowledge is perceived as *meaningful* information [2]. In a dynamic business environment, where an organisation faces unexpected and novel problems, a computational platform can be used, at best, as an *enabler* to turn data into information, but it is only through people—hence, considering the STS *as a whole*—that information is *interpreted* and turned into knowledge.

Following [2], *Knowledge Management* (KM) is a complex sociotechnical process encompassing knowledge creation, validation, distribution, presentation, and application, each facet bringing along its own issues and computational challenges

Creation—Refers to the ability of an organisation to develop *novel* and *useful* information, processes, best practices, solutions, etc. Knowledge creation is an *emergent* process in which experimentation and pure *chance* play an important role. Providing the means to undertake trial-and-error experiments, and to spot knowledge creation opportunities, is a great computational challenge for a KM platform.

Validation—Refers to the extent to which a firm can reflect on knowledge and evaluate its *relevance*, pertinency, and effectiveness for the existing organisational environment and business goals. Knowledge validation is a painstaking process of continually monitoring, evaluating, and *refining* the knowledge base to suit the existing, potential, or foresee realities. As the realities change, so may arise the need to convert parts of knowledge back into information, then data, which may finally be *discarded*. Designing computational techniques seamlessly integrating with users workflows, while transparently assisting them in all the stages involved in knowledge validation, is far from trivial.

Distribution—Refers to the distribution of organisational knowledge in different locations, embedded into different artefacts and procedures, and stored into different storage media—which is challenging by itself. Furthermore, *interactions* between organisational technologies, techniques, and people can have *direct bearing* on knowledge distribution, introducing the need to deal with some degree of *uncertainty*—about, e.g. where to find a relevant piece of information—and demanding for adaptation techniques supporting continuous and *autonomous* knowledge redistribution.

Presentation—Refers to each storage medium requiring its different means of knowledge *(re)presentation*, thus, organisational members often find it difficult to reconfigure, recombine, and *integrate* knowledge from these distinct and disparate sources. Though organisational members may find the relevant pieces of information by organising data into separate databases, they will still find it difficult to integrate and interpret information without a common representation.

Application—Refers to making knowledge more *active* for the firm in creating value. The criteria for evaluating relevance of knowledge are not often readily apparent, however, the technological platform could provide means of experimentation to assess the potential of knowledge and readily exploit it.

Two main strategies for KM are employed by early adopters of the principle [14], striving to address the above challenges

- the *process-centred* approach, which understands KM as a *social*, communication based process. Here knowledge is closely tied to the person who developed it and is shared mainly through person-to-person contacts. The main purpose of information technology is then to *enable* people communicate knowledge, not to store it
- the *product-centred* approach, focussing on knowledge *reification* into documents, then on their creation, storage, and reuse in computer-based corporate memories

Whatever the approach, the connections that KM software must facilitate are between people as much as they are between people and information systems. In particular, the software must support fruitful exchange of knowledge, and transformation from *tacit* to *explicit* knowledge [14].

Yet again, the whole process of KM, in most if not all of its facets, can be approached from a *coordination perspective*, where coordination policies and mechanisms may be applied not solely to the agents (either software or human) participating the management process, but also to the raw data subject of the process. This way, data may become organised information *autonomously*, guided by coordination mechanisms seamlessly integrating knowledge workers' own workflows with the organisation long-term goals—e.g. creation, validation, and distribution, may be (partially) delegated to the coordination infrastructure underlying the KM platform. In turn, knowledge workers may find knowledge patterns more easily by having the KM platform (thus, the underlying coordination mechanisms) assist them, by, e.g. presenting the right information at the right time in the right place.

One possible way to do so, in the broad sense of taking coordination as the ground upon which to build KM processes in STS, is outlined in the following subsection, and the subject of the other sections within this chapter.

5.1.3 Research Roadmap

Among the issues just described, many can be tackled by exploiting existing coordination abstractions and mechanisms. E.g., the need for *awareness* manifested by STS can be directly supported through the notion of *coordination artefacts*, as provided by the A&A meta-model for MAS [26]—see Sect. 5.2.2. There, artefacts are computational resources at agents' disposal, featuring, among the many properties, *observability* of interactions, which directly enables peripheral awareness.

Also, *malleability* of artefacts, that is, their ability to change behaviour dynamically, may be fruitfully exploited to support *adaptation* of the functionalities provided by the system, as well as of other non-functional properties, according to users' interactions and ever-changing needs.

KM processes may be engineered on top of coordination abstractions and mechanisms. Both traditional approaches to KM, that is, process-centred and product-centred, may be conveniently integrated through the notion of artefact: coordination artefacts as enablers of people communication—for the former approach—and resource artefacts as reification of (possibly implicit) knowledge—for the latter. Issues of KM may be then readily delegated to artefacts, exploiting their distinguishing features. In the case of knowledge distribution, e.g. the *linkability* feature comes in hand [20], by allowing delegation of distribution of knowledge, as well as of the computational load needed to make it accessible, to the KM platform.

Besides the A&A meta-model, other coordination-related frameworks may deal with the challenges described in previous section. For example, *stigmergic interaction* [23] leads to a *emergent* phenomena of global coordination arising from *local* interactions, which tolerates quite well *uncertainty* of information and *unpredictability* of behaviour—besides directly supporting peripheral awareness, if not on actions on their post-hoc traces.

For all these reasons, and many more that are detailed in dedicated paragraphs in the following, next section reviews the aforementioned literature—that is, the A&A meta-model and stigmergic interaction—and more, shaping the conceptual framework on top of which a novel approach to *user-driven coordination* is built, as sketched in Sect. 5.3.

Besides this, the conceptual framework is exploited in the $\mathcal{M}$olecules *of* $\mathcal{K}$nowledge model described in Part II of this book.

5.2 From Activity Theory to Behavioural Implicit Communication

In this section the research roadmap outlined in Sect. 5.1.3 is more thoroughly discussed, with the goal of gradually guiding the reader towards the general idea of "smart environment" envisioned by the $\mathcal{M}o\mathcal{K}$ model thoroughly described in Part II of the book.

5.2.1 Activity Theory for Multi-agent Systems

Activity Theory (AT) is a social psychological theory born in the context of Soviet Psychology [33]. Nowadays, it is widely applied in computer science, especially in Computer Supported Cooperative Work (CSCW) and Human Computer Interaction (HCI) [15]. AT is a general framework for conceptualising human activities: according to AT, any activity carried on by one or more participants (agents) of an organisation (MAS) cannot be understood without considering the tools, or *artefacts*, enabling actions and mediating interaction [19].

Thus, on the one side, artefacts mediate interaction among individuals, as well as between individuals and their environment; on the other side, artefacts represent that part of the (computational) *environment* the individuals want/have to deal with. Artefacts are not only *physical*, such as shelves, doors, phones, and whiteboards, but may also be *cognitive*, such as operating procedures, heuristics, scripts, individual and collective experience, or even both, such as operating manuals and computers.

Adopting AT as a conceptual framework for MAS leads to the fundamental recognition that agents are not the sole abstraction to design MAS: artefacts, too, are necessary [19]. As developed by Ricci et al. while defining the A&A meta-model for MAS [26], then, activity theory promotes the notion of *coordination artefact* to identify those artefacts used specifically for coordination purpose. Along this line, coordination artefacts represent a straightforward generalisation of the notion of *coordination medium* [6], coming from the fields of coordination models and languages—including abstractions like tuple spaces, channels, pheromone infrastructures [24], among the many.

> AT defines the artefact abstraction, complementing that of agent, and providing MAS engineers with a broader conceptual space where to look for solutions to design problems. In fact, the artefact abstraction has been readily adopted for engineering MAS environments, and more, as detailed in next section.

5.2.2 The A&A Meta-Model

The A&A meta-model is characterised in terms of three basic abstractions [19]:

Agents—Representing pro-active components of the MAS, encapsulating the *autonomous* execution of some kind of activities inside some sort of environment.

Artefacts—Representing reactive components of the MAS, intentionally constructed, shared, manipulated, and used by agents (or by the MAS designer), to support agents activities—either cooperatively or competitively—and/or MAS non-functional properties.

Workspaces—As the computational containers of agents and artefacts, useful for defining the *topology* of the environment, and providing a way to define a notion of *locality*.

5.2.2.1 Agents

From a computational viewpoint, autonomy means that agents encapsulate (their thread of) control. So, agents never give up control, nor are controlled by anything, unless they deliberate to do so—"agents can say no", according to Odell [17]. Only data (information, knowledge) crosses agent boundaries. As a result, the interpretation of a MAS is that of a multiplicity of distinct loci of control, interacting with each other by exchanging information [19].

Literally, the etymology of the word "agent"—from Latin "agens"—means "the one who acts", thus, the agent notion should come equipped, by definition, with a notion of *action*. Whatever the model, the notion of action is intrinsically connected to the notion of *change*: an agent acts in order to change something, which, in the context of a MAS, can be either another agent, or the environment [34, 35]. The only way to directly affect another agent state is usually thought to be through direct information exchange, that is, through a speech act—or communication action. Instead, change to the MAS environment is more easily thought of as the result of physical actions—which may be undertaken on a computational, or simulated environment, too, of course.

Any ground model of action is strictly coupled with the context where the action takes place. In this sense, autonomous agents are essentially *situated* entities, since any agent is strictly coupled with the environment where it lives and (inter)acts [19].

5.2.2.2 Artefacts

Artefacts, on the contrary, are not autonomous: since they are designed to serve some purpose for agents, artefacts do not follow their own course of action. As such, artefacts are (computationally) reactive, that is, they behave in response to agents use, and their function just needs to emerge when they are used by an agent [19].

Also, their function is expressed in terms of change to the environment, that is, what the artefact actually does when used by an agent, which makes artefacts intrinsically *situated*, too. Finally, since they are situated, artefacts are easy to be thought of as reactive to changes in the environment.

Among the main properties of artefacts, one could list [27]: *(i) inspectability* and controllability, that is, the capability of observing and controlling artefacts structure, state and behaviour at run-time; *(ii) malleability* (or, forgeability), that is, the capability of changing/adapting artefacts function at run-time, according to new requirements or unpredictable events occurring in the open environment; and *(iii) linkability*, that is, the capability of composing distinct artefacts at run-time as a form of service composition, so as to scale up with complexity of the function to be provided.

5.2.2.3 Workspaces

Workspaces conceptually contain agents and artefacts, and computationally provide MAS with a notion of *locality*—that is, agents and artefacts locally available in a given computational node—useful to shape the MAS *topology*—in terms of neighbourhood relations between workspaces. Besides this, definition of workspaces has been never further detailed, basically because according to the A&A meta-model, anything interesting inside a workspace has to be represented by a dedicated artefact.

In Sect. 5.2.5 the notion of *smart environment* introduced in [32] is discussed, and taken as a possible enhancement to the notion of A&A workspace, integrating ingredients borrowed from AT, stigmergy, and BIC (all described in following sections).

It is apparent how the A&A meta-model may prove extremely useful as a reference framework for conceiving and designing the computational part of a STS devoted to KM: agents are the goal-directed/-oriented, active components of the system, such as human users and software agents, undertaking (epistemic) actions aimed at reaching their own business goals; artefacts are the (computational) tools in their hands, including those services devoted to KM and collaboration, as well as the documents subject of the management process; workspaces are the working environments providing the coordination services necessary to deal with the issues outlined in Sect. 5.1—e.g. programmability for adaptiveness & unpredictability, self-organisation for emergence & non-determinism, observability for awareness, and so on.

5.2.3 Stigmergy and Cognitive Stigmergy

5.2.3.1 Stigmergy

The notion of *stigmergy* generally refers to a set of coordination mechanisms mediated by the *environment* [18]. For instance, in ant colonies chemical substances (pheromone) act as environment *markers* for specific social activities, and drive both the individual and the social behaviour of ants. While the notion of stigmergy undergone a large number of generalisations/specialisations/extensions [23, 27] w.r.t. the original definition [9], and even a larger number of implementations in systems of many sorts, its main features are always the same. In short, *stigmergic coordination* requires that

- some interacting agents perform some actions on the environment that leave some *traces*, or markers, which can then be *perceived* by other agents and *affect* their subsequent behaviour
- all interactions among agents are mediated by the environment, through traces—like ant's pheromones
- emission of traces is *generative* [8], thus once they are produced, traces' life is independent of the producer
- traces evolution over time depends on their relation with the environment—as in the case of pheromone diffusion, aggregation, and evaporation in ant colonies

Such a sort of interaction among agents is what produces *self-organisation*: whereas it occurs on a *local* basis, its effect is *global* in terms of the system's global structures and behaviours it originates, by *emergence* [29].

5.2.3.2   Cognitive Stigmergy

A number of relevant works in the field of cognitive sciences point out the role of stigmergy as a fundamental coordination mechanism also in the context of human societies and organisations [28, 31]. As noted in [27]

- modifications to the environment (e.g. traces) are often amenable of an *interpretation* in the context of a shared, conventional system of signs
- the interacting agents feature *cognitive* abilities that can be used in stigmergy-based interactions

Based on this, the notion of *cognitive stigmergy* is introduced in [27] as a first generalisation of stigmergic coordination exploiting agents' cognitive capabilities to enable and promote *self-organisation* of social activities: when traces become signs, stigmergy becomes cognitive stigmergy. There, self-organisation is based on signs amenable of a symbolic interpretation, and involves intelligent agents, able to correctly interpret signs in the environment, so as to react properly.

Under a cognitive perspective, the (working) environment in stigmergy can be interpreted as a set of shared, observable tools (artefacts), providing specific functionalities, that are useful for agents while performing their individual work for both empowering their capabilities and for sharing information—through the environment itself.

Thus, artefacts in cognitive stigmergy are aimed, first of all, at promoting *awareness*, that is, making agents seamlessly aware of the work and practises of other agents, which could in turn *affect*, either driving or improving, their own activities. Awareness is a key aspect to support *emergent* forms of *coordination*, where there is no preestablished plan defining exactly which are the dependencies and interactions among ongoing activities [12] and how to manage them—on the contrary, the plan emerges along with the activities themselves.

Stigmergy and cognitive stigmergy directly and efficiently support both *awareness* and *peripheral awareness* in STS, be it by simply associating reactive behaviours to changes in the shared working environment (e.g. in the form of traces deposit) if non-intelligent agents are considered (e.g. simple software components), or by true signification of signs (e.g. traces amenable of symbolic interpretation) undertaken by intelligent agents (e.g. humans or BDI agents [3]).

Besides awareness, it is apparent that stigmergic coordination is well suited for many facets of KM in STS, e.g. (i) as far as *knowledge creation* is concerned, attaching traces of past activities to managed information items may undoubtedly help further interpretation by collaborative agents; (ii) for *validation*, traces of activities may be exploited by the KM platform to autonomously spot stale, obsolete, wrong, or simply no longer relevant information, then discard it; (iii) as far as *distribution* is concerned, the literature about stigmergic coordination is full of examples of emergent spatial organisation of information items or emergence of spatial patterns among ensembles of cooperating agents—see [23] for some.

Finally, the connection between (cognitive) stigmergy and the A&A metamodel, thus activity theory, too, is obviously represented by the definition of artefact as the means to model and design computational environments within a MAS. Accordingly, (cognitive) artefacts may be the targets of agents practical/epistemic actions, and may react to actions by changing their own state—or that of *linked* artefacts—so as to reflect the traces (interpreted as, e.g. side effects) of the undertaken actions.

5.2.4 Behavioural Implicit Communication

Behavioural Implicit Communication (BIC) is a cognitive theory of communication stemming from the essential idea that usual, *practical*, even non-social behaviour can *contextually* be used as a message for communicating, and that behaviour can be communication by itself, without any modification or any additional signal or mark [5]. The adjective *behavioural* is because it is just simple, non-codified behaviour. *Implicit*, because, not being specialised nor codified, its communicative character is unmarked, undisclosed, *not manifest*. In other words, in BIC communication is just a use, and at most a destination, not the shaping function [7].

On the contrary, communication actions are normally carried on by specialised behaviours (e.g., speech acts, and gestures). Therefore, a BIC action is a *practical action* primarily aimed at reaching a practical goal, which may additionally be interpreted as aimed at achieving a communicative goal, without any predetermined (conventional or innate) specialised meaning.

BIC can be taken as a reference for different modalities of *observation-based coordination* [25]. In [32] five are identified

Unilateral—X intends to coordinate with Y by observing Y's actions.

Bilateral—The unilateral form of coordination but for both agents, so: X intends to coordinate with Y by observing Y's actions, and, viceversa, Y intends to coordinate with X by observing X's actions.

Unilateral-AW—A unilateral form of coordination, improved with a first degree of *awareness*: X intends to coordinate with Y by observing Y's actions, and Y is aware of it—that is, it knows to be observed.

Reciprocal—A bilateral form of observation-based coordination with awareness of both the involved agents: X intends to coordinate with Y by observing Y's actions, being Y aware of it, and Y intends to coordinate with X by observing X's actions, being X aware of it.

Mutual—Extends the reciprocal form by introducing the explicit awareness of each other intention to coordinate (*awareness*^{2}): X intends to coordinate with Y by observing Y's actions, being Y aware of it, Y intends to coordinate with X by observing X's actions, being X aware of it, and also X is aware of Y's intention to coordinate, while Y is aware of X's intention to coordinate.

BIC is necessary for mutual coordination, while it is possible and undoubtedly useful in the other forms of observation-based coordination.

It should be noted that *stigmergy* seems very similar to BIC. However, definition of the former is unable to distinguish between the communication and the *signification* processes. Put in other words, according to [32], one does not want to consider an escaping prey as doing communicative actions to its predator, notwithstanding that the effects of the actions of the former elicit and influence the actions of the latter.

Nevertheless, as in BIC, stigmergic communication does not exploit any specialised communicative action, but just usual practical actions. Therefore, [32] considers stigmergy as a subcategory of BIC, being communication via *long term traces*, physical practical outcomes, useful environment modifications, which preserve their practical end, but acquire a communicative function.

Under this perspective, stigmergy amounts to a special form of BIC where the addressee does not perceive the behaviour during its performance, but post-hoc traces and outcomes of it.

5.2.4.1 Tacit Messages

Tacit messages are proposed, along with the notion of BIC, to describe the messages a practical action (and its traces) may implicitly send to observers [4]:

1. *informing about the presence.* "Agent *A* is here". Since an action, an activity, a practical behaviour (and its traces), is observable in the computational environment, any agent therein—as well as the environment itself—becomes aware of *A* existence—and, possibly, contextual information such as *A* location. Think about

turning the lights on, when going out, in a room clearly visible from the outside. It is a signal left for a potential intruder to persuade him that somebody is at home. The light in itself has not a conventional meaning, but a possible inference that can be drawn by observing it is exploited to send a deceiving message. In this case, although the actual goal of the practical action is informative, the acting agent does not really want to be understood as being communicating

2. *informing about the intention.* "Agent A plans to do action β". If the agents' workflow determines that action β follows action α, peers (as well as the environment) observing A doing α may assume A next intention to be "do β". Consider the phenomenon of trust dynamics, where the fact that an agent trusts another one increases the latter trustworthiness. The trusting agent may intentionally exploit this process by, e.g., delegating to a subordinate agent a critical task: the trace is an implicit signal of the intention to trust

3. *informing about the ability.* "A is able to do ϕ_i, $i \in \mathbb{N}$". Assuming actions ϕ_i, $i \in \mathbb{N}$ have similar preconditions, agents (and the environment) observing A doing ϕ_i may infer that A is also able to do $\phi_{j \neq i}$, $j \in \mathbb{N}$. In the context of supervised learning (e.g. teacher–scholar relationship), each action (of the scholar) is also a message to the supervisor (teacher), implicitly communicating improvements and acquired abilities. For teamwork activities, the ability of agents to signal their own abilities is a crucial message that can be used to speed up team formation

4. *informing about the opportunity for action.* "p_i, $i \in \mathbb{N}$ is the set of preconditions for doing α". Agents observing A doing α may infer that p_i, $i \in \mathbb{N}$ hold, thus, they may take the opportunity to do α as soon as possible. Think about lines in, e.g. a post office: they are evident signs informing about which are the active counters—which are the condition for action. The queue line also informs about the fact that the others are waiting to act, thus: the condition for acting is there, but not available yet. Finally, the physical shape of the line also informs about who is the last person waiting, back to whom the newcomer has to wait

5. *informing about the accomplishment of an action.* "A achieved S". If S is the state of affairs reachable as a consequence of doing action α, agents observing A doing α may infer that the system is now in state S. Consider a child showing her mother she is eating a given food, or a psychiatric patient showing the nurse he is drinking his drug. It is not the ability of eating or drinking that is relevant here, but that the eating or drinking action is being accomplished. This kind of message is particularly important in satisfaction of social commitments, expectations, obligations, and the like

6. *informing about the goal.* "A has goal g". By observing A doing action α, peers of A may infer A's goal to be g, e.g., because action α is part of a workflow aimed at achieving g—likewise for the environment. In the context of a team sport, e.g., football, by kicking the ball in one direction (action), a player is communicating with a team member to sprint in that precise direction (goal)

7. *informing about the result.* "Result R is available". If peer agents know that action α leads to result R, whenever agent A does α they can expect result R to be soon available—in case action α completes successfully. Suppose that while doing the

dishes, a glass is dropped and breaks into pieces. You decide not to remove the fragments in order to let your husband understand that, although he was convinced that they were unbreakable glasses, this glass being struck, it breaks. A trace thus, can be an implicit signal not only when it is the result of an action, but also a consequence of abstaining from acting

The above categorisation is general enough to suit several different business domains and practical actions. In fact, it is used in Sect. 5.3.2 to categorise tacit messages devised out by analysing real-world STS.

BIC is taken as the reference framework for approaching the issue of coordination in knowledge-intensive STS. The reason is that BIC provides a sound cognitive and social model of action and interaction w.r.t. to both human agents and computational agents. Furthermore, as clarified in next section, BIC can be applied to computational environments as well, fully supporting environment-mediated, observation-based coordination. Also, the interpretation of BIC referenced so far, that is, the one described in [32], encompasses stigmergic coordination, too, and is deeply intertwined with the notion of (cognitive) artefact [32].

As regards KM in STS, BIC is obviously well suited to improve existing approaches to KM, be them process-centred or product-centred, partly due to its roots in activity theory and stigmergy, partly thanks to its notion of non-manifest, non-codified communication, reified by tacit messages. Furthermore, the notion of computational smart environment discussed in next section, is directly enabled by BIC, and is a solid reference for the kind of self-organising KM system envisioned by the $\mathcal{M}$olecules of $\mathcal{K}$nowledge model described in Part II.

5.2.5 Towards Computational Smart Environments

The nature of a *working environment* (computational workspace)—which depends on the tools (artefacts) shaping it—determines the effectiveness of the activities of the actors (agents, users) that are immersed in it [32]. Then, the purpose of an activity is not merely to change the environment in a way that (presumably) leads to goal satisfaction, as typically assumed in the literature.

In general, people (software agents) undertake actions to save attention, memory and computation; people recruit external elements to reduce their own cognitive (computational) effort by distributing load; and so on. This makes sense only if agents (either software or humans) and their activities are conceived as *situated* [32], that is, strongly coupled with their environment.

As a result, environment design should not merely be aimed at helping agents to achieve their goals, but also to make other actions as easy as possible—such as *epistemic*, and *coordinative* actions.

Also, [32] notices that cognitive processes exist in MAS that do not belong to individual agents: the MAS environment may participate, too, by enabling and mediating individual agent actions as well as social agent interaction, through the knowledge it embeds either implicitly or explicitly. Thus, knowledge is distributed in the environment and is encapsulated within cognitive artefacts, and the structure of the environment, as well as of the knowledge it contains, affects the activities of agents within the MAS.

According to [30], "computer supported collaborative work (CSCW) seems to be pursuing two diverging strategies", leading to distinct trends in CSCW research: the first, stemming from workflow management systems, tends to privilege *automatisation* of coordination; the second, takes *flexibility* of interaction as its main goal. That is, the former approach stresses the role of computational entities prescribing the rules of collaboration (like workflow engines), the latter mostly leverages the intelligent coordination capabilities of collaborative entities (like humans, or intelligent agents). So, there is a gap between two strategies, that [30] proposes to close by dealing with two key issues: *mutual awareness* and *coordinative artefacts*.

Mutual awareness means that actors of a collaboration activity *affect* and mutually *perceive* others' activities in the common field of work—the shared workspace—which can (partially) reveal/conceal them. Mutual awareness is then the basis for opportunistic, ad hoc alignment and improvisation, which ensures flexibility to collaborative activities. Coordinative (or, coordination) artefacts instead, encapsulate those portions of the coordination responsibilities that is better to automatise, e.g. for the sake of efficiency. So, on the one hand, coordinative artefacts define and govern the space of the admissible interaction, while, on the other hand, they do not impose a predefined course of actions unnecessarily reducing flexibility (they do not work as commanders) [32].

BIC and (cognitive) stigmergy seem to provide the necessary mutual awareness envisioned by [30], while (cognitive) coordination artefacts the required coordinative capabilities. But in order for a computational work environment to fully support BIC-based coordination, at least three different conditions have to hold [32]:

1. *observability* of practical actions and their traces must be a property of the environment where agents live. The environment can enable visibility of others, or constrain it—in the same way that sunny or foggy days affect perception. It could also enable agents to make themselves observable or hide their presence on purpose
2. agents should be able to *understand* and *interpret* (or to learn to react to) a practical action. A usual practical action becomes then a (implicit) message when the acting agent knows others are observing and will understand his behaviour
3. agents should be able to understand the *effect* that their actions have on others, so as to begin acting in the usual way also/only to obtain a desired/expected reaction

Based on these requirements, two types of *computational smart environment* are defined in [32]: common environment and shared environment.

Agents that live in a *common environment* (*c-env*) are agents whose actions and goals interfere (positively or negatively), thus need coordination to manage this interference. Agents can observe just the state of the environment and act on that basis, without having access to the actions of their peers. Even a trace is seen as part of the environment and not as a product of other agents. A general property of a c-env is that it enables agents to modify the environment state while keeping track of it. A *shared environment* (*s-env*) instead, is a particular case of a c-env that enables *(i)* different forms of observability of each other actions execution, as well as *(ii)* awareness of this observability.

It is exactly this kind of smart environment, leveraging BIC and (cognitive) stigmergy through coordination artefacts, that is envisioned in Part II of this book with the $\mathcal{M}$olecules *of* $\mathcal{K}$nowledge model and technology for self-organisation of knowledge in knowledge-intensive STS. There, shared workspaces act as active repositories of information, autonomously and continuously monitoring users' activity with the aim of exploiting their tacit messages and traces of actions so as to enable anticipatory coordination [25], while assisting usual workflows related to KM by autonomously dealing with some of the aforementioned facets of KM.

5.3 Behavioural Implicit Communication in Real-World STS

In this section a survey of a few real-world STS, heterogeneous in goals, architecture, and functionalities, is discussed, seeking for the practical (virtual) actions they provide (Sect. 5.3.1). Then, in Sect. 5.3.2, the pool of actions the STS have in common, that is, those actions having different names but the same (epistemic) goal, is devised out, as well as the tacit messages the common actions may convey and the consequent perturbation actions they may bring along.

The purpose of the section is to bridge the gap between theory and practice, showing that BIC is not only a fancy cognitive theory, but a pervasive facet of everyday technological activities.

5.3.1 Survey of Actions

It should be noted that the following list is not comprehensive: for each STS covered by the survey, the focus is solely on those actions which could more easily be interpreted in *epistemic terms*, and which could be defined *positive*, in the sense of adding information and connections, not removing them—e.g. the "post" action versus the opposite, "delete post" action. Also, features not available to the average user are ignored, e.g. companies, groups, public pages and profiles, premium services.

5.3.1.1 Facebook (http://facebook.com)

As far as Facebook is concerned, actions considered are:

Post—Publish something on Facebook wall, e.g. a text, an image, a video, or an hyperlink. The published piece of information may be publicly visible, or its visibility can be constrained with a fine granularity.
Like—Manifest interest in a piece of information, e.g. a post, a repost, or a comment. It should be noted that interest is usually positive, meaning that the user liking the post (or a comment to a post) enjoys or agrees with the information, but could also be negative, if the opposite is true, depending on the acting user habits and shared conventions among his/her friends.
Comment—Comment a post with information, e.g. text, an image, a video, or hyperlinks.
Reply—Reply to a comment with another comment. The difference w.r.t. a comment, is that the subject of a comment is a post, while the subject of a reply is a comment.
Share—Share someone else's post, either with an additional comment, or as it is—the source is automatically cited. The target audience is limited by the original post visibility constraints.
Save—Store a post for later retrieval. The saved piece of information is placed in a special section of a user workspace, and is periodically rebrought to user attention.
Tag friends—Explicitly bring to a given friend attention the piece of information he/she is tagged in. As a consequence, an explicit notification is sent to the tagged friend.
Add friend—Include a given person in the list of friends, that is, the list of observable people who can in turn observe the acting user. Observability potentially includes anything visible on the activity registry each Facebook user has—fine grained visibility details may be tuned at will.
Search—Search for any information, including posts, public pages, interest groups, people.

5.3.1.2 Twitter (http://twitter.com)

As far as Twitter is concerned, actions considered are

Tweet—Post something to Twitter wall. Besides text, pictures, hyperlinks, and Facebook-like items, also a poll can be published.
Retweet—Republish someone else's tweet, either with an additional comment, or as it is—the source is automatically cited.

Reply—Reply to a tweet with another tweet specifically directed to the author of the replied tweet, and referring to the original tweet—the author is automatically tagged and the source tweet included.

Favourite—Manifest interest in a tweet. Similarly to Facebook "like", interest is usually positive.

Share privately—Send the link to a tweet to a friend with a private message.

Follow—Include a given profile in the list of followed profiles, that is, the list of observable profiles you get notifications from. Differently from Facebook friendship, Twitter "following" relationship is not symmetric.

Search—Search for free terms, profiles, hashtags.

5.3.1.3 Google$^+$ (http://plus.google.com)

As far as Google$^+$ is concerned, actions considered are

Post—Post something on Google$^+$ wall.

Share—Share someone else's post, either with an additional comment, or as it is—the source is automatically embedded in the new post.

+1—Manifest interest in a piece of information, e.g. a post or a comment. As for Facebook and Twitter, usually a positive interest.

Comment—Comment a post with text, or hyperlinks.

Reply—Reply to a comment with another comment.

Add people—Add people to the network of friends, that is, the list of observable people who can in turn observe the acting user.

Search—Search for people, profiles, communities, collections of information.

5.3.1.4 LinkedIN (http://linkedin.com)

As far as LinkedIN is concerned, actions considered are

Post—Post something on your LinkedIN profile, e.g. text, an hyperlink, a picture.

Suggest—Manifest interest in a piece of information, e.g. a post or a comment.

Comment—Comment a post with other information, e.g. text or hyperlinks.

Share—Share someone else's post, either with an additional comment, or as it is—the source is automatically cited.

Connect—Include a given person in the list of connections, that is, the list of observable people who can in turn observe the acting user.

Search—Search for people, job offers, firms, groups, universities, posts, even personal mail.

5.3.1.5 Mendeley (http://mendeley.com)

As far as Mendeley is concerned, actions considered are

Publish—Publish a paper. The paper becomes available in the acting user's profile, and searchable through Mendeley search facilities.

Post—Publish something on Mendeley news feed, e.g. text or hyperlinks.

Like—Manifest interest in a piece of information, e.g. a publication, or a post.

Comment—Comment a post with other information, e.g. text or hyperlinks.

Cite—Share someone else's publication, either with an additional comment, or as it is, while preserving authorship.

Download—Download the publication, if made available by the author.

Follow—Include a given author in the list of followed profiles, that is, the list of observable authors you get notifications from. Similarly to Twitter following relationship, this is not symmetric.

Search—Search for people, papers, or interest groups.

5.3.1.6   Academia.edu (http://academia.edu)

As far as Academia.edu is concerned, actions considered are:

Publish—Publish a paper, either already published, or new. The paper becomes available in the acting user's profile, and searchable through Academia.edu search facilities.

Bookmark—Store a publication in a special, public bookmarks section for later retrieval.

Download—Download the publication, if made available by the author, otherwise ask for a private copy.

Follow—Include a given author in the list of followed profiles, that is, the list of observable authors you get notifications from. As for Mendeley following relationship, this is not symmetric.

Search—Search for papers, people, universities.

5.3.1.7   ResearchGate (http://researchgate.net)

As far as ResearchGate is concerned, actions considered are:

Publish—Publish a piece of information, whose type can be dynamically designed. Supported publication types are, among the many, article, book, code, dataset, patent, presentation, thesis, and so on. Published information becomes available from the publisher profile, and searchable through ResearchGate search facilities.

Comment—Comment a published item with other information, e.g. text or hyperlinks.

Download—Download a given piece of information, if made available by the author, otherwise ask for a private copy.

Follow—Follow an author, a publication, or a question. Regardless of the subject of the follow action, the follower now gets updates regarding modification of the followed source of information—e.g., new publications from authors, new comments on publications, new answers to questions. The following relationship is not symmetric, whichever the involved entity is.

Ask—Publish a question on your profile, which anybody can publicly answer to.

Answer—Publicly answer a published question.

Vote—Publicly up-vote or down-vote either a question or an answer.

Endorse—Publicly endorse a given skill of a given person.

Search—Search for people, publications, questions, job offers.

5.3.1.8 Storify (http://storify.com)

As far as Storify is concerned, actions considered are

Add source—Add a source of information to your story. The admissible sources are, among the many, other Storify elements, Twitter tweets and user profiles, Instagram[1] posts and users, YouTube videos, any Google search result, and many more.

Add content—Add content to your story, taken from one of the already added sources.

Comment story—Add comments to a specific content of a given story.

Publish story—Publish a story. From now on, the story can be publicly used as a source of information into other stories of other users.

Like story—Manifest interest in a story.

Share story—Share someone else's story.

Search stories—Search for stories based on free terms.

Follow—Include a given storyteller in the list of followed profiles, that is, the list of observable profiles you get notifications from. Like in the case of Twitter, the relation is not symmetric.

5.3.2 Factorisation of Common Actions

Based on the extensive survey just described, a core set of common actions shared by almost all the heterogeneous STS just described are identified, whose goals, despite their diversity, are almost identical—at the level of abstraction suggested by BIC theory

Share—The share action encompasses posting novel information, sharing or citing someone else's posts, publishing papers or stories, asking questions, and so on. Namely, any action whose effect is that of adding information to the system.

Mark—The mark action encompasses liking a post, voting a question/answer, bookmarking a publication, giving +1 to a post, and so on. Namely, any action whose

---

[1]http://www.instagram.com.

effect is that of marking information as relevant or not, qualitatively or quantitatively.

Annotate—The annotate action encompasses, besides the obvious annotation to stories, comments to existing posts, replies to comments, answers to questions. Namely, any action whose effect is that of attaching a piece of information to an existing information.

Connect—The connect action encompasses adding friends, following people or sources of information, and adding content and sources to stories. Namely, any action expanding the network of relationships between a user and other users or sources of information.

Harvest—The harvest action encompasses all kinds of search actions, whatever their target is. Namely, any action aimed at acquiring knowledge about either potential sources of information or potentially relevant pieces of information.

5.3.2.1 Tacit Messages from Actions

Each common action may convey different tacit messages, depending on a number of factors, such as the context within which the action occurred, the source and target of the action, and the degree of mutual awareness the specific platform supports.

In the following, a few tacit messages are sketched for each action, so as to give the reader a clue about how BIC may be used in real-world scenarios—tacit messages are referred to using their numbers, assigned in Sect. 5.2.4.

Share—Re-publishing or mentioning someone else's information can convey, e.g. tacit messages 1, 3, 5. If X shares Y's information through action a, every other agent observing a becomes aware of existence and location of both X and Y (1). The fact that X is sharing information I from source S lets X's peers infer X can manipulate S (3). If X shared I with Z, Z may infer, e.g., that X expects Z to somehow use it (5).

Mark—Marking as relevant a piece of information can convey, e.g. tacit messages 1, 4. If the sociotechnical platform lets X be aware of Y marking information I as relevant, X may infer that Y exists (1). If Y marks as relevant I belonging to X, X may infer that Y is interested in her work, perhaps seeking for collaborations (4).

Annotate—Annotating a piece of information can convey, e.g. tacit messages 5, 6. Since X annotated, e.g. Y's post, any agent observing X may infer she just finished reading that post (5). Furthermore, by interpreting the content of the annotation, agents peers of X may infer the motivation behind X's annotation (6).

Connect—Subscribing for updates regarding some piece of information or some user can convey tacit messages 2, 4. Since X manifested interest in Y's work through subscription, Y may infer X intention to use it somehow (2). Accordingly, Y may infer the opportunity for, e.g. collaboration (4).

Harvest—Performing a search query to retrieve information can convey, e.g., tacit
  messages 1, 2, 4.[2] If X search query is observable by peer agents, they can infer
  X existence and location (1). Also, they can infer X goal to acquire knowledge
  related to its search query (2). Finally, along the same line, they can take the
  chance to provide matching information (4).

5.3.2.2   Perturbation Actions from Tacit Messages

The last step still missing to bridge the gap between theory and practice regarding
BIC in real-world STS, is to answer the question: how can a coordination middleware,
underlying the sociotechnical platform for KM, take advantage of all the possible
tacit messages, just ascribed to (inter-)actions, for the benefit of the coordination
process? The answer proposed in the following is: through *perturbation actions*.

Perturbation actions are computational functions/processes changing the state of
a STS in response to users' interactions, but *transparently* to them [13]. Perturbation
actions exploit the implicit information conveyed by tacit messages, leveraging the
mind-reading and *signification* abilities ascribed to agents (either software or human),
as well as to the (smart) computational environment, with the aim of *tuning* the
coordination process so as to better support the ever-changing KM related needs of
the sociotechnical platform, and its users.

Accordingly, perturbation actions may, e.g. *(i)* spread discovery messages informing agents about the presence and location of others (tacit message *presence*), *(ii)*
establish privileged communication channels between frequently interacting agents
(*opportunity*), *(iii)* encourage/obstruct some desirable/dangerous interaction protocols or situated actions (*intention*, *ability*, *goal*), *(iv)* recommend to users novel,
potentially interesting information as soon as it is available (*accomplishment, result*).

> Not by chance, perturbation actions are one essential abstraction of the
> $\mathcal{M}$olecules of $\mathcal{K}$nowledge model, as described in Chap. 6 in Part II of this
> book, where their role and how they work in a concrete middleware is thor-
> oughly described.

To conclude the survey, here follows some clues about which possible perturbation actions may be put to work by the aforementioned real-world sociotechnical
platforms, based on the devised pool of common actions. However, what follows is
a speculation on what could be possibly done behind the scenes of these platforms,
since for many of them no public disclosure of, e.g. ranking algorithms is available.

Share—Provided by Facebook, Twitter (retweet), G+, LinkedIN, Mendeley (post),
  Storify, Academia.edu (publish), ResearchGate (publish), etc. It is likely to help
  the STS platform, underlying the social network application, in

---

[2]It should be noted, however, that which assumptions to make about a search action heavily depends
on which search criteria are supported.

- suggesting novel connections, based on common interests
- ranking feeds in the newsfeed timeline, based on similarity
- tuning personalised advertising policies, based on topic of posts
- recommending content (e.g. job offers, publications, news stories), based on similarity

Mark—Provided by Facebook (like), Twitter (like), G+ (+1), LinkedIN (suggest), Mendeley (like), Academia.edu (bookmark), ResearchGate (follow/download), Storify, etc. It is likely to influence the STS similarly to what described above, with the addition of enabling/strengthening notifications for the marked items.

Annotate—Provided by almost any STS, it is likely to help the STS platform by

- suggesting novel connections, based on shared annotations
- recommending content (e.g. job offers, publications, news stories), based on annotated items
- enabling/strengthening notifications for the annotated items

Connect—Provided by Facebook (add friend), Twitter (follow), G+ (add), LinkedIN, Mendeley (follow), Academia.edu (follow), ResearchGate (follow), etc. It is likely to help the STS platform by

- suggesting further connections
- activating/ranking feeds in the newsfeed timeline
- enabling/strengthening notifications for new/old connections

Harvest—Provided by almost every social network, it is the epistemic action by its very definition, thus may be exploited by the STS platform in a wide number of ways, heavily depending on which are the searchable information items, and which are the searching parameters. Among the many possible reactions

- reorganise the knowledge graph internally used by the STS
- tune the algorithm providing suggestions
- improve personalised advertising policies
- suggest novel connections, based on search terms
- ranking feeds in the newsfeed timeline, based on search results

As already pointed out, *mutual awareness* (including peripheral awareness, too), as well as the ability to delegate activities to *coordinative artefacts*—according to terminology in [30]—is the only path toward bridging the gap between current approaches to KM. For all these reasons, the $\mathcal{M}$olecules of $\mathcal{K}$nowledge model discussed in the upcoming Part II is heavily centred around the notions of tacit message (*traces* in $\mathcal{MoK}$) and perturbation action.

References

1. Ackerman, M.S.: The intellectual challenge of cscw: the gap between social requirements and technical feasibility. Hum. Comput. Interact. **15**(2–3), 179–203 (2000)
2. Bhatt, G.D.: Knowledge management in organizations: Examining the interaction between technologies, techniques, and people. J. Knowl. Manag. **5**(1), 68–75 (2001)
3. Castelfranchi, C.: Modelling social action for AI agents. Artif. Intell. **103**(1–2), 157–182 (1998). doi:10.1016/S0004-3702(98)00056-3
4. Castelfranchi, C., Pezzullo, G., Tummolini, L.: Behavioral implicit communication (BIC): Communicating with smart environments via our practical behavior and its traces. Int. J. Ambient Comput. Intell. **2**(1), 1–12 (2010). doi:10.4018/jaci.2010010101
5. Castlefranchi, C.: From conversation to interaction via behavioral communication: For a semiotic design of objects, environments, and behaviors. Theories and practice in interaction design, pp. 157–79 (2006)
6. Ciancarini, P.: Coordination models and languages as software integrators. ACM Comput. Surv. **28**(2), 300–302 (1996). doi:10.1145/234528.234732
7. Conte, R., Castelfranchi, C. (eds.): Cognitive and Social Action. Routledge (1995). http://books.google.com/books?isbn=1857281861
8. Gelernter, D.: Generative communication in Linda. ACM Trans. Program. Lang. Syst. **7**(1), 80–112 (1985). doi:10.1145/2363.2433
9. Grassé, P.P.: La reconstruction du nid et les coordinations interindividuelles chez Bellicositermes natalensis et Cubitermes sp. la théorie de la stigmergie: Essai d'interprétation du comportement des termites constructeurs. Insectes Soc. **6**(1), 41–80 (1959). doi:10.1007/BF02223791
10. Hudson, S.E., Smith, I.: Techniques for addressing fundamental privacy and disruption tradeoffs in awareness support systems. In: Proceedings of the 1996 ACM Conference on Computer Supported Cooperative Work, CSCW '96, pp. 248–257. ACM, New York, NY, USA (1996). doi:10.1145/240080.240295
11. Hutchins, E.: Cognition in the Wild. MIT Press (1995)
12. Malone, T.W., Crowston, K.: The interdisciplinary study of coordination. ACM Comput. Surv. **26**(1), 87–119 (1994). doi:10.1145/174666.174668
13. Mariani, S., Omicini, A.: Anticipatory coordination in socio-technical knowledge-intensive environments: Behavioural implicit communication in MoK. In: M. Gavanelli, E. Lamma, F. Riguzzi (eds.) AI*IA 2015, Advances in Artificial Intelligence, Lecture Notes in Computer Science, vol. 9336, Chap. 8, pp. 102–115. Springer International Publishing (2015). doi:10.1007/978-3-319-24309-2. XIVth International Conference of the Italian Association for Artificial Intelligence, Ferrara, Italy, September 23–25, 2015, Proceedings
14. Mentzas, G., Apostolou, D., Young, R., Abecker, A.: Knowledge networking: a holistic solution for leveraging corporate knowledge. J. Knowl. Manag. **5**(1), 94–107 (2001)
15. Nardi, B.: Context and Consciousness: Activity Theory and Human-computer Interaction. MIT Press (1996)
16. O'Day, V.L., Bobrow, D.G., Shirley, M.: The social-technical design circle. In: Proceedings of the 1996 ACM Conference on Computer Supported Cooperative Work, pp. 160–169. ACM (1996)
17. Odell, J.J.: Objects and agents compared. J. Object Technol. **1**(1), 41–53 (2002). http://www.jot.fm/issues/issue_2002_05/column4
18. Omicini, A.: Agents writing on walls: Cognitive stigmergy and beyond. In: Paglieri, F., Tummolini, L., Falcone, R., Miceli, M. (eds.) The Goals of Cognition. Essays in Honor of Cristiano Castelfranchi, *Tributes*, vol. 20, Chap. 29, pp. 543–556. College Publications, London (2012)
19. Omicini, A., Ricci, A., Viroli, M.: Artifacts in the A&A meta-model for multi-agent systems. Auton. Agent. Multi-Agent Syst. **17**(3), 432–456 (2008). doi:10.1007/s10458-008-9053-x
20. Omicini, A., Ricci, A., Zaghini, N.: Distributed workflow upon linkable coordination artifacts. In: Ciancarini, P., Wiklicky, H. (eds.) Coordination Models and Languages, LNCS, vol. 4038, pp. 228–246. Springer (2006). doi:10.1007/11767954

21. Orlikowski, W.J.: The duality of technology: Rethinking the concept of technology in organizations. Organ. Sci. **3**(3), 398–427 (1992)
22. Ossowski, S., Omicini, A.: Coordination knowledge engineering. Knowl. Eng. Rev. **17**(4), 309–316 (2002). doi:10.1017/S0269888903000596
23. Parunak, H.V.D.: A survey of environments and mechanisms for human-human stigmergy. In: Weyns, D., Parunak, H.V.D., Michel, F. (eds.) Environments for Multi-Agent Systems II, LNCS, vol. 3830, pp. 163–186. Springer (2006). doi:10.1007/11678809
24. Parunak, H.V.D., Brueckner, S., Sauter, J.: Digital pheromone mechanisms for coordination of unmanned vehicles. In: Castelfranchi, C., Johnson, W.L. (eds.) 1st International Joint Conference on Autonomous Agents and Multiagent systems, vol. 1, pp. 449–450. ACM, New York, NY, USA (2002). http://dx.doi.org/10.1145/544741.544843
25. Piunti, M., Castelfranchi, C., Falcone, R.: Anticipatory coordination through action observation and behavior adaptation. In: Proceedings of AISB (2007)
26. Ricci, A., Omicini, A., Denti, E.: Activity Theory as a framework for MAS coordination. In: Petta, P., Tolksdorf, R., Zambonelli, F. (eds.) Engineering Societies in the Agents World III, LNCS, vol. 2577, pp. 96–110. Springer (2003). doi:10.1007/3-540-39173-8. 3rd International Workshop (ESAW 2002), Madrid, Spain, 16–17 Sep. 2002. Revised Papers
27. Ricci, A., Omicini, A., Viroli, M., Gardelli, L., Oliva, E.: Cognitive stigmergy: Towards a framework based on agents and artifacts. In: Weyns, D., Parunak, H.V.D., Michel, F. (eds.) Environments for MultiAgent Systems III, LNCS, vol. 4389, pp. 124–140. Springer (2007). doi:10.1007/978-3-540-71103-2. 3rd International Workshop (E4MAS 2006), Hakodate, Japan, 8 May 2006. Selected Revised and Invited Papers
28. Schmidt, K., Wagner, I.: Ordering systems: Coordinative practices and artifacts in architectural design and planning. Comput. Support. Coop. Work (CSCW) **13**(5–6), 349–408 (2004)
29. Serugendo, G.D.M., Foukia, N., Hassas, S., Karageorgos, A., Mostéfaoui, S.K., Rana, O.F., Ulieru, M., Valckenaers, P., Van Aart, C.: Self-organisation: Paradigms and applications. Springer (2003)
30. Simone, C., Schmidt, K.: Mind the gap! towards a unified view of cscw. In: Fourth International Conference on Design of Cooperative Systems (COOP2000), Sophia-Antipolis (Fr) (2000)
31. Susi, T., Ziemke, T.: Social cognition, artefacts, and stigmergy: A comparative analysis of theoretical frameworks for the understanding of artefact-mediated collaborative activity. Cogn. Syst. Res. **2**(4), 273–290 (2001)
32. Tummolini, L., Castelfranchi, C., Ricci, A., Viroli, M., Omicini, A.: "Exhibitionists" and "voyeurs" do it better: A shared environment approach for flexible coordination with tacit messages. In: Weyns, D., Parunak, H.V.D., Michel, F. (eds.) Environments for Multi-Agent Systems, LNAI, vol. 3374, pp. 215–231. Springer (2005). doi:10.1007/b106134
33. Vigotsky, L., et al.: Mind in Society (1978)
34. Viroli, M., Holvoet, T., Ricci, A., Schelfthout, K., Zambonelli, F.: Infrastructures for the environment of multiagent systems. Auton. Agent. Multi-Agent Syst. **14**(1), 49–60 (2007). doi:10.1007/s10458-006-9001-6
35. Weyns, D., Omicini, A., Odell, J.J.: Environment as a first-class abstraction in multi-agent systems. Auton. Agent. Multi-Agent Syst. **14**(1), 5–30 (2007). doi:10.1007/s10458-006-0012-0
36. Whitworth, B.: Socio-technical systems. Encycl. Hum. Comput. Interact. pp. 533–541 (2006)

Part II
Self-organisation of Knowledge in $\mathcal{M}$olecules of $\mathcal{K}$nowledge

In the second part of this book, the $\mathcal{M}$olecules of $\mathcal{K}$nowledge ($\mathcal{MoK}$) model and technology for *self-organisation of knowledge* in knowledge-intensive sociotechnical systems are thoroughly described. $\mathcal{MoK}$ is the result of the integration of all the different, but complementary, research works discussed so far, in Part I of this book. In fact:

- it is a self-organising *biochemical coordination* model, where coordination laws are biochemical reactions, information items are molecules, and the agents to coordinate are the chemists working with a "knowledge-based chemical solution"— Chap. 3

- it has been prototyped as a middleware layer for knowledge management applications, by implementing it upon the TuCSoN coordination infrastructure, fully exploiting its *situated architecture*, for distribution, and the ReSpecT language, for *spatiotemporal awareness* and adaptiveness—Chap. 4

- it integrates a socio-cognitive theory of action and interaction since its very foundation, adopting the *behavioural implicit communication* perspective over *anticipatory coordination* via tacit messages and stigmergic coordination—Chap. 5.

Chapter 6
$\mathcal{M}$olecules of $\mathcal{K}$nowledge: Model

Abstract In this chapter the $\mathcal{M}$olecules of $\mathcal{K}$nowledge model for self-organising coordination of knowledge-intensive sociotechnical systems is thoroughly described: its basic abstractions (Sect. 6.2), its chemical-inspired computational model (Sect. 6.3), its BIC-based interaction model (Sect. 6.4), and its modelling of information (Sect. 6.5).

6.1 Motivation, Context, Goal

Nowadays, ICT systems have gone far beyond pure, *algorithmic* Turing Machine computation, as Turing himself anticipated long ago with o-machines and c-machines [28], and Wegner later highlighted [30] with its equation "computation = algorithm + *interaction*". The question "how to manage interaction?" then, originated a whole research landscape, branded *coordination models and languages*, which is devoted to understanding how to *manage dependencies* arising from interacting activities in systems of any sort [19]. However, in recent years a plethora of novel *open*, *pervasive*, highly *dynamic*, and mostly *unpredictable* systems have surged, presenting brand-new challenges which demand for innovative coordination approaches [23].

Sociotechnical Systems (STS) and *Knowledge-Intensive Environments* (KIE), as described in Chap. 5, are both blatant examples of such a sort of systems, being them conceived and designed to combine business processes, technologies, and people's skills [31] to store, handle, and make accessible large repositories of information [4]. By definition, both KIE and STS are heavily interaction-centred, thus, managing their *interaction space* is of paramount importance for ensuring their functionalities, as well as for providing desirable non-functional properties [27]—e.g. scalability, fault-tolerance, self-* properties in general. However, engineering coordination mechanisms and policies accordingly is far from trivial, mostly due to a few peculiar features of the aforementioned systems [2, 4]:

- people may behave within a STS in ways completely *unpredictable* from the designer's standpoint. In particular, it is almost impossible to globally foresee and influence the space of potential interactions. Most probably, users, as well as

© Springer International Publishing AG 2016

S. Mariani, *Coordination of Complex Sociotechnical Systems*,
Artificial Intelligence: Foundations, Theory, and Algorithms,
DOI 10.1007/978-3-319-47109-9_6

software components, will behave in a self-interested fashion, which may help to anticipate some of their actions, and may provide some clues on how to design coordination strategies at the micro-level [24]

- both (mutual) *awareness*—that is, knowing who is present—and *peripheral aware-ness*—that is, monitoring of others' activity—are fundamental in STS [14] because visibility of information flow—thus *observability* of dependencies—enables learning and greater efficiency [15]—as well as *observation-based coordination* [25]
- knowledge creation is an *emergent* process in which experimentation and pure *chance* play an important role. Providing the means to undertake trial-and-error experiments, and to spot knowledge creation opportunities, is a great computational challenge for a Knowledge Management (KM) platform
- *interactions* between organisational technologies, techniques, and people can have *direct bearing* on knowledge distribution, introducing the need to deal with some degree of *uncertainty*—about, e.g. where to find a relevant piece of information— and demanding for *adaptation* techniques supporting continuous and *autonomous* knowledge re-distribution

The *data-driven approach* to coordination [7], such as tuple-based models [9], aims at coordinating interacting agents by properly managing access to information, rather than by directly *commanding* the parties about what to do, and when. A similar approach is apparently suitable for knowledge-intensive STS, where data, information, and knowledge drive both the business goals of the organisation as a whole, and the everyday activities of the co-workers sharing the computational platform in charge of data, information, and knowledge management.

In fact, as already highlighted in Sect. 5.1.2, the whole process of KM in STS, in most if not all of its facets, can be approached from a *coordination perspective*, where coordination policies and mechanisms may be applied not solely to the agents (either software or human) participating the management process, but also to the raw data subject of the process.

Therefore, a possibly novel research thread originates from the question: why should we stick with the view of data as passive, "dead" things to run algorithms upon in the traditional I/O paradigm? Why not to foster a novel interpretation of both knowledge management and data-driven coordination in general, where *data is alive*, spontaneously and continuously evolving so as to better serve the ever-changing needs of the organisation? This chapter is precisely devoted to explore this research line, by describing a model for *self-organising*, *user-centric* coordination in knowledge-intensive STS: the *Molecules of Knowledge* model (*MoK* for short).

Accordingly, the *MoK* model fosters a novel way to approach, model, and design computational platforms supporting *information and knowledge management* in STS, where users interact with information as usual, while the software exploits their interactions to continuously and spontaneously *(self-)organise* information, and to *adapt* such an organisation to their ever-changing needs. This way, the technological platform is no longer perceived as a mere tool in the hands of users, but more as an active part in users' own workflows, constantly striving to autonomously improve the service it provides to the users.

To this end, $\mathcal{M}o\mathcal{K}$ conveniently builds on existing research regarding, e.g. *self-organisation* [8, 29, 32] and *cognitive stigmergy* [6, 22]. Thus $\mathcal{M}o\mathcal{K}$ relies on:

- a *biochemical metaphor* to design the computational model in charge of applying coordination laws to information pieces, so as to spontaneously self-organise information [20]
- a *cognitive theory* of social action to design the interaction model, suitably interpreted and extended for representing and exploiting users' actions, as well as their side effects, so as to devise out appropriate *anticipatory coordination* actions to undertake [21]

6.2 Core Abstractions

The $\mathcal{M}o\mathcal{K}$ model is built around the biochemical metaphor.

Accordingly, a $\mathcal{M}o\mathcal{K}$-coordinated system is a network of $\mathcal{M}o\mathcal{K}$ *compartments* (representing information repositories), where $\mathcal{M}o\mathcal{K}$ *seeds* (representing information sources) continuously and spontaneously inject $\mathcal{M}o\mathcal{K}$ *atoms* (representing atomic information chunks). $\mathcal{M}o\mathcal{K}$ atoms may then aggregate into *molecules* (representing composite information chunks), diffuse to neighbouring compartments, lose relevance as time flows, gain relevance upon users interactions, or have their properties modified—everything as a consequence of user agents' interactions.

Such autonomous and decentralised processes are enacted by $\mathcal{M}o\mathcal{K}$ biochemical *reactions* (the coordination laws dictating how the system evolves), and are influenced by $\mathcal{M}o\mathcal{K}$ *enzymes* (reification of user agents' actions) as well as by $\mathcal{M}o\mathcal{K}$ *traces* (actions' side effects). Both enzymes and traces are transparently, and possibly unintentionally, left within the working environment by $\mathcal{M}o\mathcal{K}$ *catalysts* (representing users, either human or software agents) while performing their activities.

6.2.1 Atoms

As $\mathcal{M}o\mathcal{K}$ elementary units of information, atoms are meant to represent any piece of information that can be regarded as being *atomic*, that is which cannot be further decomposed in smaller chunks. The granularity of information is set by the agents, either software or human, that create atoms from information sources. Thus, atoms may represent table cells of a relational DB, nodes in a graph DB, document content, or metadata in a document-oriented DB; hyperlinks of a web page, feeds of an RSS channel, posts or comments in a blog; word, phrases, or paragraphs in an article; and so on.

Atoms are *continuously* and *spontaneously* injected by sources of information into suitable repositories, where they become susceptible to $\mathcal{M}o\mathcal{K}$ biochemical reactions (computational processes, see Sect. 6.2.8) in charge of system evolution—e.g., they can be aggregated into more complex information heaps, exploited to inference novel knowledge, or shared with other compartments.

Atoms are formally defined as follows:

$$\texttt{atom}(\mathit{Src},\mathit{Content},\mathit{Meta\text{-}info})_c, \quad c \in \Re^+$$
$$\mathit{Src} :: = \texttt{URI}$$
$$\mathit{Content} :: = \texttt{raw information}$$
$$\mathit{Meta\text{-}info} :: = \texttt{(semantic) metadata}$$

where

- *Src* is meant to provide an always up-to-date reference to the original source of information, wherever it is, and in whichever format it is persistently stored—e.g. the URL of a web page, or, the absolute path of a file on disk
- *Content* is the raw piece of atomic information the atom conveys—e.g. records of a DB, comments in a blog, sentences within an article
- *Meta-info* is meant to store any kind of metadata, related to the atom content, supporting knowledge inference and discovery—e.g. the DB schema the content must comply to, a set of synonyms for a set of words, the categorisation of an article topic based on a dedicated ontology
- *c* is the concentration value of the atom, resembling its *relevance*—according to whatever definition of "relevance" best suits the application at hand

6.2.2 Seeds

As *MoK sources of information*, seeds are meant to represent any facet of a source of information and to make available any information therein contained that may be useful for the application at hand. Sources of information reified by seeds may be: legacy DBs, web pages, RSS channels, files on disk, sensor devices, and so on—namely anything capable of generating raw data or (un)structured information.

Seeds generate information continuously and spontaneously (through *MoK* biochemical reactions), that is: *(i)* any data chunk is produced by a seed multiple times, not once, at a *rate* depending on heterogeneous and dynamic *contextual information*—e.g. predicted relevance of the information, users' preferences, and so on; *(ii)* any data chunk is produced proactively by the seed, with no need for external intervention—still allowed for agents willing to influence atoms generation process.

Seeds are formally defined as follows:

$$\texttt{seed}(\mathit{Src},\mathit{Atoms})_c, \quad c \in \Re^+$$
$$\mathit{Atoms} :: = \mathit{atom}^i_{c_i} \mid \mathit{atom}^i_{c_i}, \mathit{Atoms}, \quad c_i \in \Re^+, \ i \in \mathbb{N}$$

where

- `Atoms` is the set of information pieces to be released into the information repository where the seed lives
- `Src` and c retain their meaning

6.2.3 Molecules

As $\mathcal{MoK}$ *composite units of information*, molecules are meant to represent any piece of information that is not considered as atomic. Accordingly, molecules may represent: table rows in a relational DB, sub-graphs in a graph DB, a collection of documents in a document-oriented DB; hyperlinks chains in a web page, related feeds of an RSS channel, posts with comments in a blog; similar words, related phrases, or sections in an article, and so on.

As such, molecules are, in general, *collections of (semantically) related atoms*, where the semantics underlying the aggregation process depends on the specific domain of the application at hand—e.g. for a citizen journalism IT platform, the driving force may be the similarity of news articles based on word counts or a given ontology.

Molecules are continuously and spontaneously generated by $\mathcal{MoK}$ biochemical reactions, to whom they are susceptible likewise atoms—still, either software or human agents, too, can create, manipulate, and share molecules.

Molecules are formally defined as follows:

$$\texttt{molecule}(Atoms)_c, \quad c \in \mathfrak{R}^+$$
$$Atoms ::= \texttt{atom}^i \mid \texttt{atom}^i, Atoms, \quad i \in \mathbb{N}$$
$$\{Atoms \mid \mathcal{F}_{\mathcal{MoK}}(\texttt{atom}^i, \texttt{atom}^j) = \delta \geq th\}, \quad i \neq j \in \mathbb{N}, \quad \delta, th \in (0, 1] \in \mathfrak{R}$$

where

- $\mathcal{F}_{\mathcal{MoK}}$ is $\mathcal{MoK}$ similarity-based *matchmaking function*, assigning a similarity score δ to pairs of atoms—or pairs of other, possibly heterogeneous $\mathcal{MoK}$ entities (more on $\mathcal{F}_{\mathcal{MoK}}$ in Sect. 6.5)
- *th* is a similarity threshold, indicating the minimum similarity two atoms must have in order to be aggregated into a molecule—or, in general, indicating for whichever pair of (possibly heterogeneous) $\mathcal{MoK}$ entities when they do match.

Put in other words, the atoms aggregated by a molecule have to be, according to $\mathcal{F}_{\mathcal{MoK}}$, sufficiently ($\delta$) related—the threshold *th* defining "sufficiently" being necessarily application specific. It is worth to note that each atom within the molecule must be unique—it is considered meaningless to aggregate identical atoms—and that atoms lose their own relevance when joining a molecule—only the relevance of the molecule matters.

6.2.4 Catalysts

As $\mathcal{M}o\mathcal{K}$ *knowledge workers*, catalysts in $\mathcal{M}o\mathcal{K}$ represent the agents—either software or human—which undertake *(epistemic) actions* on the information living within the $\mathcal{M}o\mathcal{K}$ system, in order to achieve their business goals.

As a side effect of their activity, catalysts *influence*—intentionally or not—both the way in which $\mathcal{M}o\mathcal{K}$ processes apply to information and knowledge, and information properties—such as relevance, and location. Influence is based on the *epistemic nature* of the activity taking place—e.g. a "annotate" action versus a "share" action—as well as on contextual information regarding the action itself—e.g. which information is involved, where it is, who is doing the action, when, and so on.

As long as the goal is that of improving quality of information—whatever this means in the specific application scenario—promoting knowledge inference and discovery, and supporting effective information sharing, any system property and any information available to $\mathcal{M}o\mathcal{K}$ may be affected—e.g. tuning biochemical reactions rate, manipulating information content and location, and so on (more on this in Sect. 6.4).

Catalysts are formally defined as follows:

$$Catalyst = (\alpha \dagger [\![\cdot]\!]_i).Catalyst, \quad i \in \bigcup_i [\![\cdot]\!]_i$$
$$\alpha \in \{\text{share }(Reactant) \mid \text{mark }(Reactant) \mid \text{annotate }(Reactant) \mid$$
$$\text{connect }(Reactant) \mid \text{harvest }(Reactant)\}$$
$$Reactant :: = seed \mid atom \mid molecule$$

where

- α denotes one among the actions available to the catalyst
- symbol $\dagger$ denotes application of the action within one among the information repositories available to the catalyst
- brackets $[\![\cdot]\!]$ denote a $\mathcal{M}o\mathcal{K}$ compartment—defined in Sect. 6.2.9
- notation $Y = x.Y$ is the usual process algebraic definition of recursive behaviour

Put in other words, a catalyst is modelled as the sequence of actions she performs within all the different information repositories at her disposal—description of each action α is provided in Sect. 6.4.

6.2.5 Enzymes

As $\mathcal{M}o\mathcal{K}$ *reification of actions*, enzymes in $\mathcal{M}o\mathcal{K}$ reify *(i)* the *epistemic nature* of all the actions available to agents for information handling and knowledge discovery, as well as *(ii)* any *contextual information* related to actions.

The former is vital to $\mathcal{M}o\mathcal{K}$ because it enables *adaptiveness*, that is, the ability of $\mathcal{M}o\mathcal{K}$ biochemical reactions to dynamically change their functioning according to

what the agents are doing—e.g. search queries for a given keyword may increase the
frequency at which related information is shared from neighbouring repositories.

The latter is fundamental because it enables *situatedness* and *awareness*, that is,
the ability of $\mathcal{MoK}$ to precisely characterise actions in space, time, and w.r.t. any
other property of the computational environment they are taking place within—e.g.
who is taking action, where (e.g. in which repository), when, and so on.

Enzymes are automatically and transparently (to agents) produced by $\mathcal{MoK}$ within
the repository where the action is taking place, which means that *(i)* agents need to do
nothing else beyond their usual actions to generate enzymes—thus there is no cogni-
tive/computational overhead for them— and that *(ii)* it is not necessary for agents to
be aware of enzymes being released whenever they undertake actions—nevertheless,
awareness may help them gain better assistance from $\mathcal{MoK}$, as discussed in Sect. 6.4.

Enzymes are formally defined as follows:

$$\texttt{enzyme}(\textit{Species}, s, \textit{Reactant}, \textit{Context})_c, \quad c, s \in \Re^+,$$
$$\textit{Species} :: = \texttt{share} \mid \texttt{mark} \mid \texttt{annotate} \mid \texttt{connect} \mid \texttt{harvest}$$
$$\textit{Reactant} :: = \textit{seed} \mid \textit{atom} \mid \textit{molecule}$$
$$\textit{Context} :: = \texttt{contextual info}$$

where

- *Species* denotes the epistemic nature of the action the enzyme reifies, and contributes to determine the activities $\mathcal{MoK}$ undertakes to enact the influences of the
  action's (and its side effects) on the $\mathcal{MoK}$ system
- *s* depends on both *Species* and *Context*, and denotes the strength of the enzyme,
  that is, the magnitude of the relevance boost brought to the involved seed, atom,
  or molecule
- *Context* is meant to track any contextual information regarding the action which
  may be useful for $\mathcal{MoK}$ system evolution—e.g. time of execution, outcome, previous and following action, etc.

6.2.6 Traces

As $\mathcal{MoK}$ *reification of actions' (side) effects*, traces reify within $\mathcal{MoK}$ any (side)
effect, either practical or communicative, that any action could cause—that is any
modification to $\mathcal{MoK}$ computational environment, which is due to the action but
may be not its intentional primary effect. A category of communicative side effects
of actions particularly interesting for $\mathcal{MoK}$ is that of *tacit messages* [6], thoroughly
discussed in Sect. 6.4. Briefly, tacit messages are a special kind of message which is
implicitly—and possibly, *unintentionally*—communicated by an agent undertaking
any form of *practical action*—which may also be a communicative act itself—to any
other agent able to *observe* such action and *understand* the message, as well as to
the computational environment where the action took place.

Traces are *automatically* and *transparently* (to agents) produced by *MoK* within the repository where the action took place, similarly and consequently to enzymes.

Traces are formally defined as follows:

$$\texttt{trace}(\textit{Msg}, \texttt{Context}, \textit{Subject})_c, \quad c \in \Re^+$$

$$\textit{Msg} :: = \texttt{presence} \mid \texttt{intention} \mid \texttt{ability} \mid \texttt{opportunity} \mid \texttt{accomplishment} \mid$$
$$\texttt{goal} \mid \texttt{result}$$
$$\textit{Subject} :: = \textit{seed} \mid \textit{atom} \mid \textit{molecule} \mid \asymp \mid \textit{Reaction}$$

where

- *Msg* is the tacit message conveyed by the trace, depending on the corresponding enzyme's species and action context, and (possibly) modulating the way the trace affects the system state—see Sect. 6.4 for a description of which enzyme generates which trace
- *Subject* is what could be affected by the trace, depending on the species and reactant of the involved enzyme (symbol $\asymp$ and term *Reaction* are defined in Sects. 6.2.10 and 6.2.8, respectively)

Along with *Msg*, any additional information regarding the tacit message may be stored in a *MoK* trace (within *Context*)—e.g. the acting agent location—to be later retrieved and exploited by *MoK* reactions upon need.

6.2.7 Perturbations

As *MoK reactions to interactions' side effects*, perturbations are the *computational functions* in charge of applying (application specific, custom defined) reactions to (side effects of) agents' interactions with *MoK*, actually enacting the *influence* on information lifecycle—as well as on knowledge inference, discovery and sharing— *MoK* agents may have.

Accordingly, perturbation actions may affect both *(i)* *MoK* biochemical reactions functioning—e.g. their application rate, their targets, and so on—and *(ii)* information and system properties—e.g. content, location, relevance, and so on.

Perturbation actions are associated to *MoK* traces—deposited by enzymes, in turn—and *spontaneously* carried out by *MoK* as soon as possible, which means, when *(i)* the trace causing the perturbation is available, and *(ii)* the body of knowledge or the system property subject of the perturbation is available.

Summing up, perturbation actions enact the influence of agents on the body of knowledge in *MoK*, coherently w.r.t. the side effects of agents' interactions as represented by traces, which are automatically generated from the original (epistemic) action as reified by enzymes.

Perturbation actions are formally defined as follows:

$$\texttt{perturbation}(\textit{P}, \textit{Subject})$$
$$\textit{P} :: = \texttt{attract} \mid \texttt{repulse} \mid \texttt{approach} \mid \texttt{drift-apart} \mid \texttt{strengthen} \mid \texttt{weaken} \mid$$
$$\texttt{boost} \mid \texttt{wane}$$
$$\textit{Subject} :: = \textit{seed} \mid \textit{atom} \mid \textit{molecule} \mid \asymp \mid \textit{Reaction}$$

where P is the perturbation action caused by the trace, depending on the trace tacit message and its subject, as well as (indirectly) from the original enzyme species and context—see Sect. 6.4 for details on correspondences.

> Description of the meaning and purpose of each perturbation action is detailed in Sect. 6.4, nevertheless, a brief overview is undoubtedly useful: attract perturbation action brings information closer to where the original action took place (repulse does the opposite); approach facilitates exchange of information between information repositories (the one where the action took place and the one where the trace ends up being, drift-apart does the opposite); strengthen increases concentration of information (weaken does the opposite); boost increases rate of a $\mathcal{MoK}$ biochemical reaction (wane does the opposite).

6.2.8 Reactions

As $\mathcal{MoK}$ *knowledge dynamics processes*, reactions are the *autonomous* and *decentralised* computational processes supporting (meta) information handling as well as knowledge inference, discovery, and sharing in $\mathcal{MoK}$.

Autonomous, because reactions are scheduled and executed by $\mathcal{MoK}$ according to *dynamic rate expressions*—inspired by rate expressions of natural chemical reactions—which are meant to support *awareness* of the contextual information (possibly) affecting reactions application. This in turn enables *adaptiveness* to the external influences put by interacting agents.

Decentralised, because $\mathcal{MoK}$ reactions may apply to seeds, atoms, molecules, as well as enzymes and traces, depending on their nature and purpose, but anyway they only rely on *local* information—that is, information present in the repository where the reaction executes—and can only affect *neighbouring* information repositories, at most—many reactions are confined within a single information repository.

The rationale driving reactions application to seeds, atoms, etc., that is, to which specific seed, atom, etc., a given reaction is applied to, is $\mathcal{F}_{\mathcal{MoK}}$ *similarity* between the reactant *templates* used in the reaction and the actual reactants available in the reacting information repository.

The semantics underlying this similarity measure is business-domain specific: e.g. in the case of a IT platform for collaboration and sharing of papers between researchers, documents similarity measures such as squared Euclidean distance, cosine similarity, and relative entropy are all reasonable alternatives.

Details regarding the structure and purpose of each $\mathcal{MoK}$ reaction, as well as description of $\mathcal{F}_{\mathcal{MoK}}$ similarity measure, are given in Sects. 6.3 and 6.5, respectively.

6.2.9 Compartments

As $\mathcal{MoK}$ *information repositories* and knowledge containers, compartments are the *computational* abstraction in $\mathcal{MoK}$ responsible for: *(i)* handling the whole information life cycle—from storage to sharing, to knowledge inference; *(ii)* provisioning information to agents; *(iii)* scheduling and executing $\mathcal{MoK}$ biochemical reactions, that is, the processes manipulating information and supporting knowledge inference, discovery, and sharing.

As such, compartments act as *active repositories of knowledge*, not merely storing information persistently to make it available to agents upon need, but also *spontaneously* evolving information—possibly improving its quality and inferring novel knowledge—and proactively sharing information with other neighbouring compartments—possibly moving it closer to where it is needed more.

Compartments are formally defined as follows:

$$Compartment = [\![Seeds,\ Atoms,\ Molecules,\ Enzymes,\ Traces,\ Reactions]\!]$$

where brackets $[\![\cdot]\!]$ denote the compartment boundaries, defining a notion of *locality*—$\mathcal{MoK}$ reactions are confined therein, and affect only local information.

6.2.10 Membranes

As $\mathcal{MoK}$ *interaction channels*, membranes are the *communication* abstraction in $\mathcal{MoK}$, as well as its *topological* abstraction.

In fact, on the one hand, membranes enable exchange of information between compartments; on the other hand, by establishing 1:1 communication channels, membranes implicitly define the notions of *locality* and *neighbourhood* in $\mathcal{MoK}$. Locality, because they forbid interaction between compartments which are not coupled by any membrane, thus confine the computational processes therein—e.g. $\mathcal{MoK}$ biochemical reactions. Neighbourhood, because they allow $\mathcal{MoK}$ biochemical reactions to involve more than one compartment, given they are coupled by a membrane—e.g. sharing of information necessarily involves a sending compartment and, at least, a receiving compartment.

Membranes are formally defined as follows:

$$Compartment_i \asymp Compartment_j, \quad i \neq j \in \mathbb{N}$$

where symbol $\asymp$ denotes the membrane connecting compartments i and j.

6.3 Computational Model: Artificial Chemical Reactions

As briefly described in Sect. 6.2, reactions are $\mathcal{MoK}$ *autonomous* and *decentralised* processes supporting (meta) information handling as well as knowledge inference, discovery, and sharing: essentially, they determine the global behaviour of a $\mathcal{MoK}$ system, together with agents' interactions. Accordingly, $\mathcal{MoK}$ features injection, aggregation, diffusion, decay, reinforcement, deposit, and perturbation reactions.

> To enhance readability and avoid redundancy, from the kinetic rate expressions of each reaction has been omitted a multiplicative parameter h, meant to represent a hook for tuning $\mathcal{MoK}$ reactions' application rates—e.g. through $\mathcal{MoK}$ perturbation reaction. This parameter is initially set to 1, thus does not affect the effective rate of execution. Then, as the $\mathcal{MoK}$ system evolves, it may be either increased or decreased so as to speed up or slow down the reaction rate upon need—e.g. due to catalysts interactions.

6.3.1 Injection

$\mathcal{MoK}$ *injection reaction* generates atoms from seeds, at a given rate, putting them into the compartment where the seed lives. Injection reaction is formally defined as follows:

$$\texttt{seed}(\textit{Src},\textit{Atoms}) \xrightarrow{r_{inj}} \texttt{seed}(\textit{Src},\textit{Atoms}) + atom_{c+c_i}^i, \quad \forall atom_{c_i}^i \in \textit{Atoms}$$
$$r_{inj} = \tfrac{1}{1+\texttt{time}} * \texttt{diff}(\sharp seed, \sharp atom)$$

where:

- superscript i denotes the i-th atom in the set of atoms $\texttt{Atoms}$—and, accordingly, its concentration value (relevance), denoted by subscript c_i
- $\sharp$ is the operator returning concentration of its operand
- $\texttt{diff}(\cdot,\cdot)$ is a function computing any one notion of difference between concentrations (e.g. subtraction)
- $\texttt{time}$ is a variable tracking the flow of time

Put in other words, given a seed able to generate a set of atoms, each of them is injected in the local compartment with its own relevance—possibly increasing its relevance, by adding up to the concentration of identical atoms possibly already present—every $\frac{1}{r_{inj}}$ time steps.[1]

The dynamic rate expression of the injection reaction represents a trade-off between two contrasting needs: on one hand, atoms should be *perpetually* injected into a $\mathcal{MoK}$ system, since there is no reasonable way to know a-priori *when* some information will be useful the most; on the other hand, it is desirable to avoid *flooding* the system without any control on the quantity of atoms—thus the size of the knowledge base—in play.

Accordingly, r_{inj} is designed to: *(i)* slower the injection process as time passes, thus as the compartment likely becomes more and more congested, *(ii)* comply to a threshold enforcing an upper bound on the concentration of injected atoms—as soon as saturation is reached, the injection reaction stops until the atoms' concentration lowers.

> Chap. 8 reports on the *simulate-then-tune* loop carefully undertaken to come up with the rate expressions presented in this whole section.

6.3.2 Aggregation

$\mathcal{MoK}$ *aggregation reaction* ties together *(semantically) related* atoms into molecules, or molecules into other molecules, at a given rate. Aggregation reaction is formally defined as follows:

$$Reactant' + Reactant'' \xrightarrow{r_{agg}}$$
$$(Reactant' \oplus Reactant'') + (Reactant' \ominus Reactant'')$$

$$\left.\begin{aligned} \oplus = \{Reactants \mid \mathcal{F}_{\mathcal{MoK}}(Reactant', Reactant'') = \delta \geq th\} \\ \ominus = \{Reactants \mid \mathcal{F}_{\mathcal{MoK}}(Reactant', Reactant'') = \delta < th\} \end{aligned}\right\} \; \delta, th \in (0, 1] \in \Re$$

$$Reactant :: = atom \mid molecule$$
$$Reactants :: = Atoms \mid Molecules$$
$$r_{agg} = \frac{time}{\sharp Reactant^{lhs}}$$

---

[1]Approximately, due to the stochastic nature of the scheduling algorithm used by $\mathcal{MoK}$ compartments to execute reactions, detailed in Sect. 7.1.

where:

- same apices (′ or ″) denote same reactants
- $\oplus$ is the operator returning the set of reactants obtained by extracting from the two input sets only those reactants for which $\mathcal{F}_{MoK}$ result is above (or equal to) the threshold
- $\ominus$ is the operator returning the set of reactants obtained by extracting from the two input sets only those reactants for which $\mathcal{F}_{MoK}$ result is below the threshold—thus, it is the dual operator of $\oplus$
- superscript *lhs* denotes the left-hand side of the reaction—notation $\sharp Reactant^{lhs}$, therefore, returns the concentration of the reactants
- *th* and $\mathcal{F}_{MoK}$ retain their usual meaning (described for the molecule abstraction in Sect. 6.2)

and concentration values are not specified because they all equal 1. Put in other words, given two molecules—or two atoms, or one atom and a molecule—every $\frac{1}{r_{agg}}$ time steps they are joined into a new one, binding together (semantically) related atoms while non-related ones are released back into the reacting compartment—the one they currently live in.

The dynamic rate expression of the aggregation reaction is meant to enforce a direct proportionality between the size of a molecule and the speed of aggregation: the bigger a molecule is—that is, the more knowledge a molecule is conveying— the faster it aggregates—that is, the more frequently it attracts other (semantically) similar atoms/molecules. Such a choice is motivated mainly by two considerations: on the one hand, as time passes by, it is likely that more and more atoms roam compartments, thus, it is desirable to aggregate more, so as to have different forms of more concise information—for many reasons, such as memory occupation; on the other hand, since molecules decay, and since non-similar atoms are released back into the compartment during aggregation, it is unlikely for molecules to keep growing endlessly—unless they are really exploited by catalysts.

It is worth to note that the products of MoK aggregation reaction—that is, terms in the right-hand side of the reaction formalisation—may specify *arbitrary expressions* over reactants as their own *instantiation rules*, besides simple operators $\oplus$ and $\ominus$. This is necessary to, e.g. support complex forms of information aggregation, such as filtering, merging, etc.

6.3.3 Diffusion

MoK *diffusion reaction* moves atoms, molecules, and traces among *neighbouring* compartments, at a given rate. Diffusion reaction is formally defined as follows:

$$\llbracket Reactants' \cup Reactant\rrbracket_i \asymp \llbracket Reactants''\rrbracket_j \xrightarrow{r_{diff}} \llbracket Reactants'\rrbracket_i \asymp$$
$$\llbracket Reactants'' \cup Reactant\rrbracket_j, \quad i \neq j \in \mathbb{N}$$
$$Reactant :: = atom \mid molecule \mid trace$$
$$Reactants :: = Atoms \mid Molecules \mid Traces$$
$$r_{diff} = d * \texttt{diff}(\llbracket \sharp Reactant\rrbracket_i, \llbracket \sharp Reactant\rrbracket_j), \quad d \in (0, 1] \in \mathfrak{R}$$

where:

- brackets $\llbracket \cdot \rrbracket$ delimit compartments
- subscripts i, j identify a specific compartment
- symbol $\asymp$ denotes membranes connecting compartments
- d is an arbitrary weight factor tuning diffusion strength

Put in other words, given two compartments connected by a membrane, a molecule, an atom, or a trace is removed from either of the two and sent to the other—one unit of concentration at a time—at the rate given by r_{diff} dynamic rate expression.

The rate expression is meant to *(i)* provide an upper bound to diffusion, avoiding unbounded proliferation of foreign (meta) information pieces in compartments which are not their origin—here, diffusion asymptotically tends to balance distribution of reactants among neighbouring compartments—*(ii)* provide a hook to fine-tune the extent to which reactants are diffused—here, only a fraction of the reactants are allowed to diffuse.

6.3.4 Decay

MoK decay reaction decreases the relevance of atoms, molecules, enzymes, and traces as *time flows*. Decay reaction is formally defined as follows:

$$Reactant_c \xrightarrow{r_{dec}} Reactant_{c-1}, \quad c \in \mathfrak{R}^+$$
$$Reactant :: = atom \mid molecule \mid enzyme \mid trace$$

$$r_{dec} = \begin{cases} \texttt{fMA}(a) * \texttt{log(1+time)}, & a \in \mathfrak{R}^+, \quad Reactant \setminus trace \\ \texttt{diff}(\sharp trace^{\Uparrow}, \sharp trace) * \texttt{log(1+time)} \end{cases}$$

where:

- fMA is the function implementing the *law of mass action* [5], that is the mathematical model explaining and predicting the behaviour of solutions in dynamic equilibrium
- a is the *affinity constant* needed by fMA—which, here, can be diverse for each Reactant type as well as dynamically adapted
- superscript $\Uparrow$ denotes where a *MoK* abstraction comes from—in this case, it states that $\sharp trace^{\Uparrow}$ is the concentration of the enzyme who deposited the trace actually decaying

Put in other words, given an atom, molecule, enzyme, or trace, its concentration (thus, relevance) is decreased by 1 at the rate given by r_{dec} dynamic rate expression.

This rate expression is designed by recognising that time dependency alone is not enough for a meaningful decay behaviour: it would simply end-up slowing down the dual saturation process provided by injection/aggregation/deposit reactions. Hence, on the one hand, logarithmic time dependency guarantees a smoother decay process, on the other hand, dependency on reactants' concentration makes the process asymptotically tend to homogenise (meta) information relevance.

> The *law of mass action* [5] states that the rate of an elementary reaction (r_f)—a reaction that proceeds through only one transition state, that is, one mechanistic step—is proportional (k_f) to the product of the concentrations of the participating molecules (R^1, R^2): $r_f = k_f[R^1][R^2]$. k_f is called *rate constant* and, in chemistry, is a function of participating molecules affinity.

6.3.5 Reinforcement

$\mathcal{MoK}$ *reinforcement reaction* increases the relevance of atoms and molecules according to $\mathcal{MoK}$ agents' *interactions*, at a given rate. Reinforcement reaction is formally defined as follows:

$$\texttt{enzyme(species,s,Reactant,Context)} + \texttt{Reactant}'_c \xrightarrow{r_{reinf}}$$
$$\texttt{enzyme(species,s,Reactant,Context)} + \texttt{Reactant}'_{c+s}, \quad c, s \in \Re^+$$
$$\mathcal{F}_{\mathcal{MoK}}(\texttt{Reactant}, \texttt{Reactant}') = \delta \geq th, \quad \delta, th \in (0, 1] \in \Re$$
$$\texttt{Reactant} :: = \texttt{atom} \mid \texttt{molecule}$$
$$r_{reinf} = \texttt{diff(}\sharp\texttt{Reactant}^\Uparrow, \sharp\texttt{Reactant)}$$

where, in this case, symbol $\Uparrow$ states that $\sharp \texttt{Reactant}^\Uparrow$ is either the concentration of the seed source of the atom to reinforce, or an average of the concentrations of the seeds sources of the atoms aggregated by the molecule to reinforce.

Put in other words, given an enzyme and a (semantically) related atom or molecule, the concentration value of the reactant (thus, its relevance) is increased according to enzyme's specification (in particular, to s) every $\frac{1}{r_{reinf}}$ time steps.

The dynamic rate expression of the reinforcement reaction is meant to enforce *situatedness* and *awareness* of the feedback that $\mathcal{MoK}$ agents implicitly provide to $\mathcal{MoK}$. Thus, feedback should: *(i)* be prompt, that is, rapidly and considerably increase concentration despite decay; *(ii)* be bounded, in both time and space—accordingly, enzymes do not diffuse, and reinforcement does not consider neighbourhoods; *(iii)* depend on the nature of interactions, that is, on enzymes' epistemic nature (their *species*)—e.g. different *species* may imply different values for s.

6.3.6   *Deposit*

MoK deposit reaction generates traces from enzymes, at a given rate, putting them into the compartment where the *(inter-)action* originally releasing the enzyme took place. Deposit reaction is formally defined as follows:

$$\text{enzyme}(species, s, Reactant, Context) \xrightarrow{r_{dep}}$$
$$\text{enzyme}(species, s, Reactant, Context) + \text{trace}(Msg, Context, Subject)_{c+s}$$
$$r_{dep} = \tfrac{1}{1+\text{time}} * \text{diff}(\natural enzyme, \natural trace)$$

Put in other words, given an enzyme of a certain species, thus able to generate that species of traces, *s* concentration of the trace is deposited every $\frac{1}{r_{dep}}$ time steps in the *local* compartment—the one where the enzyme lives.

The dynamic rate expression of the deposit reaction is the same as that of the injection reaction, thus represents the same trade-off between *flooding* and *availability*. Nevertheless, seeds do not decay while enzymes do, thus, the run-time dynamics of the two reactions are similar but not identical.

6.3.7   *Perturbation*

MoK perturbation reaction carries out the *(side) effects* of (interaction) activities undertaken by *MoK* catalysts, at a given rate, considering both the enzymes' species and the traces' tacit message. Perturbation reaction is formally defined as follows:

$$\text{trace}(Msg, Context, Subject) + Subject' \xrightarrow{r_{pert}}$$
$$\text{perturbation}(P, Subject) \dagger Subject'$$
$$Subject :: = seed \mid atom \mid molecule \mid \times \mid Reaction$$
$$r_{pert} \propto (p, Subject', trace)$$

where:

- symbol † denotes application of perturbation action *p* to *Subject'*
- symbol ∝ denotes some kind of proportionality—in this case, it states that the dynamic rate expression of perturbation reaction should be a function of the kind of perturbation action (as stemming from the enzyme *species* and the trace tacit message), of any property of the matching *Subject'*, and of any property of the trace itself

Put in other words, given a trace conveying a tacit message and stemming from a certain species, and its subject, the perturbation action corresponding to that species and tacit message is started, at the rate given by r_{pert} dynamic rate expression. This rate expression depends on the specific perturbation action the trace applies, nevertheless, it is likely to also depend on the concentration of the trace and the subject involved.

The autonomous computational process started by the perturbation action may affect any property of its subject—e.g. increasing/decreasing reactants' relevance, or changing their location in the neighbourhood—as well as any property of the $\mathcal{MoK}$ system—e.g. tuning rate expressions.

A detailed description of perturbation actions and their relationships with traces and enzymes is provided in the upcoming section (Sect. 6.4).

6.4 Interaction Model: Epistemic Actions, Tacit Messages, and Perturbation Actions

Interaction, thus *coordination* of interactions, in $\mathcal{MoK}$ is interpreted from the socio-cognitive perspective of BIC [6], where communication does not occur through any specialised signal, but through the *practical behaviour* observed by the recipient(s). Then, actions themselves—along with their (side) effects—become the message, possibly intentionally (implicitly) sent in order to obtain a desired reaction—either by the computational environment where the action takes place, or by other agents who can observe the action and its effects.

This perspective leads to the argument that self-organising coordination can be based on the *observation* and *interpretation* of actions as wholes, that is, both the practical behaviour and its (side) effects—rather than solely of their effects, or traces, on the environment, as happens, e.g. for *stigmergic coordination* [10].

Tacit messages have been already described in Chap. 5, along with the notion of BIC. Here follows a brief recap:

1. *informing about the presence.* "Agent A is here". Since an action, an activity, a practical behaviour (and its traces), is observable in the computational environment, any agent therein—as well as the environment itself—becomes aware of A existence—and, possibly, contextual information such as A location

2. *informing about the intention.* "Agent A plans to do action β". If the agents' workflow determines that action β follows action α, peers (as well as the environment) observing A doing α may assume A next intention to be "do β"

3. *informing about the ability.* "A is able to do ϕ_i, $i \in \mathbb{N}$". Assuming actions ϕ_i, $i \in \mathbb{N}$ have similar preconditions, agents (and the environment) observing A doing ϕ_i may infer that A is also able to do $\phi_{j \neq i}$, $j \in \mathbb{N}$

4. *informing about the opportunity for action.* "p_i, $i \in \mathbb{N}$ is the set of pre-conditions for doing α". Agents observing A doing α may infer that p_i, $i \in \mathbb{N}$ hold, thus, they may take the opportunity to do α as soon as possible
5. *informing about the accomplishment of an action.* "A achieved S". If S is the state of affairs reachable as a consequence of doing action α, agents observing A doing α may infer that A is now in state S
6. *informing about the goal.* "A has goal g". By observing A doing action α, peers of A may infer A's goal to be g, e.g. because action α is part of a workflow aimed at achieving g—likewise for the environment
7. *informing about the result.* "Result R is available". If peer agents know that action α leads to result R, whenever agent A does α they can expect result R to be soon available—in case action α completes successfully

Within $\mathcal{M}o\mathcal{K}$ the factorisation of common actions described in Chap. 5, along with the discussion about the possible *tacit messages* and *perturbation actions* they may convey, is exploited to define precise associations between $\mathcal{M}o\mathcal{K}$ enzymes' species, traces' messages, and perturbation actions. This enables to evaluate $\mathcal{M}o\mathcal{K}$ behaviour in response to users interactions in a more rigorous way, e.g. through simulations and demo deployments—see Chap. 9.

Accordingly, here follows the list of $\mathcal{M}o\mathcal{K}$ actions outlined in Chap. 5, now completed by a description of *(i)* the enzyme they (transparently) release within $\mathcal{M}o\mathcal{K}$, *(ii)* the traces the enzyme may (autonomously) deposit within $\mathcal{M}o\mathcal{K}$, and *(iii)* the perturbation actions these traces may bring along.

6.4.1 Share

The share action is reified by enzymes with `Species` = share. Then, depending on the `Context` within which the action took place, share enzymes may deposit the following different sorts of traces:

- `presence` traces, that is, traces having `Msg` = presence, indicating to $\mathcal{M}o\mathcal{K}$ presence, location, and any other available property of the acting agent
- `ability` traces, indicating to $\mathcal{M}o\mathcal{K}$ the acting agent's capabilities, in terms of both what she can do, and what she can perceive about others—e.g. what actions are available to her, on which targets, which of her traces other catalysts are perceiving, etc.
- `accomplishment` traces, indicating to $\mathcal{M}o\mathcal{K}$ which state of affairs the acting agent may have reached upon successful completion of the action—e.g. which information has been manipulated and how

which, according to *(i)* their species, *(ii)* the context within which the original enzyme was released, and *(iii)* their `Subject`, may lead to the following perturbation actions:

- `approach` perturbations, that is, perturbation actions having $P = $ `approach`, stemming from the `presence` tacit message (and indirectly from the `share` action), aimed at bringing closer to each other the compartments of those agents interacting more often with each other information items. "Closer" here means "logically closer", that is, interactions between compartments, and the users working with them, are facilitated and promoted—e.g. diffusion rate is increased. Nevertheless, it is possible to imagine a more physical interpretation, according to which, the involved compartments are physically migrated in geographically closer hosts, so as to, e.g. lower the communication latency
- `attract` perturbations, stemming from the `ability` tacit message, aimed at bringing to the compartment where the action took place—thus, not necessarily the one where the trace is at a given time, being traces able to diffuse whereas enzymes are not—information similar to the one target of the `share` action—according to any notion of similarity implemented through function $\mathcal{F}_{MoK}$. The opposite perturbation, `repulse`, may also be undertaken for those information items recognised as being dissimilar to the shared information
- `boost`/`wane` perturbations, stemming from the `accomplishment` tacit message, aimed at increasing/decreasing the rate of $\mathcal{MoK}$ reactions so as to facilitate the acting agent's workflow—e.g. $\mathcal{MoK}$ reinforcement and decay reactions' rates may be respectively increased and decreased for information items similar to those target of the original `share` action

6.4.2   Mark

The mark action is reified by enzymes with $Species = $ `mark`. Then, depending on the $Context$ within which the action took place, `mark` enzymes may deposit the following different sorts of traces:

- `presence` traces, that is traces having $Msg = $ `presence`
- `opportunity` traces, indicating to $\mathcal{MoK}$ that a new opportunity for action is now available, enabled by the action just completed successfully—e.g. a collaboration between co-workers, exploitation of additional information, etc.

which, according to *(i)* their species, *(ii)* the context within which the original enzyme was released, and *(iii)* their $Subject$, may lead to the following perturbation actions:

- `approach` perturbations, that is, perturbation actions having $P = $ `approach`, stemming from the `presence` tacit message (and indirectly from the `mark` action)
- `strengthen` perturbations, stemming from the `opportunity` tacit message, aimed at increasing relevance (concentration) of information (semantically) related to the one target of the original `mark` action. If marking information is allowed to bear a negative meaning—e.g. disliking information as opposed to liking—the opposite perturbation action, that is `weaken`, is to be considered

Also `attract` and `boost` (or `wane`) perturbation actions may be considered, stemming from the `opportunity` tacit message, based on the `Context` of the original enzyme, and the `Subject` of the trace.

6.4.3 Annotate

The annotate action is reified by enzymes with *Species* = `annotate`. Then, depending on the `Context` within which the action took place, `annotate` enzymes may deposit the following different sorts of traces:

- `accomplishment` traces, that is, traces having *Msg* = `accomplishment`
- `goal` traces, indicating to *MoK* which could be the motivations behind the acting agent's behaviour, in terms of the state of affairs she aims to achieve in the medium to long term

which, according to *(i)* their species, *(ii)* the context within which the original enzyme was released, and *(iii)* their *Subject*, may lead to the following perturbation actions:

- `boost`/`wane` perturbations, that is, perturbation actions having *P* = `boost` / `wane`, stemming from the `accomplishment` tacit message (and indirectly from the `annotate` action)
- `attract`/`repulse` perturbations, stemming from the `goal` tacit message

Also `strengthen` (or `weaken`) perturbation actions may be considered, stemming from both tacit messages, based on the `Context` of the original enzyme, and the `Subject` of the trace.

6.4.4 Connect

The connect action is reified by enzymes with *Species* = `connect`. Then, depending on the `Context` within which the action took place, `connect` enzymes may deposit the following different sorts of traces:

- `intention` traces, that is, traces having *Msg* = `intention`, indicating to *MoK* the immediate cause of agent's action, in terms of the state of affairs she aims to achieve in the short-term—right after the action completes
- `opportunity` traces

which, according to *(i)* their species, *(ii)* the context within which the original enzyme was released, and *(iii)* their `Subject`, may lead to the following perturbation actions:

- `approach` perturbations, that is, perturbation actions having `P = approach`, stemming from the `intention` tacit message
- `strengthen` perturbations, stemming from the `opportunity` tacit message

> Also `attract` and `boost` (or `wane`) perturbation actions may be considered, respectively stemming from the `intention` and `opportunity` tacit messages, based on the `Context` of the original enzyme, and the `Subject` of the trace.

6.4.5 Harvest

The harvest action is reified by enzymes with `Species = harvest`. Then, depending on the `Context` within which the action took place, `harvest` enzymes may deposit the following different sorts of traces:

- `presence` traces, that is, traces having `Msg = presence`
- `intention` traces
- `opportunity` traces

which, according to *(i)* their species, *(ii)* the context within which the original enzyme was released, and *(iii)* their `Subject`, may lead to the following perturbation actions:

- `approach` perturbations, that is, perturbation actions having `P = approach`, stemming from the `intention` tacit message
- `attract` perturbations, stemming from the `intention` tacit message
- `strengthen` perturbations, stemming from the `opportunity` tacit message

It should be noted that the harvest action is the quintessential epistemic action, potentially conveying every sort of tacit message, thus enabling any sort of inference leading to any sort of perturbation action. Therefore, based on the `Context` of the original enzyme, and the `Subject` of the trace, any other perturbation action may be considered.

> In Sect. 9.1 some of the above described associations, thus the whole idea of BIC-driven coordination in the very end, are evaluated by simulating a citizen journalism scenario, where user agents' interactions within a $\mathcal{MoK}$-coordinated infrastructure for content search and sharing are simulated to investigate how enzymes, traces, and perturbation actions may affect $\mathcal{MoK}$ coordination capabilities, therefore the system behaviour.

6.5   Information Model: Representation and Similarity-Based Matchmaking

As already mentioned in Sect. 6.3, $\mathcal{MoK}$ relies on function $\mathcal{F}_{MoK}$ for *measuring similarity* between information items, as well as for selecting which specific $\mathcal{MoK}$ entities $\mathcal{MoK}$ reactions should be applied to—namely, for matchmaking. Since $\mathcal{F}_{MoK}$ is likely to depend on the application scenario at hand, it cannot be defined once and for all. However, for the sake of concreteness, in the following some viable, specific text-mining techniques for $\mathcal{F}_{MoK}$ are described, that turned out to be effective in an academic papers clustering scenario—as reported in Sect. 9.2.

Generally speaking, measuring similarity between $\mathcal{MoK}$ entities requires first of all to decide which kind of content atoms and molecules convey. *Text-based knowledge* is already identified as the kind of information $\mathcal{MoK}$ aims at dealing with, thus what is missing is to decide the *granularity* of text-based knowledge, that is, namely, whether atoms convey words and molecules sentences, or atoms sentences and molecules collections of them—possibly even whole documents—or something else similar.

In the experiments described in Sect. 9.2, the choice is to put BIBTEX[2] records first—suitably edited to remove fields not useful for the purpose—then abstracts, finally full academic papers, into atoms, then to exploit $\mathcal{MoK}$ *aggregation reaction* to cluster similar atoms into molecules. It is worth noting that *hierarchical clustering* may be achieved, e.g. by clustering similar molecules into the same compartment, whereas dissimilar molecules into different compartments. Furthermore, depth of the hierarchy may be increased by recursively considering neighbourhoods of compartments, neighbourhoods of neighbourhoods, and so on—however, such an interesting perspective is left for future investigation. As a side note, it is interesting to recognise that this kind of *topological clustering* is similar to the clustering approach based on *self-organising maps* [17].

The vast majority of *similarity measures* (or, *correlation functions*) are based on the *vector space* representation of documents (or, more generally, text snippets), according to which each document is represented by a vector where each cell stores a word of the document and its *weight* inside the document. For the experiments in Sect. 9.2, weights are computed based on [18], which combines Okapi's *tf* score [26] and INQUERY's normalised *idf* score [3] as follows:

$$v_{i,j} = \frac{tf_{i,j}}{tf_{i,j} + 0.5 + 1.5 \frac{doclen_j}{avgdoclen}} \cdot \frac{log(\frac{colsize+0.5}{docf_i})}{log(colsize + 1)} \tag{6.1}$$

where $v_{i,j}$ is the weight of ith term within jth document, $tf_{i,j}$ is the frequency of term i in document j, $docf_i$ the number of documents in which term i is, $doclen_j$ the number of terms in document j, $avgdoclen$ the average of documents' length.

---

[2]http://www.bibtex.org.

The simplest method to measure similarity between text snippets is to count the co-occurrences of words, that is, the number of words appearing in both snippets, and possibly how many times, normalising the obtained value according to the length of the text within the involved snippets.

A slightly more refined and widely used method is to rely on *cosine similarity* [13]:

$$Sim(C_1, C_2) = \frac{\sum_{k=1}^{n} c_i(t_k) \cdot c_j(t_k)}{\sqrt{\sum_{k=1}^{n} c_i(t_k)^2 \cdot \sum_{k=1}^{n} c_j(t_k)^2}} \qquad (6.2)$$

where $C_i = \{c_i(t_1), \ldots, c_j(t_n)\}$ and C_j are the weight vectors of the documents to compare, and t_k represents the kth word. $Sim(C_1, C_2) \in [-1, 1]$, meaning that text snippets C_1, C_2 are identical (1), totally dissimilar (-1), unrelated (0), or anything in-between.

Another method, emphasising big differences in weights, is the *mean squares difference* [11]:

$$d(C_i, C_j) = \frac{\sum_{k=1}^{n} (c_i(t_k) - c_j(t_k))^2}{n}$$

Yet another possibility, is to exploit *euclidean distance* [12]:

$$dist(C_i, C_j) = \sqrt{\sum_{k=1}^{n} | c_i(t_k) - c_j(t_k) |^2}$$

Furthermore, in [16], a *concept-based* similarity measure is proposed, considering three different levels: sentences, whole documents, collections of documents. For each sentence (or document, or corpus), *part-of-speech* tagging [1] is used to semantically interpret the content of the text, so as to define and assign concepts to that portion of text. The authors introduce three novel measures of frequency:

- for sentences, the conceptual term frequency (*ctf*), that is, the number of occurrences of a concept in that sentence
- for documents, the concept-based term frequency (*tf*), that is, the number of occurrences of a concept within the whole document
- for documents collections, the concept-based document frequency (*df*), that is, the number of documents which contain the concept

Based on these, as well as many other factors, a new similarity measure is defined [1].

In Sect. 9.2, some of these similarity measures are put to test in an actual exemplary deployment of academic papers clustering—in particular, the basic method counting co-occurrences, cosine similarity, and concept-based similarity.

References

1. Abney, S.: Part-of-Speech Tagging and Partial Parsing, pp. 118–136. Springer Netherlands, Dordrecht (1997). doi:10.1007/978-94-017-1183-8
2. Ackerman, M.S.: The intellectual challenge of cscw: the gap between social requirements and technical feasibility. Hum. Comput. Inter. **15**(2–3), 179–203 (2000)
3. Allan, J., Callan, J., Croft, W.B., Ballesteros, L., Byrd, D., Swan, R., Xu, J.: Inquery does battle with trec-6. NIST SPECIAL PUBLICATION SP, pp. 169–206 (1998)
4. Bhatt, G.D.: Knowledge management in organizations: Examining the interaction between technologies, techniques, and people. J. Knowl. Manag. **5**(1), 68–75 (2001)
5. Cardelli, L.: On process rate semantics. Theor. Comput. Sci. **391**(3), 190–215 (2008)
6. Castelfranchi, C., Pezzullo, G., Tummolini, L.: Behavioral implicit communication (BIC): Communicating with smart environments via our practical behavior and its traces. Int. J. Ambient Comput. Intell. **2**(1), 1–12 (2010). doi:10.4018/jaci.2010010101
7. Di Pierro, A., Hankin, C., Wiklicky, H.: Probabilistic Linda-based coordination languages. In: de Boer, F.S., Bonsangue, M.M., Graf, S., de Roever, W.P. (eds.) 3rd International Conference on Formal Methods for Components and Objects (FMCO'04), LNCS, vol. 3657, pp. 120–140. Springer, Berlin, Heidelberg (2005). doi:10.1007/11561163
8. Fernandez-Marquez, J.L., Di,: Marzo Serugendo, G., Montagna, S., Viroli, M., Arcos, J.L.: Description and composition of bio-inspired design patterns: a complete overview. Nat. Comput. **12**(1), 43–67 (2013). doi:10.1007/s11047-012-9324-y
9. Gelernter, D.: Generative communication in Linda. ACM Trans. Program. Lang. Syst. **7**(1), 80–112 (1985). doi:10.1145/2363.2433
10. Grassé, P.P.: La reconstruction du nid et les coordinations interindividuelles chez Bellicositermes natalensis et Cubitermes sp. la théorie de la stigmergie: Essai d'interprétation du comportement des termites constructeurs. Insectes Soc. **6**(1), 41–80 (1959). doi:10.1007/BF02223791
11. Herlocker, J.L., Konstan, J.A., Borchers, A., Riedl, J.: An algorithmic framework for performing collaborative filtering. In: Proceedings of the 22nd Annual International ACM SIGIR Conference on Research and Development in Information Retrieval, pp. 230–237. ACM, New York, NY, USA (1999)
12. Hotho, A., Nürnberger, A., Paaß, G.: A brief survey of text mining. LDV Forum—GLDV Journal for Computational Linguistics and Language Technology **20**(1), 19–62 (2005). http://www.kde.cs.uni-kassel.de/hotho/pub/2005/hotho05TextMining.pdf
13. Huang, A.: Similarity measures for text document clustering. In: Proceedings of the Sixth New Zealand Computer Science Research Student Conference (NZCSRSC2008), Christchurch, New Zealand, pp. 49–56 (2008)
14. Hudson, S.E., Smith, I.: Techniques for addressing fundamental privacy and disruption tradeoffs in awareness support systems. In: Proceedings of the 1996 ACM Conference on Computer Supported Cooperative Work, CSCW '96, pp. 248–257. ACM, New York, NY, USA (1996). doi:10.1145/240080.240295
15. Hutchins, E.: Cognition in the Wild. MIT Press (1995)
16. Jadhav, M.A., Shinde, S.K.: A concept based mining model for nlp using text clustering. In: International Journal of Engineering Research and Technology, vol. 2. ESRSA Publications, ESRSA Publications (2013)
17. Lagus, K., Honkela, T., Kaski, S., Kohonen, T.: Self-organizing maps of document collections: A new approach to interactive exploration. KDD **96**, 238–243 (1996)
18. Leuski, A.: Evaluating document clustering for interactive information retrieval. In: Proceedings of the Tenth International Conference on Information and Knowledge Management, CIKM '01, pp. 33–40. ACM, New York, NY, USA (2001). doi:10.1145/502585.502592
19. Malone, T.W., Crowston, K.: The interdisciplinary study of coordination. ACM Comput. Surv. **26**(1), 87–119 (1994). doi:10.1145/174666.174668
20. Mariani, S.: On the "local-to-global" issue in self-organisation: Chemical reactions with custom kinetic rates. In: Eighth IEEE International Conference on Self-Adaptive and Self-Organizing

Systems Workshops, SASOW 2014, Eighth IEEE International Conference on Self-adaptive and Self-organizing Systems Workshops, SASOW 2014, pp. 61–67. IEEE, London, UK (2014). doi:10.1109/SASOW.2014.14. Best student paper award

21. Mariani, S., Omicini, A.: Anticipatory coordination in socio-technical knowledge-intensive environments: Behavioural implicit communication in MoK. In: Gavanelli, M., Lamma, E., Riguzzi, F. (eds.) AI*IA 2015, Advances in Artificial Intelligence, Lecture Notes in Computer Science, vol. 9336, Chap. 8, pp. 102–115. Springer International Publishing (2015). doi:10.1007/978-3-319-24309-2. XIVth International Conference of the Italian Association for Artificial Intelligence, Ferrara, Italy, September 23–25, 2015, Proceedings

22. Omicini, A.: Agents writing on walls: Cognitive stigmergy and beyond. In: Paglieri, F., Tummolini, L., Falcone, R., Miceli, M. (eds.) The Goals of Cognition. Essays in Honor of Cristiano Castelfranchi, *Tributes*, vol. 20, Chap. 29, pp. 543–556. College Publications, London (2012)

23. Omicini, A., Viroli, M.: Coordination models and languages: From parallel computing to self-organisation. Knowl. Eng. Rev. **26**(1), 53–59 (2011). doi:10.1017/S026988891000041X

24. Ossowski, S., Omicini, A.: Coordination knowledge engineering. Knowl. Eng. Rev. **17**(4), 309–316 (2002). doi:10.1017/S0269888903000596

25. Piunti, M., Castelfranchi, C., Falcone, R.: Anticipatory coordination through action observation and behavior adaptation. In: Proceedings of AISB (2007)

26. Robertson, S.E., Walker, S., Jones, S., Hancock-Beaulieu, M.M., Gatford, M., et al.: Okapi at trec-3. NIST Spec. Publ. SP **109**, 109 (1995)

27. Simone, C., Schmidt, K.: Mind the gap! towards a unified view of cscw. In: Fourth International Conference on Design of Cooperative Systems (COOP2000), Sophia-Antipolis (Fr) (2000)

28. Turing, A.M.: Systems of logic based on ordinals. Proc. Lond. Math. Soc. **2**(1), 161–228 (1939)

29. Viroli, M., Casadei, M.: Biochemical tuple spaces for self-organising coordination. In: Field, J., Vasconcelos, V.T. (eds.) Coordination Languages and Models, LNCS, vol. 5521, pp. 143–162. Springer, Lisbon, Portugal (2009). doi:10.1007/978-3-642-02053-7

30. Wegner, P.: Why interaction is more powerful than algorithms. Commun. ACM **40**(5), 80–91 (1997). doi:10.1145/253769.253801

31. Whitworth, B.: Socio-technical systems. Encycl. Hum. Comput. Interact. pp. 533–541 (2006)

32. Zambonelli, F., Omicini, A., Anzengruber, B., Castelli, G., DeAngelis, F.L., Di Marzo Serugendo, G., Dobson, S., Fernandez-Marquez, J.L., Ferscha, A., Mamei, M., Mariani, S., Molesini, A., Montagna, S., Nieminen, J., Pianini, D., Risoldi, M., Rosi, A., Stevenson, G., Viroli, M., Ye, J.: Developing pervasive multi-agent systems with nature-inspired coordination. Pervasive Mob. Comput. **17**, 236–252 (2015). doi:10.1016/j.pmcj.2014.12.002. Special Issue "10 years of Pervasive Computing" In Honor of Chatschik isdikian

Chapter 7
$\mathcal{M}$olecules *of* $\mathcal{K}$nowledge: Technology

Abstract In this chapter an overview of the current state of $\mathcal{MoK}$ technology is provided. Accordingly, Sect. 7.1 discusses the $\mathcal{MoK}$ prototype designed on top of the TuCSoN coordination infrastructure, whereas Sect. 7.2 describes the full-fledged $\mathcal{MoK}$ ecosystem.

7.1 Prototype on TuCSoN

The TuCSoN coordination middleware is an ideal candidate for the implementation of a $\mathcal{MoK}$-like middleware, most of all thanks to *(i)* its situated architecture, enabling definition of a *topology* of distinct, *situated computational loci*—thus, providing a notion of *locality*, too—, and *(ii)* programmability of the ReSpecT tuple centres it distributes over the network.

By relying on TuCSoN, $\mathcal{MoK}$ compartments can be straightforwardly mapped to ReSpecT tuple centres, suitably programmed so as to execute the Gillespie algorithm for stochastic simulation of a chemical solution [5]. Tuple centres are then spread over a network according to an *application-specific* topology, defined again in ReSpecT—ultimately providing the notion of *neighbourhood*.

> In the following the ReSpecT implementation of the Gillespie algorithm is referred to as "the chemical engine" (of a $\mathcal{MoK}$ compartment). Also, the terms "$\mathcal{MoK}$ reaction" and "chemical law" can be used interchangeably, being the latter the implementation of the former within the prototype.

For the above reasons, a prototype implementation of the $\mathcal{MoK}$ model upon the TuCSoN coordination middleware [12], specialised on $\mathcal{MoK}$ computational model and middleware services, is publicly available[1] and has been used for early testing of $\mathcal{MoK}$, as well as for some of the experimental deployments discussed in Chap. 9.

---

[1] http://bitbucket.org/smariani/tucson/branch/MoK-proto.

© Springer International Publishing AG 2016
S. Mariani, *Coordination of Complex Sociotechnical Systems*,
Artificial Intelligence: Foundations, Theory, and Algorithms,
DOI 10.1007/978-3-319-47109-9_7

TuCSoN is exploited to distribute across a network of connected devices a number of *MoK* compartments, implemented as suitably programmed ReSpecT tuple centres [10, 11]. There, information atoms and molecules are packaged into TuCSoN first-order logic tuples and manipulated by both catalysts (TuCSoN agents) and *MoK* reactions (ReSpecTspecifications and *chemical law tuples*). Finally, BIC-related aspects—such as reification of actions as enzymes, traces deposit, as well as perturbation actions application—are implemented as ReSpecT specifications and TuCSoN spawned activities.

Accordingly, Sect. 7.1.1 overviews how *MoK* main abstractions are mapped on TuCSoN and ReSpecT ones, whereas Sect. 7.1.2 briefly describes how *MoK* compartments are implemented on top of ReSpecT tuple centres.

7.1.1 Core Abstractions Mapping

In the ReSpecT specification implementing the chemical engine of *MoK* compartments, three are the main abstractions upon which the Gillespie simulation algorithm is based—thus, which *MoK* model abstractions are mapped upon: *reactants*, *chemical laws*, *neighbourhoods*. Since TuCSoN first-order logic tuples are the only data structure ReSpecT can manipulate, each abstraction is actually implemented as a different sort of tuple.

7.1.1.1 Reactants

Each reactant is represented as a TuCSoN tuple with the following syntax:

```
reactant(Kind, Amount)
```

where *Kind* is a placeholder for the actual reactant, and *Amount* indicates its quantity, resembling *relevance*—e.g. concentration or multiplicity.

> The term "reactant" here is used to denote atoms, molecules, enzymes, traces, and also seeds.

7.1.1.2 Chemical Laws

The chemical laws exploited by the chemical engine to implement *MoK* reactions are essentially of three sorts: *ordinary*, *temporal*, and *instantaneous*.

Ordinary laws are those whose scheduling is driven by a *rate expression*, determining the likelihood they are actually executed, as well as time taken to complete execution. Besides this, in order to be executed, they need the correct amount of reactants to be present in the tuple centre where they are installed, at the time they are scheduled.

Chemical laws are reified as TuCSoN tuples having the following structure:

$$\texttt{law([Reactants], Rate, [Products])}$$

where

- *[Reactants]* represents the set of reactants necessary for the reaction to be selected for scheduling, and *consumed* by the reaction if successfully applied
- *Rate* is the rate expression of the reaction, that is, the (stochastic) likelihood that a specific law is actually selected for execution among many *competing* ones
- *[Products]* represents the set of reactants produced by the reaction as a result of its successful execution

Temporal laws are those with no execution rate associated, to be executed instead according to a dynamically configurable time interval—still, if and only if all the necessary reactants are available, in the right amount, when the period expires.

These laws are reified as TuCSoN tuples as follows:

$$\texttt{timedLaw([Reactants], Period, [Products])}$$

where terms *Reactants* and *Products* retain their usual meaning, while term *Period* indicates the time interval according to which the reaction should be executed.

Instantaneous laws are those having no associated rate or time interval, dictating their scheduling. Instead, they are scheduled for execution as soon as the required reactants are available within the tuple centre where they are installed.

Their representation as TuCSoN tuples is the same as other laws, provided term *Rate/Period* is specified by the constant inf:

$$\texttt{law([Reactants], inf, [Products])}$$

7.1.1.3 Neighbourhood

The term "neighbourhood" denotes the set of tuple centres which are reachable from a given tuple centre, according to an application-specific *reachability criterion*.

Usual network-based reachability, in fact, is of no help in the context of a TuCSoN-based middleware, because TuCSoN tuple centres can communicate with any other tuple centre belonging to any other TuCSoN node, provided it has a known network address. Thus, without some form of reachability constraint, any $\mathcal{MoK}$ compartment would be able to interact with any other compartment within a given $\mathcal{MoK}$ system.

Accordingly, $\mathcal{MoK}$ administrators are free to define application-specific neighbourhoods through a special kind of tuple *neighbour*, to be put in a tuple centre for each reachable tuple centre. The tuple is structured as follows:

$$\texttt{neighbour(Id, Address, Port)}$$

where

- `Id` represents the *locally unique* identifier of the *MoK* compartment in the neighbourhood—equal to the name of the **ReSpecT** tuple centre acting as *MoK* compartment
- `Address` is the IP address of the **TuCSoN** node hosting the neighbour tuple centre
- `Port` is the TCP port number where the mentioned **TuCSoN** node is listening to incoming requests

Once that neighbourhood relationships are defined, a special kind of tuple—or better, of tuple wrap—is provided to indicate the chemical engine that the wrapped tuple has to be fired to a (*uniformly probabilistically* chosen) neighbour:

$$firing(Reactant)$$

where `Reactant` is a placeholder for the actual reactant to be sent to the selected neighbour among the pool of available ones.

7.1.2   The Chemical Engine Logic

The *logic* of the chemical engine implemented by **ReSpecT** specifications may be conceptually split in two distinct stages, to be iterated until no more *triggerable laws* can be found:

1. selection of the chemical law to schedule for execution

    a. match reactant *templates* against available reactants, to collect *triggerable* laws
    b. compute *effective* rates for all the triggerable laws
    c. randomly select a triggerable law, *stochastically* chosen according to the effective rates just computed

2. execution of the selected chemical law, following *Gillespie algorithm* for chemical solution dynamics simulation [5]

    a. instantiate products
    b. update reactants and products quantity in the space
    c. enqueue firing reactants ready to be moved (if any)
    d. update the state of the system—e.g. Gillespie exponential decay

7.1.2.1   Reactants Matching (Step 1.*a*)

In Step 1.*a*, the engine verifies, for each chemical law, whether the required reactants are available within the local compartment, that is whether the local **ReSpecT** tuple centre contains *at least* one reactant tuple matching each of the reactant templates specified in each chemical law, with at least the desired amount. Then, for each chemical law whose above condition is satisfied, the engine marks the law as *triggerable*, that is suitable to be scheduled and executed.

According to the $\mathcal{MoK}$ model, matching of reactant templates against actual reactants should be based on $\mathcal{F}_{\mathcal{MoK}}$ similarity function, so as to leverage some sort of *semantic* capabilities. In this prototype implementation, however, $\mathcal{F}_{\mathcal{MoK}}$ is simply an improved version of Prolog syntactical *unification*, considering also simple Java regular expressions and WordNet synsets [9].

Also, according to the $\mathcal{MoK}$ model, the matching process should be influenced by the *relevance* of reactants in the compartment, that is, by some value representing the (relative) amount of a given reactant (w.r.t. all the other matching reactants available in the compartment). This guarantees that the more relevant a given reactant is, the *more likely* it will win matching.

Nevertheless, in the current prototype implementation, relevance is approximated by *multiplicity* of the tuple representing the reactant, and matching consequently affected by this multiplicity—still probabilistically.

7.1.2.2 Effective Rates (Step 1.*b*)

In Step 1.*b*, the engine computes the *effective rate* of $\mathcal{MoK}$ triggerable reactions based on their *nominal* rate. The former is the rate as dynamically computed according to the system state—e.g. reactants multiplicity—, actually driving *probabilistic selection* of the chemical law to be executed. The latter is the rate expression as defined within the chemical law implementing a $\mathcal{MoK}$ reaction.

According to the $\mathcal{MoK}$ model, the nominal rate of a reaction can be specified by an *arbitrary rate expression*, so as to enable a wide range of stochastic emergent behaviours—as clarified by the simulations discussed in Chap. 8.

Nevertheless, in this prototype implementation, nominal rates ar assumed to be continuous values, which are then automatically multiplied for the product of the concentrations of the reactants to be consumed. This way, rate expressions in the prototype are restricted to be a simple parametrisation of the law of mass action [1], which can be adjusted at run-time. Ultimately, this ensures a fair degree of expressiveness regarding the range of behaviours achievable by the prototype, while the implementation is kept simple, thus efficiency high.

7.1.2.3 Law Selection (Step 1.*c*)

In Step 1.*c*, the chemical engine applies the Gillespie chemical solution dynamics simulation algorithm to choose the chemical law to schedule for execution [5].

Conceptually, selection and execution can be accomplished as a single process proceeding as follows:

- each triggerable law is conceptually associated to a timer, whose value is (uniformly) probabilistically set at a random value between 0 and the inverse of the effective rate of the reaction
- then, timers are started in parallel so that a *critical race* begins among the competing chemical laws
- finally, the chemical law whose associated timer expires first, is executed with a stochastic, *exponentially distributed delay*, based on the summation of the concentrations of all reactants considered

However, in the prototype, selection and execution are two distinct steps. While execution is discussed below, selection proceeds as follows: based on the effective rates computed as described above, the chemical engine (uniformly) probabilistically chooses a random reaction to schedule for execution.

In this prototype, the role of timers is played by *spawned activities*, which are TuCSoN implementation of LINDA `eval` primitive [4]—see the official TuCSoN documentation for details.[2]

7.1.2.4   Products Instantiation (Step 2.*a*)

In Step 2.*a*, the products of the chemical law selected for execution are *instantiated* based on the matching reactants actually sampled from the MoK compartment. This means, if any product contained variables corresponding to other variables specified in reactant *templates*, Prolog-based unification (and propagation) ensures they now contain ground terms.

According to the MoK model, a product may specify *arbitrary expressions* over reactants as its own *instantiation rules*. This is necessary to, e.g. support complex forms of information aggregation, such as filtering, merging, etc.

Nevertheless, in this prototype implementation, products are restricted to be composed by Prolog values or variables, simple arithmetic expressions involving variables and values, simple string operators such as concatenation or substitution (built-in in tuProlog [2], the Prolog engine exploited in TuCSoN), or simple list operations such as replacement and concatenation (again, built-in in tuProlog).

This way, a fair degree of expressiveness regarding products is provided, while the implementation is kept simple, thus efficiency high.

7.1.2.5   Compartment Update (Step 2.*b*)

In Step 2.*b*, reactants and products are, respectively, *withdrawn* from the compartment and *injected* into it, that is, the corresponding tuples consumed and put into the ReSpecT tuple centre acting as MoK compartment.

---

[2]http://www.slideshare.net/andreaomicini/the-tucson-coordination-model-technology-a-guide.

This is done as a single atomic operation, despite implying multiple `in` and `out` LINDA operations, thanks to the transactional execution semantics of ReSpecT specifications [10].

7.1.2.6 Firing Queue (Step 2.*c*)

In Step 2.*c*, the chemical engine prepares *firing tuples* for being sent to a *uniformly probabilistically chosen neighbour.*

TuCSoN tuples representing products of, e.g. a $\mathcal{MoK}$ diffusion reaction, are wrapped as firing tuples, then put into a *firing queue* waiting for their target ReSpecT tuple centre to be defined. Then, the ReSpecT program implementing the chemical engine retrieves the set of *application-specific neighbours*, and randomly picks one according to a uniform probability distribution: this is the tuple centre receiving the firing tuple currently at the top of the firing queue.

7.1.2.7 Engine Update (Step 2.*d*)

In Step 2.*d*, the engine takes care of updating its state, that is, the state of the simulation according to Gillespie algorithm [5]. Among the many operations to be done, encompassing cleaning up temporary tuples, updating tuples tracking systems properties, and the like, one deserves special attention: enforcement of reaction *execution delay*. According to Gillespie in fact, besides the critical race among triggerable reactions, also the execution step involves time accounting.

In particular, between actual execution of a reaction and the next scheduling step, a *Poisson-distributed time delay* has to expire. The reason for doing this is to faithfully emulate the physical nature of a chemical solution, enabling well-founded formal investigation of asymptotical *convergence* to a desired *emergent* behaviour—as done, e.g. with the simulations discussed in Chap. 8.

7.1.3 Spotlight on Engine Implementation

In this section some details regarding ReSpecT implementation of the chemical engine behind $\mathcal{MoK}$ compartments are provided.

$\mathcal{MoK}$ abstractions are mapped to TuCSoN tuples, so as to be conveniently handled by ReSpecT specifications implementing $\mathcal{MoK}$ reactions. For instance, a $\mathcal{MoK}$ enzyme may be represented by the following tuple:

```
reactant(enzyme(species(Sp), strength(St), reactant(R), context(Ctx)), C)
```

where:

- term Sp denotes the species of the enzyme

- St is the strength of the reinforcement brought by the enzyme, according to its species
- R is the reactant actually targeted by the enzyme
- Ctx is meant to store any contextual information regarding the action reified by the enzyme, potentially relevant for coordination purpose
- C is the concentration of the enzyme

Then, an enzyme may be exploited by MoK reinforcement reaction, which can be encoded as a **TuCSoN** tuple as follows:

```
law([reactant(enzyme(Sp, St, R1, Ctx), C1), reactant(R2, C2)],
                             Rate,
    [reactant(enzyme(Sp, St, R1, Ctx), C1), reactant(R2, C2 + St)])
```

meaning that the relevance of reactant $R2$ matching the enzyme's target $R1$, according to $\mathcal{F}_{MoK}$, is increased by St.

Another interesting example is that of the **TuCSoN** tuple implementing MoK decay reaction:

```
law([reactant(R, 1)], Rate, [])
```

meaning that 1 unit of concentration of reactant R is destroyed.

As a last example, consider MoK diffusion:

```
law([reactant(R, C)], Rate, [firing(reactant(R, C))])
```

meaning that, at a pace given by $Rate$—whose effective value is computed at runtime—an amount C of reactant R is made available for diffusion.

At this point, a legitimate question may arise: who takes care of selecting the compartment target of diffusion? How the choice is made?

Here is were **ReSpecT** comes to the rescue. The above tuples are nothing more than a convenient way of representing MoK reactions within the **TuCSoN** framework, that is first-order logic Prolog terms. Then, suitable **ReSpecT** specifications, besides those implementing the chemical engine, take care of interpreting and executing the computation corresponding to this representation.

In the case of diffusion, an ad hoc **ReSpecT** reaction probabilistically picks a `neighbour` tuple, exploiting uniform primitives thoroughly described in Chap. 3, so as to select the destination compartment based on a uniform probability distribution. Then, it sends the `firing` tuple by relying on **TuCSoN** communication facilities.

Another example of the need for **ReSpecT** is while matching reactant templates, used in the left-hand side of chemical laws, against the actual reactant tuples present in the local tuple centre. There, in fact, matching is based on $\mathcal{F}_{MoK}$ similarity measure, thus tuProlog engine [2] cannot be used as is.

Accordingly, then, suitable **ReSpecT** reactions are dedicated to perform $\mathcal{F}_{MoK}$ based matching, by exploiting the already mentioned **TuCSoN** *spawned activities*.

7.2 Software Ecosystem

A comprehensive $\mathcal{MoK}$ *ecosystem* is currently under development.[3] The aim of such a development effort is that of making a *full-fledged platform* for self-organisation of knowledge available, including not just the implementation of the $\mathcal{MoK}$ core model—e.g. the chemical-like machinery—, but also all the additional features that $\mathcal{MoK}$ demands, such as:

- automatic *information retrieval* and *extraction*
- automatic *semantic enrichment* and representation of unstructured text
- document-oriented persistent *storage layer* and graph-based in-memory representation layer
- networking facilities such as automatic *discovery* of compartments for dynamic re-configuration of network topology, mechanisms for *adaptive routing* of information such as digital pheromones [8] or swarming algorithms [15], etc.
- automatic *knowledge inference* and *discovery*, either ontology-based or not
- suitable *user interface* assisting knowledge inference and discovery through BIC inspired mechanisms—e.g. in the spirit of [13]

Accordingly, the $\mathcal{MoK}$ ecosystem is designed according to the architecture depicted in Fig. 7.1, composed of the following logical layers:

Information harvesting—It provides searching facilities for information retrieval, as well as text mining-related techniques for information extraction—e.g. *part of speech* tagging, named entity recognition, etc.

Knowledge representation & persistency—It is devoted to knowledge representation formats and languages, in particular, concerning technologies for building *ubiquitous knowledge bases* on resource-constrained devices [14]. Also, memorisation of data, information, and knowledge, is handled here, both persistent and in-memory—e.g. *document-oriented* DB for persistent storage and *on-memory graph* DB for run-time manipulation of $\mathcal{MoK}$ abstractions.

Networking & communication—It provides both low-level networking (discovery services, heartbeat, point-to-point and multicast data transfer, etc.) and high-level communication services (gossiping, routing, etc.).

Self-organisation—It is devoted to chemical-inspired self-organisation mechanisms ($\mathcal{MoK}$ reactions), semantics-related aspects ($\mathcal{F}_{\mathcal{MoK}}$-based matchmaking), as well as to users' interactions exploitation ($\mathcal{MoK}$ perturbation actions).

User interaction—It provides users with the means to interact with the system, and the $\mathcal{MoK}$ system with the ability of reifying actions, their side effects, the context within which they take place, and so on—so as to enable and promote BIC-based coordination.

In the upcoming sections, an overview of some of the software modules implementing the above layers is provided, which are available in the $\mathcal{MoK}$ working

---

[3]Code publicly available under LGPL license at http://bitbucket.org/smariani/mok and http://bitbucket.org/smariani/mok-projects.

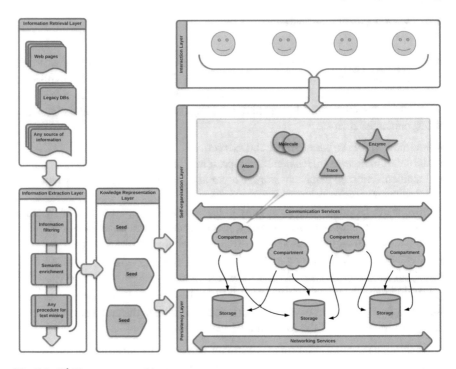

Fig. 7.1 MoK ecosystem architecture

prototype—the information harvesting layer, the networking and communication layer, and the user interaction layer.

It is worth mentioning that, although software modules implementing the self-organisation layer exists within MoK ecosystem, they offer similar functionalities as those provided by the chemical engine described in Sect. 7.1.2—part of the MoK middleware prototype. Implementation is considerably different—e.g. not on top of the TuCSoN coordination middleware—but the design rationale is the same: for each MoK compartment, a chemical engine is in charge of scheduling and executing MoK reactions. In particular, w.r.t. the prototype discussed in Sect. 7.1:

- reactants matching is based on $\mathcal{F}_{MoK}$, considering *cosine similarity* [7], WordNet[4]-based *synsets* [9], and allowing reactant templates to specify *regular expressions* [6]
- reaction rates are arbitrary mathematical expressions providing the required expressiveness for fully supporting custom kinetic rates—described in Sect. 6.3 and evaluated through simulation in Chap. 8
- diffusion of reactants follows the API provided by the communication and networking modules described in Sect. 7.2.2

---

[4]http://wordnet.princeton.edu.

7.2.1 Information Harvesting Layer

Two software modules offer the functionalities expected for this layer: the first one is a *distributed information retrieval system*, including a simple search engine and a web crawling module; the second one is an *information extraction component*, featuring a Natural Language Processing (NLP) service and a module for building $\mathcal{MoK}$ atoms.

7.2.1.1 Information Retrieval System

The first component of the system is a very simple custom *search engine* built on top of the *Google Custom Search* platform,[5] which lets developers build their own custom search facilities by providing API for, e.g. choosing which websites to search in, ranking results, etc.

Here, Google Custom Search is used to implement a *personalised search* within the APICe website,[6] storing publications, course material, thesis, software products, and other stuff related to academic activities undertaken by the APICe research group. Such a choice is easily modifiable, and has been made to support experimental deployment of $\mathcal{MoK}$ in an academic papers clustering scenario, used for evaluating, e.g. function $\mathcal{F}_{\mathcal{MoK}}$—see Sect. 9.2.

The second component is a *web crawler* module based on the `crawler4j` library,[7] providing Java API for implementing a multi-threaded crawler. Crawling is quite straightforward: given a set of pages retrieved through a keyword-based search by the above described custom search engine, the crawler starts processing them in parallel with the aim of *(i)* downloading their textual content, and *(ii)* acquiring further links to other pages also containing the keywords. Depth of the search may be configured, as well as other performance-related parameters, likewise the opportunity of extending the search to *synsets* of the given keywords, based on WordNet [9].

Since `crawler4j` does not provide any support for distributing crawlers over an infrastructure of networked hosts, a dedicated *distribution layer* has been implemented, working as follows:

1. a (set of) server component(s) wait(s) on a well-known network address for dynamic registration of crawlers
2. as soon as a custom search provides some results, the server component distributes the retrieved pages to the registered crawlers
3. then, crawlers begin to process pages, sending to the server component text snippets and further links found

---

[5]http://developers.google.com/custom-search/.

[6]http://apice.unibo.it.

[7]http://github.com/yasserg/crawler4j.

4. finally, the server component stores the received snippets persistently—for resilience reasons, e.g. in a remote DB—and further dispatches the new links to the pool of crawlers

Summing up, by using *MoK* ecosystem information retrieval layer, it is possible to retrieve text documents—e.g. web pages, there attached PDF files, etc.—given a set of keywords and considering their synsets.

7.2.1.2   Information Extraction System

The first component of the system is a *NLP module* implemented on top of the *Apache OpenNLP* library.[8] In particular, two functionalities provided by the library are especially welcome for *MoK*: *part of speech* (POS) tagging and *named entity recognition*.

Part of speech tagging is useful to give a first degree of semantics to snippets of text by, e.g. recognising verbs, subjects of a dialogue, etc., based mostly on grammatical rules. Named entity recognition, instead, is useful to give another bit of semantics to unstructured text, by locating and classifying elements of text based on pre-defined *categories*, e.g. names of persons, organisations, locations, expressions of times, quantities, etc.

The NLP module fetches text snippets from the information retrieval system presented in previous section—e.g. from the DB fed by the server component as soon as crawlers finish processing—then, it applies POS and named entity recognition algorithms to feed the second component of this module: the *MoK atoms builder*.

As the name suggests, the component is in charge of *(i)* implementing the data structure representing *MoK* atoms, as well as *(ii)* the mechanisms automatically filling this data structure based on information provided by both the NLP module—such as tagged sentences—and the information retrieval component—e.g. the URL of the web page where the text comes from.

The component as a whole is widely configurable to, e.g. generate different kinds of atoms based on NLP outcomes—e.g. person atoms, organisation atoms, sentence atoms, etc. Also, it can be *trained* to learn new tagging models for both POS and named entity recognition.

7.2.2   Networking and Communication Layer

Two software modules implement the functionalities expected for this layer: the first one is an *asynchronous networking module* meant to provide low-level API for both data transfer and network topology maintenance; the second one is an *adaptive communication module* providing higher level API meant to directly support the implementation of the *MoK* diffusion reaction.

---

[8]http://opennlp.apache.org.

7.2.2.1 Asynchronous Networking Module

The networking module is developed on top of the Netty NIO framework[9] for *channel-based*, *event-driven asynchronous* message passing, which builds on Java NIO library to provide:

Channels—Actually carrying out communications by providing an API for opening, binding to, connecting to, closing channels, as well as for reading from and writing data to channels.
Channel handlers—Interceptor of channel operations and events.
Event loops—Allowing management of channel operations.

Each channel is registered to one event loop, which processes all events from that channel within a single thread. An event loop may serve multiple channels—one thread per each. Changes in the state of channels, as well as events generated by channels, are intercepted by a dedicated channel handler.

The networking module exploits these abstractions to provide its own, higher level ones:

Compartments—The main abstraction of the module, it is meant to encapsulate the communication capabilities of $\mathcal{MoK}$ compartments—e.g. diffusion of atoms, molecules, and traces—and to manage network-related properties of the compartment, which may change at run-time—such as its network address, its neighbourhood, whether forwarding of received packets is enabled or not, etc.
Neighbourhoods—Compartments are grouped in neighbourhoods, which define the boundaries for $\mathcal{MoK}$ diffusion—if forwarding is disabled.
Membranes—Each compartment is associated to others in its neighbourhood by membranes, actually enabling and taking care of diffusion of atoms and molecules. Also membranes have application-specific properties to track, which may change at run-time—e.g. diffusion likelihood, distance between connected compartments, etc.

A compartment should first of all *join* a $\mathcal{MoK}$ system to receive its neighbourhood in the form of a set of membranes. Then, in order to communicate with the compartments in its neighbourhood, it utilises the appropriate membranes, which provide methods for *point-to-point*, *multicast*, and *broadcast* data transfer. Each data transfer is marked by a *globally unique ID*, enabling implementation of *retransmission* mechanisms, and necessary to avoid *flooding* the network when compartments forward received information.

Each networking operation within the framework is asynchronous and follows a callback model, thus, any compartment invokes operations with a "fire-and-forget" semantics, to be later notified upon their completion—either successful or not. Accordingly, notifications for compartments joining the neighbourhood, reception of data, failures, etc. are available.

---

[9]http://netty.io/index.html.

The networking module also includes *hotspot* components, meant to support *openness* of the $\mathcal{MoK}$ system, and dynamic (re)configuration and maintenance of network *topology*. Hotspots are passive components reachable on a well-known address, on which they listen to incoming connection requests by $\mathcal{MoK}$ compartments. As soon as the request arrives, the hotspot computes the neighbourhood the newcomer should be assigned to, based on the properties of the requesting compartment—e.g. its geographical location, average latency, application-specific preferences—and its own configured *policies* for neighbourhood association. Then, it sends the neighbourhood to the joining compartment, and notifies the compartments therein about the newcomer.

It should be noted that joining the $\mathcal{MoK}$ system by contacting multiple hotspots is perfectly fine, and enables complex topologies to be built, since each hotspot may have different neighbourhood association policies and different *partial views* of the network.

Hotspots are also in charge of *gracefully* releasing connections when compartments leave the $\mathcal{MoK}$ system, that is of informing compartments in the neighbourhood about the leaving one. Even in the case of an abrupt disconnection, e.g. due to network issues or device failure, the system is guaranteed to keep a consistent (partial) view over the network: as soon as compartments attempt to communicate with the no longer available peer, disconnection is detected and promptly communicated to the hotspot, which propagates information to the interested compartments—those in the neighbourhood of the leaving one.

Besides handling join/leave of compartments, and topology-related aspects, hotspots take no role in communication between compartments: in fact, after the join phase, communication is *completely p2p*.

7.2.2.2 Adaptive Communication Module

The communication module is developed on top of the networking module just described, thus, exploits its abstractions and services to provide *direct support* to $\mathcal{MoK}$ high-level communication requirements. In particular, the module provides an API to *(i)* carry out $\mathcal{MoK}$ *diffusion*—that is, sharing of atoms, molecules, or traces between compartments in the same neighbourhood—according to a few different modalities, and *(ii)* undertake $\mathcal{MoK}$ *harvest* actions to seek for information within the whole space of networked $\mathcal{MoK}$ compartments, despite the actual compartment where the action takes place.

As far as the harvest action is concerned, two modalities are supported:

- one takes as input parameter a set of *keywords* and searches matching information by exploiting function $\mathcal{F}_{\mathcal{MoK}}$, here implemented as the *cosine similarity* measure [7] extended to consider *sysnsets* [9]—many other parameters can be specified, e.g., whether to restrict searching to the current neighbourhood
- another takes as input parameter an atom or a molecule, and searches information matching that piece of information—still based on $\mathcal{F}_{\mathcal{MoK}}$ similarity measure

Whichever is the chosen modality, a few features are supported by the current implementation which are worth to be mentioned:

- whenever a compartment receives a search request, regardless of the fact it can provide matching information or not, it tracks that the requesting compartment is looking for information matching the given keywords/atom/molecule
- whenever the compartment where the search action took place receives a reply from a remote compartment, within its neighbourhood or not, it tracks that the compartment has matching information (for that keywords/atom/molecule)
- whenever a compartment receives a search request, regardless of the fact it can provide matching information or not, it forwards the request to its neighbours—flooding is automatically avoided by the underlying networking module described in previous section
- replies to search actions imply movement of a fraction of the matching atoms and molecules concentration, not their copy

As far as $\mathcal{MoK}$ diffusion is concerned, four modalities for transmitting information are currently supported:

Random—The diffusing item (atom, molecule, or trace) is sent to a neighbour compartment chosen at random, each compartment having the same probability.
Probabilistic—The diffusing item is sent to a neighbour compartment chosen at random, each compartment having a probability depending on properties of the membrane connecting it to the sender compartment—e.g. their distance, according to application-specific metrics.
Broadcast—The diffusing item is sent to all the compartments in the neighbourhood.
Focussed—The diffusing item is sent to a specific compartment.

Both diffusion and search generate *gradients* [3], which are used to route *(i)* search replies, *(ii)* further search requests, and *(iii)* focussed diffusions. More in general, forwarding of data packets is implemented on top of gradients *dynamically created* by the above described actions, which provide a sort of *adaptive routing list* to every networked compartment.

Routing lists are data structures tracking compartments connecting a source compartment to a destination compartment. Routing lists are incrementally and cooperatively filled by the compartments themselves, which add their reference to the list prior to passing it while forwarding data packets.

Routing lists may provide more alternatives to reach a given destination: strictly worse alternatives are eliminated—e.g. those with more compartments to traverse—whereas equivalent ones are chosen probabilistically, so as to support *graceful degradation* of routing performance in case of topology changes—e.g. compartments disconnections breaking a routing path.

Spreading of search requests is actually implemented on top of diffusion, where the items diffused are not atoms nor molecules, but traces (deposited by the `harvest` enzyme, in turn released by the homonym action).

All the features described so far are meant to cooperatively support *adaptive communications* within MoK. Compartments track each other requests to improve their performance, e.g. by attracting information which is more frequently requested by neighbour compartments. Complementarily, compartments track each other replies to improve their efficiency, e.g. by autonomously switching diffusion modality to focussed diffusion when a compartment is recognised as the best source for a given kind of information.

7.2.3   User Interaction Layer

A single software module provides the functionalities expected for this layer, which are basically three: *(i)* exposing an API for making MoK actions available to catalysts, *(ii)* modelling MoK enzymes, traces, and perturbations, and *(iii)* handling (part of) their lifecycle[10]—e.g. enzymes production, perturbations execution, etc.

MoK actions are those described in Sect. 6.4, that is, *share, mark, annotate, connect,* and *harvest.* Being the whole MoK ecosystem implemented in Java, they are modelled as Java `Runnable` objects, whose method `run()` implements the goal of the action—e.g. for action `share` it actually handles sharing of the information target of the action with neighbouring compartments. Besides this, action objects also track those *action properties* useful for MoK *adaptive* and *self-organising* processes, such as who performed the action, when, within which compartment, which actions came before the current one, and so on.

Enzymes and traces are modelled by simple Java objects reifying the structures formalised in Sect. 6.2. Accordingly, enzymes have a species and a reference reactant field, as well as a key-value map storing contextual information similarly to actions; traces have a tacit message field, a subject field indicating what could be affected, and the usual key-value map for the context—this time regarding trace generation.

Enzymes are generated as soon as actions are undertaken, *transparently* to the acting catalyst, by the machinery underlying the exposed API, which is also in charge of actually executing the action. Traces instead are deposited by MoK homonym reaction, which exploits the methods provided by this interaction module to query enzymes' content and build traces accordingly.

Perturbation actions are modelled as Java `Runnable` objects, whose method `run()` implements the goal of the perturbation action—e.g. for a `attract` perturbation actually handles collecting information from neighbouring compartments. Besides this, perturbation objects also have a key-value map storing properties regarding application of the perturbation action which may be conveniently configured at run-time— e.g. the strength of a `boost` perturbation. Furthermore, for convenience reasons,

---

[10]Part is handled through MoK reactions, thus by the dedicated self-organisation layer.

perturbation objects also track some contextual information and action properties inherited by enzymes and traces, so as to enable the *context-awareness* required to reach *flexibility* and *expressiveness*—e.g. the same tacit message sent by different catalysts and regarding different information pieces may lead to the same perturbation but with a different tuning of its aforementioned properties.

Perturbations are actually executed by $\mathcal{MoK}$ homonym reaction, which exploits perturbation properties to dynamically tune its effects on the $\mathcal{MoK}$ entity affected.

The machinery underlying the exposed API is associated to a compartment, thus handles interactions of all the catalysts sharing that compartment. Whenever a catalyst executes an action, the machinery *(i)* generates the corresponding enzyme, and *(ii)* actually carries out action execution—e.g. in case of an `harvest` action, it interacts with the communication layer to trigger the computations described in Sect. 7.2.2.2. Being catalysts allowed to interact from anywhere (e.g. remotely) with their compartment, their concurrent interactions are ordered according to when invocation of actions reaches the compartment. There, a Java `Executor` takes care of *asynchronously* executing actions and dispatching results.

References

1. Cardelli, L.: On process rate semantics. Theor. Comput. Sci. **391**(3), 190–215 (2008)
2. Denti, E., Omicini, A., Ricci, A.: tuProlog: A light-weight Prolog for Internet applications and infrastructures. In: Ramakrishnan, I. (ed.) Practical Aspects of Declarative Languages, LNCS, vol. 1990, pp. 184–198. Springer, Berlin, Heidelberg (2001). doi:10.1007/3-540-45241-9. 3rd International Symposium (PADL 2001), Las Vegas, NV, USA, 11–12 March 2001. Proceedings
3. Fernandez-Marquez, J.L., Arcos, J.L., Serugendo, G.D.M., Viroli, M., Montagna, S.: Description and composition of bio-inspired design patterns: The gradient case. In: Proceedings of the 3rd Workshop on Biologically Inspired Algorithms for Distributed Systems, BADS '11, pp. 25–32. ACM, New York, NY, USA (2011). doi:10.1145/1998570.1998575
4. Gelernter, D.: Generative communication in Linda. ACM Trans. Program. Lang. Syst. **7**(1), 80–112 (1985). doi:10.1145/2363.2433
5. Gillespie, D.T.: Exact stochastic simulation of coupled chemical reactions. J. Phys. Chem. **81**(25), 2340–2361 (1977). doi:10.1021/j100540a008
6. Habibi, M.: Java Regular Expressions: Taming the Fava. Util. Regex Engine. Springer, Berlin Heidelberg (2004)
7. Huang, A.: Similarity measures for text document clustering. In: Proceedings of the Sixth New Zealand Computer Science Research Student Conference (NZCSRSC2008), Christchurch, New Zealand, pp. 49–56 (2008)
8. Jeon, P.B., Kesidis, G.: Pheromone-aided robust multipath and multipriority routing in wireless manets. In: Proceedings of the 2Nd ACM International Workshop on Performance Evaluation of Wireless Ad Hoc, Sensor, and Ubiquitous Networks, PE-WASUN '05, pp. 106–113. ACM, New York, NY, USA (2005). doi:10.1145/1089803.1089974
9. Miller, G., Fellbaum, C.: Wordnet: An electronic Lexical Database (1998)
10. Omicini, A.: Formal ReSpecT in the A&A perspective. Electron. Notes Theor. Comput. Sci. **175**(2), 97–117 (2007). doi:10.1016/j.entcs.2007.03.006
11. Omicini, A., Denti, E.: From tuple spaces to tuple centres. Sci. Comput. Program. **41**(3), 277–294 (2001). doi:10.1016/S0167-6423(01)00011-9
12. Omicini, A., Zambonelli, F.: Coordination for Internet application development. Auton. Agents Multi-Agent Syst. **2**(3), 251–269 (1999). doi:10.1023/A:1010060322135

13. Ruotsalo, T., Jacucci, G., Myllymäki, P., Kaski, S.: Interactive intent modeling: Information discovery beyond search. Commun. ACM **58**(1), 86–92 (2014). doi:10.1145/2656334
14. Ruta, M., Scioscia, F., Di Sciascio, E., Rotondi, D.: Ubiquitous knowledge bases for the semantic web of things. In: First Internet of Things International Forum (2011)
15. Sim, K.M., Sun, W.H.: Ant colony optimization for routing and load-balancing: survey and new directions. IEEE Trans. Syst. Man. Cybern. A: Syst. Hum. **33**(5), 560–572 (2003). doi:10.1109/TSMCA.2003.817391

Chapter 8
$\mathcal{M}$olecules of $\mathcal{K}$nowledge: Simulation

Abstract In this chapter, the $\mathcal{MoK}$ computational model, that is, the set of $\mathcal{MoK}$ reactions, and its interaction model, that is, the way catalysts' actions are handled, are simulated in order to asses the extent to which they enable the kind of adaptive self-organising behaviours envisioned by $\mathcal{MoK}$. Accordingly, Sect. 8.1 reports on simulation of each $\mathcal{MoK}$ reaction, while Sect. 8.2 discusses a simulated scenario of online collaboration.

8.1 Computational Model

Simulation is widely recognised as a fundamental development and evaluation stage in the process of designing and deploying complex software systems, such as MAS and computational biology systems [5, 11], mostly due to the huge number of local interactions between components, influence of randomness and probability on system evolution, high number of system parameters. $\mathcal{MoK}$ enjoys all the aforementioned properties—being inspired to biochemistry, and devoted to the coordination of sociotechnical, knowledge-intensive MAS—thus simulation is a suitable means to evaluate its design. In particular, $\mathcal{MoK}$ computational model is likely to benefit from a simulation stage, since it is concerned with *local* computational processes ($\mathcal{MoK}$ reactions) originating *global* self-organisation by *emergence*, with the twofold goal of *(i)* qualitatively evaluate the ability of $\mathcal{MoK}$ reactions to contribute to the goals of the model, and *(ii)* ground the design of $\mathcal{MoK}$ reactions rate expressions on a solid basis.

A number of different simulation tools capable of modelling biochemical-like processes exist, either born in the biochemistry field (see [1] for a survey) or in the Multi-Agent-Based Simulation (MABS) research area (survey in [12]). Among the many, ALCHEMIST [13], PRISM [7], and BioPEPA [4] are worth to be mentioned. The choice here falls on the latter for its appealing features, which perfectly suit the purpose of evaluating $\mathcal{MoK}$ reactions.

© Springer International Publishing AG 2016   199
S. Mariani, *Coordination of Complex Sociotechnical Systems*,
Artificial Intelligence: Foundations, Theory, and Algorithms,
DOI 10.1007/978-3-319-47109-9_8

BioPEPA [4] is a language for modelling and analysis of biochemical processes. It is based on PEPA [6], a process algebra originally aimed at performance analysis of software systems, extending it to deal with some features of biochemical networks, such as *stoichiometry* (how many molecules of a given kind participate) and different kinds of *kinetic laws*—including the law of mass action. The most appealing features of BioPEPA are

- custom kinetic laws represented by means of *functional rate expressions*
- definition of stoichiometry and *role* played by the species (reactant, product, enzyme, etc.) in a given reaction
- theoretical roots in CTMC semantics [2]—behind any BioPEPA specification lies a stochastic labelled transition system modelling a CTMC

In BioPEPA, rate expressions are defined as mathematical equations involving reactants' concentrations (denoted with the reactant name and dynamically computed at run-time) and supporting mathematical operators (e.g. exp and log functions) as well as built-in kinetic laws (e.g. the law of mass action, denoted with keyword fMA) and time dependency (through variable time, changing value dynamically according to the current simulation time step).[1]

The BioPEPA Eclipse plugin is the tool allowing to simulate BioPEPA specifications of biochemical systems—in our case, *MoK* reactions.

Each of the following experiments has been performed using Gillespie's stochastic simulation algorithm in 100 independent replications. Each of the following plots has been directly generated by BioPEPA Eclipse plugin as a result of the correspondent experiment—hence, of the 100 Gillespie runs. In each chart, the *x*-axis plots the time steps of the simulation, whereas the *y*-axis the concentration level of the reactants expressed in units of molecules.

It should be noted that *MoK* deposit and perturbation reactions were left out of simulations. The motivation for ignoring the former is that it is identical to injection, except it involves different reactants. The latter, apart from being application-specific, is already the subject of the experiments in Sect. 9.1.

One reaction at a time is incrementally added to the simulated BioPEPA specification. This allows evaluation of *(i)* the interplay between the different reactions constituting the *MoK* model, and *(ii)* the whole pool of *MoK* reactions altogether—as the last step—to understand if the achievable global behaviours are enablers for the kind of self-organising behaviour desired for *MoK*.

The codebase tracking the BioPEPA specifications used in the examples is publicly available under LGPL licence at http://bitbucket.org/smariani/mok-biopepa.

---

[1]To learn more about BioPEPA syntax, please refer to [4].

8.1.1 Injection

Injection reaction is formalised in Sect. 6.3 as follows:

$$\text{seed}(src, Atoms) \xrightarrow{r_{inj}} \text{seed}(src, Atoms) + atom^i_{c+c_i}, \quad \forall atom^i_{c_i} \in Atoms$$

$$r_{inj} = \frac{1}{1 + \text{time}} * \text{diff}(\sharp seed, \sharp atom)$$

Two contrasting needs are addressed here: on one hand, atoms should be *perpetually* injected into the $\mathcal{MoK}$ system, since there is no way to know a priori *when* some information will be useful; on the other hand, one would likely avoid flooding the system without any control on how many atoms are in play. To get there, three rate expressions are simulated and evaluated:

1. one having injection rate decreasing as time passes
2. one enforcing some kind of saturation to stop injection
3. one as a combination of the two above

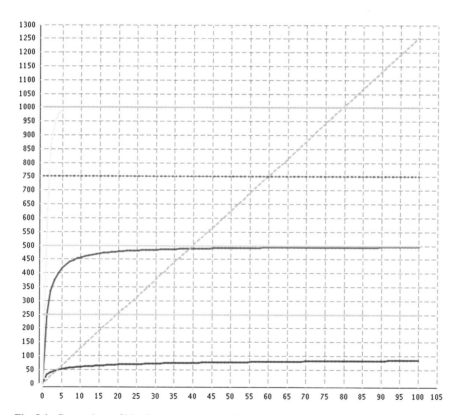

Fig. 8.1 Comparison of kinetic rate expressions for injection reaction [9]

```
1  injE = [source_economics/atom_economics * (1 / (1 + time))];  // option (1)
2  injS = [source_sports - atom_sports];                          // option (2)
3  injC = [(1 / (1 + time)) * (source_crime - atom_crime)];       // option (3)
4  injP = [fMA(0.05)];                                            // option (4)
```

Fig. 8.2 The fMA keyword calls a built-in function to compute the law of mass action [9]. Its only parameter is the rate constant. The fMA implicitly considers reactants involved in the reaction exploiting its correspondent functional rate—for the full BioPEPA specification, please refer to [8]

Figure 8.1 shows atoms evolution according to rate (1) in blue (corresponding seeds in purple dashed line), to rate (2) in yellow (seeds in pink) and to rate (3) in red (seeds in orange). The green dashed line plots the law of mass action rate (seeds in light blue). Figure 8.2 shows the BioPEPA specification implementing these rate expressions.

Using the rate expression based on the law of mass action is out of question: its behaviour follows none of the requirements for $\mathcal{MoK}$ injection reaction. Once discarded also rate (1), whose trend is clearly too slow in reaching saturation, rates (2) and (3) may seem almost identical. Actually they are not:

- rate expression (2) is saturation-driven only, thus, whenever at some point in time some atoms will suddenly decrease in concentration—e.g. due to agents consuming them—they will go back to saturation level as fast as possible, no matter how long their sources are within the system
- rate expression (3) instead, makes the saturation process time-dependant. In particular, the longer seeds are within the system, the slower saturation will be

Choosing among the two essentially depends on how fast information loses relevance compared to how frequently users are expected to interact with the system. Being knowledge-intensive STS intrinsically fast-paced ones, rate expression (3) is preferred for $\mathcal{MoK}$.

8.1.2 Decay

Decay reaction is formalised in Sect. 6.3 as follows:

$$Reactant_c \xrightarrow{r_{dec}} Reactant_{c-1}, \quad c \in \mathfrak{R}^+$$

$$r_{dec} = \begin{cases} \text{fMA}(a_R) * \log(1+\text{time}), & a_R \in \mathfrak{R}^+, \quad Reactant \setminus trace \\ \text{diff}(\sharp[\Uparrow trace], \sharp trace) * \log(1+\text{time}) \end{cases}$$

Decay is an effective way to resemble the relationship between information relevance and flow of time. In many application scenarios, in fact, information tends (on average) to lose (potential) relevance as time passes by: journalistic news do so, academic papers do so, posts in social networks, fitness data, sensor streams and so on. Furthermore, decay enforces a kind of *negative feedback* which, together with the

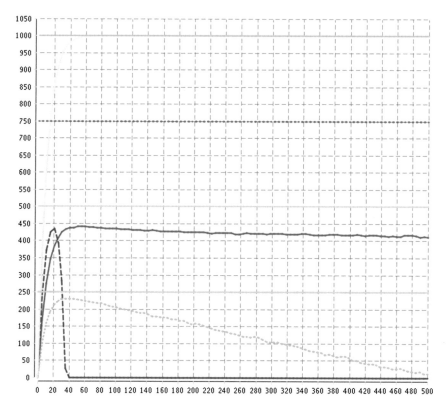

Fig. 8.3 Comparison of kinetic rate expressions for atoms decay [9]

positive feedback provided by $\mathcal{MoK}$ enzymes, e.g. through reinforcement reaction, enables the *feedback loop* peculiar of self-organising systems [3].

Nevertheless, time dependency alone seems not enough for a meaningful decay behaviour: using, e.g. a fixed rate one would end up simply slowing down the saturation process provided by injection reaction. Hence, Fig. 8.3 shows three different combinations of time dependency and concentration dependency for $\mathcal{MoK}$ decay reaction—a fourth one (yellow line), based on the law of mass action, is given for comparison purpose:

1. linear time dependency + relative concentration dependency (blue dashed line for atoms, purple dashed for corresponding seeds)
2. logarithmic time dependency + relative concentration dependency (red line for atoms, orange for seeds)
3. linear time dependency + built-in law of mass action (green dashed line, light blue for seeds)

```
1  decayE = [source_economics / atom_economics * time];   // option (1)
2  decayC = [source_crime / atom_crime * log(1+time)];    // option (2)
3  decayP = [fMA(0.05) * time];                           // option (3)
4  decayS = [fMA(0.05)];                                  // option (4)
```

Fig. 8.4 BioPEPA specification of rate expressions for MoK decay reaction [9]

Figure 8.4 shows the BioPEPA specification used.[2] The law of mass action is unsatisfactory, as well as option (1). Options (2) and (3) seem both viable instead.

The choice is mostly driven by how fast are the dynamics of the scenario in which MoK has to be deployed, thus how fast information should lose relevance. Nevertheless, it should be noted that option (3) has an additional parameter w.r.t. option (2): the law of mass action rate constant. Even if such a parameter is made dynamically adjustable—e.g. the ratio between sources and atoms concentrations as done in options (1), (2)—the trend still would not match the requirements for MoK decay reaction. Thus, the choice for MoK fell on option (2).

8.1.3 Aggregation

Aggregation reaction is formalised in Sect. 6.3 as follows:

$$Reactant' + Reactant'' \xrightarrow{r_{agg}}$$
$$(Reactant' \oplus Reactant'') + (Reactant' \ominus Reactant'')$$
$$r_{agg} = \frac{\text{time}}{\sharp Reactant^{lhs}}$$

The main responsibility of the aggregation reaction is to cluster together similar information atoms. While doing so, a fact should be considered: as time passes by, it is likely that more and more atoms will be roaming compartments, thus, it is desirable to aggregate more, so as to have different forms of more concise information[3]—for many reasons, such as memory occupation. Also, it is worth to note that molecules decay, and that non-similar atoms are released back into the compartment during aggregation, thus it is unlikely for molecules to keep growing endlessly—unless they are really exploited by catalysts.

Based on the above discussion, three rate expressions seem viable—a fourth one, based on fMA solely, is considered for comparison purpose:

---

[2] Actually, the Heaviside function is also used to counter BioPEPA tolerance to negative rates, which are meaningless—see [4].

[3] Aggregation may assume different forms, such as filtering, merging, fusing, etc.

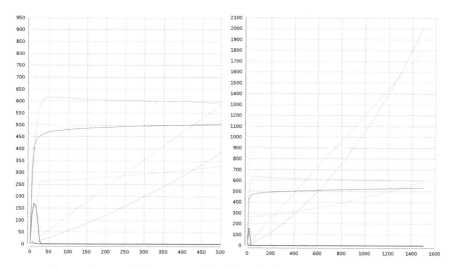

Fig. 8.5 Comparison of kinetic rate expressions for molecules aggregation

1. one featuring direct proportionality w.r.t. time
2. one combining direct proportionality w.r.t. time with inverse proportionality w.r.t. atoms, so as to make the aggregation process slower when more and more atoms are present—a motivation could be that these atoms may be relevant on their own, since they are so many and not yet aggregated
3. one combining direct proportionality w.r.t. time with inverse proportionality w.r.t. the generated molecule, so as to speed up the aggregation process when molecules lose relevance—a motivation could be that these molecules deserve a chance to be exploited by catalysts

Figure 8.5 shows the above-described rate expressions on different time horizons (shorter on the left, longer on the right).

Rate expression (1) aggregates atoms so fast that they are almost instantly depleted, and have no chance to go nowhere near their saturation level (not depicted to ease readability of the plot, but equal to previous simulations)—orange dotted line for molecules, red line for atoms. Rate expression (2) implements quite well the desiderata, being atoms kept slightly under their saturation level, and being molecules produced slightly faster as time passes by—pink dotted line for molecules, yellow line for atoms. Rate expression (3) seems almost identical to option (2) on a short time period, but in the long run (picture on the right) it exhibits a more linear trend w.r.t. option (2)—light blue line for molecules, dotted green line for atoms. Rate expression (4) is clearly out of question, in a way very similar to option (1)—purple dotted line for molecules, blue dotted line for atoms.

Figure 8.6 shows the BioPEPA specification used.[4] Once again the choice among options (2) and (3) is mostly driven by the application-specific needs $\mathcal{MoK}$ should

---

[4] Again, the Heaviside step function has been used to avoid negative rates.

```
1  aggC = [fMA(0.5) * time];                      // option (1)
2  aggS = [fMA(0.5) * time/atom_sports];          // option (2)
3  aggP = [fMA(0.5) * time/molecule_politics];    // option (3)
4  aggE = [fMA(0.5)];                             // option (4)
```

Fig. 8.6 BioPEPA specification of rate expressions for *MoK* aggregation reaction

support. According to the deployment scenarios envisioned for *MoK*, option (2) is preferred.

8.1.4 Reinforcement

Reinforcement reaction is formalised in Sect. 6.3 as follows:

$$\text{enzyme}(species, s_{species}, Reactant, Context) + Reactant'_c \xrightarrow{r_{reinf}}$$
$$\text{enzyme}(species, s_{species}, Reactant, Context) + Reactant'_{c+s}, \quad c, s \in \Re^+$$
$$r_{reinf} = \text{diff}(\sharp[\Uparrow Reactant], \sharp Reactant)$$

In order to properly engineer *MoK* reinforcement reaction rate, it should be kept in mind what enzymes are meant for, that is, *(i)* representing a *situated interest* manifested by an agent w.r.t. a piece of knowledge—an atom or a molecule—*(ii)* be exploited to reinforce knowledge relevance within the system. The word "situated" means that reinforcement should take into account the *situatedness* of agents (inter-)actions along a number of dimensions: time, space, type—a harvest action, a mark action, etc. For these reasons, *MoK* reinforcement reaction rate should

- be prompt, that is, rapidly increase molecules concentration—despite decay
- be limited in both time and space, to resemble the relationship between relevance and situatedness of (inter-)actions
- depend on the (inter-)action type—e.g. a mark action could inject more enzymes and/or reinforce atoms with greater stoichiometry w.r.t. a harvest action

Figure 8.7 clearly shows that the desiderata are fulfilled only by a reinforcement reaction having a functional dependency on the ratio between the reinforced molecule's concentration and its source own (yellow line)—option (1) in Fig. 8.8. Once again, sticking with the law of mass action alone is out of question: option (2)—dashed blue line—even if adopting a dynamic rate constant, exhibits an exceedingly high and fast peak, option (3)—red line—using a fixed rate constant (as in the law of mass action typically is), almost completely ignores the feedback—enzymes are too slowly consumed (orange line, plotting enzymes concentration).

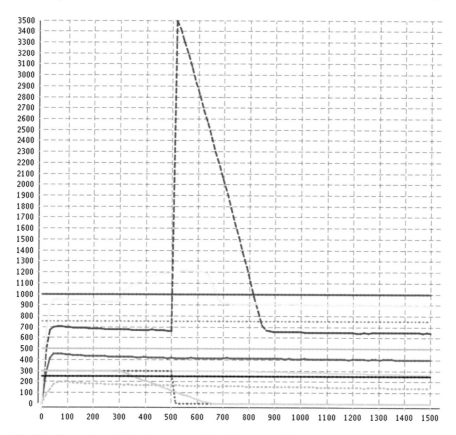

Fig. 8.7 Comparison of kinetic rate expressions for atoms reinforcement [9]

```
1 feedS = [(source_sports / atom_sports)];           // option (1)
2 feedE = [fMA(source_economics / atom_economics)];  // option (2)
3 feedC = [fMA(0.05)];                                // option (3)
```

Fig. 8.8 BioPEPA specification of rate expressions for $\mathcal{MoK}$ reinforcement reaction [9]

Furthermore, Fig. 8.9 shows how *concentration* and *stoichiometry* can influence $\mathcal{MoK}$ reinforcement reaction behaviour, effectively modelling situatedness—in particular, w.r.t. the type of (inter-)action. In fact, in Fig. 8.9 *(i)* the initial concentration of red enzymes (red line) is doubled w.r.t. yellow enzymes (yellow line) in Fig. 8.7: as a result, the duration of the feedback is doubled as well; *(ii)* the stoichiometry of red atoms (red line) in reinforcement reaction is doubled w.r.t. yellow atoms (yellow line) in Fig. 8.7: as a result, the intensity of the feedback is more than doubled. Also, Fig. 8.9 shows that the opposite holds, too: halving the initial concentration halves the duration of the feedback (yellow and blue lines).

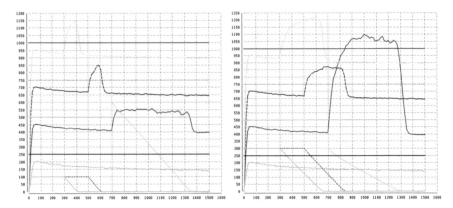

Fig. 8.9 Enzymes concentration increment effect on reinforcement (on the *left*), and atoms stoichiometry increment effect on reinforcement (on the *right*) [9]

8.1.5 Diffusion

Diffusion reaction is formalised in Sect. 6.3 as follows:

$$[\![Reactants' \cup Reactant]\!]_i \varprec [\![Reactants'']\!]_j \xrightarrow{r_{diff}} [\![Reactants']\!]_i \varprec$$
$$[\![Reactants'' \cup Reactant]\!]_j, \quad i \neq j \in \mathbb{N}$$
$$r_{diff} = d * \mathtt{diff}([\![\sharp Reactant]\!]_i, [\![\sharp Reactant]\!]_j), \quad d \in (0, 1] \in \Re$$

The topology underlying diffusion simulations simply includes four *MoK* compartments connected one to each other, allowing any molecule to move anywhere.

The main requirements for *MoK* diffusion reaction are similar to those for *MoK* injection: on one hand, one would like to perpetually spread information around, because agents working in other compartments may be interested in it; on the other hand, it is also desirable to keep some degree of control about how much information moves.

Such a degree of control is achieved by reusing the concept of saturation, as shown by Fig. 8.10: in particular, it seems reasonable to allow only a fraction of molecules to leave their origin compartment—the corresponding BioPEPA specification is shown in Fig. 8.11. In practice, one can arbitrarily decrease/increase the saturation level of the origin compartment in the destination compartment. Furthermore, they are functionally related.

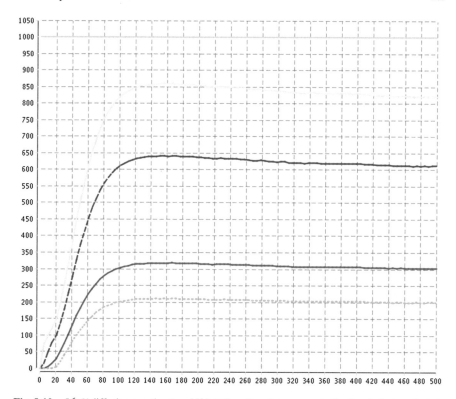

Fig. 8.10 $\mathcal{MoK}$ diffusion reaction trend [9]. *Yellow line* plots concentration level of atoms in their origin compartment (the *orange horizontal line* represents their source)

The simulations discussed in this section essentially demonstrate a few things:

- first, *feasibility* of the chemical-inspired approach w.r.t. $\mathcal{MoK}$ goals, since for each $\mathcal{MoK}$ reaction a satisfactory rate expression is achieved, which meets the requirements for that reaction behaviour
- second, *expressiveness* of the chemical-inspired approach based on custom rate expressions rather than on the law of mass action solely, which enables reaching different trends—as regards information evolution—according to how rate expressions are engineered
- third, *adaptiveness* of the approach, since rate expressions are engineered upon contextual information—e.g. concentration of reactants—which may be opportunistically influenced by either catalysts—e.g. enzymes—or $\mathcal{MoK}$ itself—e.g. through perturbation actions

```
1  // diffusion weight
2  DW = 0.75;
3  // diffusion functional rates (a@x => a@y)
4  diffSE = [DW * as@sports - as@economics];    // blue line
5  diffSC = [DW/2 * as@sports - as@crime];       // red line
6  diffSP = [DW/3 * as@sports - as@politics];    // green line
```

Fig. 8.11 BioPEPA specification for diffusion rates [9]. Notation *r* @*c* refers to the concentration of reactant *r* in compartment *c*. Previous listings did not follow this notation because there was only a single compartment

8.2   Interaction Model

Once that *MoK* computational model is simulated, it is reasonable to simulate the interaction model of *MoK*, to qualitatively evaluate to which extent users' behaviour is able to steer *MoK* autonomous coordinative behaviour. To this end a citizen journalism scenario is simulated, where users share a *MoK*-coordinated IT platform for retrieving, assembling, and publishing news stories.

Users have personal devices (smartphones, tablets, laptops) running the *MoK* middleware, they use to *(i)* *search* throughout the IT platform looking for relevant information, *(ii)* modify, *annotate*, comment, etc. information so as to shape their own news story, and finally *(iii)* *release* their story to the public, for both reading and reuse.

For a number of reasons—among which limiting bandwidth consumption, boosting security, reducing communication latency, etc.—the extent to which a search action may extend is limited by a (possibly logical, not physical) *neighbourhood* of compartments, that is, those compartments connected by a membrane to the compartment where the search action takes place—e.g. neighbourhood can be based on 1-hop network reachability.

While performing search actions, and in general while undertaking their usual business-related activities, users release (*transparently*, possibly *unintentionally*) *enzymes* within the compartment underlying the working space they are operating on, which in turn deposits *traces* which start wandering across the network of compartments constituting the news management IT platform—recall that traces are subject to diffusion whereas enzymes are not.

Then, the *MoK* middleware exploits enzymes and traces to schedule *perturbation actions* aimed at enacting some form of *anticipatory coordination* [14]. In particular, within the simulated scenario users perform harvest, mark, and share actions, which deposit, respectively, intention, opportunity, and presence traces, ultimately causing attract, strengthen, and boost perturbation actions—according to *MoK* terminology.

Thus, what happens in practice is that the *MoK* middleware exploits users' (local) interactions to improve the (global) spatial organisation of information: whenever users implicitly manifest interest in a piece of information—through harvesting, marking, and sharing actions—the $\mathcal{MoK}$ middleware interprets their *intention* to exploit information, and the *opportunity* for others to exploit it as well, *attracting* similar information towards the compartment where the action took place, *increasing* relevance of the information target of the action, and *boosting* reinforcement and diffusion reactions accordingly.

Simulation tool used is NetLogo 5.0.5, available at http://ccl.northwestern.edu/netlogo/. Videos of the simulations are available on YouTube (https://youtu.be/8ibkXdukTfk). Source code of the simulations is to be released as a NetLogo model, available at http://ccl.northwestern.edu/netlogo/models/community/. 100 $\mathcal{MoK}$ compartments are networked in a grid (4 neighbours per compartment, except border); 2500 molecules, split in 5 non-overlapping semantic categories (representing matching with different enzymes), are uniformly sampled then randomly scattered in the grid—statistically, 500 molecules per category; 250 enzymes, split in the same categories, are generated in 5 random compartments; enzymes' categories are uniformly sampled in batches consisting of 50 enzymes each, so that generated enzymes of a given category are always multiple of 50; enzymes are generated *periodically* (every 250 time steps) and subject to decay; 2 traces per enzyme are generated, coherently with enzymes' category and according to the same time interval; traces, too, are subject to decay, although at a lower rate w.r.t. enzymes—due to their different purpose: represent *long-term effects* of actions for the former, reify *situated* actions for the latter.

The simulations proceed as follows: molecules randomly diffuse among neighbouring compartments; enzymes reify, e.g. a `harvest` action which successfully collects a set of molecules from the local compartment; enzymes stand still in the compartment where the action took place until decay, depositing traces; traces, representing, e.g. tacit message `intention`, randomly diffuse among neighbouring compartments until either (i) decay or (ii) find a matching molecule to apply their perturbation action to; the perturbation action, e.g. `attract`, makes the involved molecule diffuse towards the compartment where the enzyme father of the trace belongs.

Figures 8.12, 8.13, and 8.14 showcase how the emergent *collective intelligence* phenomena enabling anticipatory coordination is effectively supported by the BIC inspired abstractions and mechanisms featured in $\mathcal{MoK}$.

The coordination infrastructure, in fact, does not know in advance the effectiveness of its coordination activities in supporting users' workflows: it only tries to react to users' activities at its best, according to its own interpretation of users' actions in epistemic terms—e.g. through tacit messages. This is exactly what anticipatory coordination is: the infrastructure tries to foresee the user coordination needs even before users do, with the aim of satisfying them at best [10].

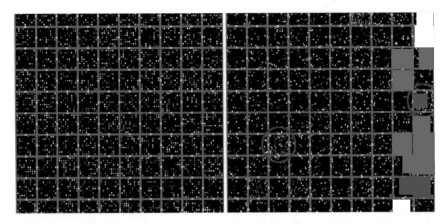

Fig. 8.12 *Self-organising, adaptive anticipatory coordination* [10]. (*left*) The simulation starts with atoms and molecules of information belonging to different topics (represented as differently coloured dots) randomly scattered across catalysts' compartments (represented as black squares, delimited by blue lines, and connected by membranes represented as light blue patches). (*right*) From time to time, users (catalysts) carry out `harvest`, `mark`, and `share` actions, releasing homonym enzymes (represented as coloured flags) within the workspace they are working on

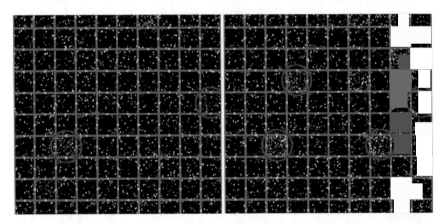

Fig. 8.13 (*left*) As soon as enzymes are released, *MoK* reinforcement reaction increases relevance of the information atoms and molecules target of the original action. (*right*) Then, `intention`, `opportunity`, and `presence` traces are deposited, free to wander between neighbouring compartments, crossing membranes, so as to apply their perturbation action potentially to any compartment in the network

Figure 8.12 (left) shows the initial configuration: information molecules (coloured dots) are randomly scattered throughout a grid of networked compartments (black squares)—light blue little squares represent membranes between compartments, allowing diffusion. Figure 8.12 (right) highlights two compartments in which enzymes (coloured flags) have just been released, thus traces begin to spawn and diffuse (coloured arrows): green enzymes in the bottom-left one, cyan enzymes in the top-right one.

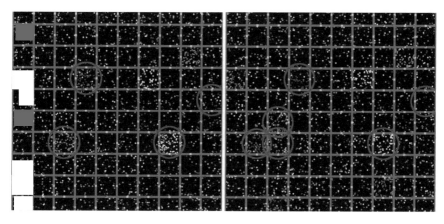

Fig. 8.14 (*left*) In fact, clusters begin to appear—as an *emergent* phenomenon—thanks to the interplay between `attract`, `strengthen`, and `boost` perturbations, both where the original action took place as well as in distant compartments, reached by the traces, and storing compatible information. (*right*) Whenever new actions are performed by catalysts, the $\mathcal{MoK}$ infrastructure *adaptively* reorganises the spatial configuration of information so as to better tackle the novel, now arising coordination needs

Colours represent semantic differences for different matches: red molecules match green enzymes/traces, orange molecules match lime enzymes/traces, yellow molecules match turquoise enzymes/traces, magenta molecules match cyan enzymes/traces, pink molecules match sky blue enzymes/traces.

Fig. 8.13 (left) showcases that the expected clusters appear: red molecules (brought by green traces' perturbation action) have the highest concentration in the bottom-left (highlighted) compartment, likewise magenta molecules (brought by cyan traces) in the top-right one. Figures 8.13 (left) and 8.14 showcase that clusters are transient, hence $\mathcal{MoK}$ coordinative behaviour *adaptive*: they last as long as users' action effects (enzymes and traces) last.

In fact, besides new clusters appearing (magenta molecules, top-left and yellow molecules, bottom-right), the previous ones either disappear (magenta cluster, top-right) or are replaced (orange cluster, bottom-left). This *adaptiveness* feature is confirmed by Fig. 8.15, plotting the oscillatory trend of clustered (still) molecules and traces.

Also, the series of pictures just described highlights other desirable features of $\mathcal{MoK}$, stemming from both its biochemical inspiration and BIC, respectively: *locality* and *situatedness* (of both computations and interactions). In fact, as neighbouring compartments can influence each other through diffusion, they can also act independently by, e.g. aggregating different molecules.

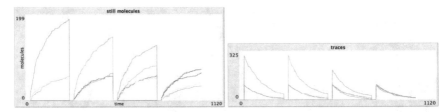

Fig. 8.15 In (*left*), concentration of still molecules over time; in (*right*), concentration of traces over time [10]. Still molecules represent molecules currently in the "right" compartment—the one storing matching enzymes. The oscillatory trend is due to periodic injection of enzymes (thus traces) which clears the still state of molecules. The different colours correspond to the different molecules. Traces move molecules to the right compartment through perturbations. The oscillatory trend is due to decay of traces over time. The different colours correspond to the different traces

The simulation discussed in this section highlights a few things:

- first, *feasibility* of the BIC-based approach to coordination w.r.t. $\mathcal{MoK}$ goals, since users' interaction effectively steers $\mathcal{MoK}$ coordinative behaviour toward, e.g. a better spatial configuration of information items despite diffusion being uniform, by stimulating $\mathcal{MoK}$ to undertake appropriate *anticipatory coordination* actions
- second, *efficiency* of the approach, from both the user and the system perspective: for the former, users may be completely *unaware* of the BIC machinery working behind the scenes, and $\mathcal{MoK}$ would still function, thus their cognitive overhead is zero; for the latter, enzymes and traces are generated from *locally* available information, and perturbation actions apply locally, or on *neighbourhoods* at most, thus they are computationally inexpensive and scalable
- third, *adaptiveness* of the approach, being clusters transiently appearing only as long as users' interest justify their existence
- fourth, possibly the most interesting property to notice, the ability of $\mathcal{MoK}$ to exhibit—to some extent—*intelligent* and *semantically driven* behaviour even despite traditional machine learning and reasoning processes being not exploited—relying instead on chemical-inspired self-organisation and behavioural implicit communication

References

1. Alves, R., Antunes, F., Salvador, A.: Tools for kinetic modeling of biochemical networks. Nat. Biotechnol. **24**(6), 667–672 (2006). doi:10.1038/nbt0606-667

2. Anderson, W.J.: Continuous-time Markov Chains: An Applications-oriented Approach. Springer Science & Business Media, New York, Philadelphia (2012)

3. Brun, Y., Marzo Serugendo, G., Gacek, C., Giese, H., Kienle, H., Litoiu, M., Müller, H., Pezzè, M., Shaw, M.: Engineering self-adaptive systems through feedback loops. In: Cheng, B., Lemos, R., Giese, H., Inverardi, P., Magee, J. (eds.) Software Engineering for Self-Adaptive Systems, Lecture Notes in Computer Science, vol. 5525, pp. 48–70. Springer, Berlin Heidelberg (2009). doi:10.1007/978-3-642-02161-9

4. Ciocchetta, F., Hillston, J.: Bio-PEPA: A framework for the modeling and analysis of biological systems. Theor. Comput. Sci. **410**(33–34), 3065–3084 (2009). doi:10.1016/j.tcs.2009.02.037. Concurrent Systems Biology: To Nadia Busi (1968–2007)

5. Gardelli, L., Viroli, M., Omicini, A.: On the role of simulations in engineering self-organising MAS: The case of an intrusion detection system in TuCSoN. In: Brueckner, S.A., Di Marzo Serugendo, G., Hales, D., Zambonelli, F. (eds.) Engineering Self-Organising Systems, LNAI, vol. 3910, pp. 153–168. Springer, Berlin, Heidelberg (2006). doi:10.1007/11734697. 3rd International Workshop (ESOA 2005), Utrecht, The Netherlands, 26 July 2005. Revised Selected Papers

6. Gilmore, S., Hillston, J.: The PEPA workbench: A tool to support a process algebra-based approach to performance modeling. In: G. Haring, G. Kotsis (eds.) Computer Performance Evaluation Modeling Techniques and Tools, Lecture Notes in Computer Science, vol. 794, pp. 353–368. Springer, Berlin, Heidelberg (1994). doi:10.1007/3-540-58021-2

7. Kwiatkowska, M., Norman, G., Parker, D.: PRISM 4.0: Verification of probabilistic real-time systems. In: G. Gopalakrishnan, S. Qadeer (eds.) Proc. 23rd International Conference on Computer Aided Verification (CAV'11), LNCS, vol. 6806, pp. 585–591. Springer, Berlin, Heidelberg (2011)

8. Mariani, S.: Analysis of the Molecules of Knowledge model with the Bio-PEPA Eclipse plugin. AMS Acta Technical Report 3783, ALMA MATER STUDIORUM–Università di Bologna, Bologna, Italy (2013). http://amsacta.unibo.it/3783/

9. Mariani, S.: Parameter engineering vs. parameter tuning: the case of biochemical coordination in MoK. In: Baldoni, M., Baroglio, C., Bergenti, F., Garro, A. (eds.) From Objects to Agents, CEUR Workshop Proceedings, vol. 1099, pp. 16–23. Sun SITE Central Europe, RWTH Aachen University, Turin, Italy (2013). http://ceur-ws.org/Vol-1099/paper5.pdf. XIV Workshop (WOA 2013). Workshop Notes

10. Mariani, S., Omicini, A.: Anticipatory coordination in socio-technical knowledge-intensive environments: Behavioural implicit communication in MoK. In: Gavanelli, M., Lamma, E., Riguzzi, F. (eds.) AI*IA 2015, Advances in Artificial Intelligence, Lecture Notes in Computer Science, vol. 9336, Chap. 8, pp. 102–115. Springer International Publishing (2015). doi:10.1007/978-3-319-24309-2. XIVth International Conference of the Italian Association for Artificial Intelligence, Ferrara, Italy, September 23–25, 2015, Proceedings

11. Merelli, E., Armano, G., Cannata, N., Corradini, F., d'Inverno, M., Doms, A., Lord, P., Martin, A., Milanesi, L., Möller, S., Schroeder, M., Luck, M.: Agents in bioinformatics, computational and systems biology. Briefings Bioinform. **8**(1), 45–59 (2007). doi:10.1093/bib/bbl014

12. Nikolai, C., Madey, G.: Tools of the trade: A survey of various agent based modeling platforms. J. Artif. Soc. Soc. Simul. **12**(2), 2 (2009). http://jasss.soc.surrey.ac.uk/12/2/2.html

13. Pianini, D., Montagna, S., Viroli, M.: Chemical-oriented simulation of computational systems with Alchemist. J. Simul. **7**(3), 202–215 (2013). doi:10.1057/jos.2012.27

14. Piunti, M., Castelfranchi, C., Falcone, R.: Anticipatory coordination through action observation and behavior adaptation. In: Proceedings of AISB (2007)

Chapter 9
$\mathcal{M}$olecules of $\mathcal{K}$nowledge: Case Studies

Abstract In this chapter, the $\mathcal{MoK}$ technology is evaluated through two exemplary use cases, documents clustering and smart news management, so as to showcase its adaptive and self-organising abilities.

9.1 Similarity-Based Clustering

Besides simulations of the $\mathcal{MoK}$ model, it is indeed useful to test at least small portions of the $\mathcal{MoK}$ technology, with the aim of evaluating in an actual deployment scenario, even if simplified, whether $\mathcal{MoK}$ is not only able to achieve the desired behaviours, but if it can do so effectively and efficiently. On purpose, here follow experiments of some of the different similarity measures presented in Sect. 6.5 in a document clustering scenario, where scientific publications on the APICe online repository[1] are taken as $\mathcal{MoK}$ seeds, the full text of papers is embedded into atoms, and clustering into molecules happens through $\mathcal{MoK}$ aggregation reaction—taking two atoms, checking their similarity, then merging them in a molecule if they are similar *enough*.

Before proceeding along that line, it is necessary to perform some preprocessing of the documents subject of the experiments. Preprocessing involves the most common steps of a typical text mining pipeline, such as text extraction, tokenisation, stemming, part-of-speech tagging, and the like. The aim is to obtain the vector space representation described in Sect. 6.5.

In the following, only three out of the many more experiments performed are described, being the most successful ones, w.r.t. both clustering results and efficiency. In particular, all the three experiments are based on full-text atoms, that is, atoms storing a vector space representation of the whole text of the paper they represent.

However, the experiments actually performed consider every combination of text snippet and similarity measure, that is, all sorts of atoms—BIBTEX,[2] abstract-based, and full-text based atoms—are aggregated according to any basic similarity

---

[1] http://apice.unibo.it.

[2] http://www.bibtex.org.

© Springer International Publishing AG 2016
S. Mariani, *Coordination of Complex Sociotechnical Systems*,
Artificial Intelligence: Foundations, Theory, and Algorithms,
DOI 10.1007/978-3-319-47109-9_9

measure—cosine similarity, mean squares difference, euclidean distance, concept-based similarity.

It should be noted that, since $\mathcal{F}_{MoK}$ similarity measure is exploited in MoK during system operation (online), rather than in a preprocessing stage (offline), the weighting formula (6.1) is adjusted to consider a bootstrap phase in which no other document is known, and to dynamically change according to new documents (atoms) being put into MoK compartments.

Experiments were run on an Intel Core i7 (3 GHz, 4MB L3 cache) machine with 16GB of DDR3 RAM 1600 MHz, using OS X 10.10.5 kernel Darwin 14.5.0 64 bit. Java VisualVM (http://visualvm.java.net) was used for profiling execution time. Slightly more than a hundred papers were considered, that is, all papers published on **APICe** between 2010 and 2013. This apparently small number is motivated by the fact that one should imagine to let MoK operate for a few hours, within a research collaboration scenario, in which researchers from a few different research teams in the same department share a MoK platform for retrieving potentially relevant scientific papers.

9.1.1   Basic Measure

In the first experiment, a very basic approach is pursued, that is

- weight assignment is simply constant, that is, each term considered for measuring similarity is assigned the constant weight $\frac{1}{n}$, where n is the number of terms in the document—or, more generally, in the text snippet
- similarity measure—that is, $\mathcal{F}_{MoK}$—is simply based on *weighted co-occurrences* of terms, that is, the more terms are in common between text snippets, the more snippets are considered similar
- co-occurrences of terms is checked syntactically—no semantics involved here

The reason to include this very basic approach into discussion of experiments stems from the online character of the clustering process adopted by MoK: being the aggregation reaction meant to continuously execute aggregations according to its dynamic rate, it is crucial that weight assignment, co-occurrences check, and similarity measure, are as *efficient* (barely speaking, *fast*) as possible—effectiveness is not substantial in MoK, due to its very nature. In this case, e.g., time taken to compute similarity for a single comparison is the lowest experienced: just ≈ 8 ms.

Figure 9.1 graphically depicts the clustering results obtained. There, coloured, smaller spheres are not atoms, but molecules, and light-blue, bigger spheres are themselves molecules, although aggregating other molecules. Each smaller molecule has a name, roughly denoting the topic of the atoms (hence papers) it aggregates, as defined by experts in the field—the authors of the papers themselves. The different

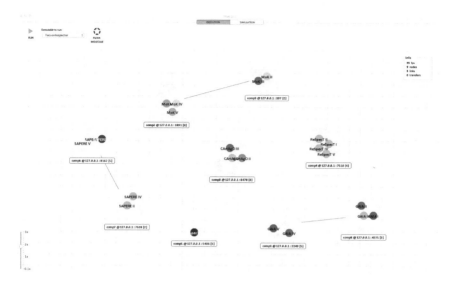

Fig. 9.1 Clustering result for most basic similarity measure

colours roughly resemble similarity as computed by $\mathcal{F}_{MoK}$ function. Links between bigger molecules are another graphical representation of similarity calculated by $\mathcal{F}_{MoK}$: linked molecules are similar enough to be considered somehow connected (correlated), but not enough to be clustered together in a single molecule—according to the application-specific threshold mentioned in Sect. 6.3.

Figure 9.1 clearly shows that MoK aggregation reaction has some success in finding similarity patterns, even in the case of $\mathcal{F}_{MoK}$ most basic implementation. For example, although no molecule includes all the papers tagged with the same topic by experts, no molecule aggregates information belonging to different topics. Furthermore, similar information aggregated by different molecules is anyway recognised to be similar by $\mathcal{F}_{MoK}$ function—a link lies between the different molecules.

9.1.2 Cosine Similarity

In this second experiment, the previous approach is refined as follows:

- weight assignment occurs according to function (6.1)
- $\mathcal{F}_{MoK}$ is based on *cosine similarity*, that is, on function (6.2)
- co-occurrences of terms is still checked syntactically

Figure 9.2 shows that the above refinements lead to an improvement in the clustering results obtained by MoK aggregation reaction featuring cosine similarity measure as $\mathcal{F}_{MoK}$. In fact, now all the papers belonging to the same topic, according to experts

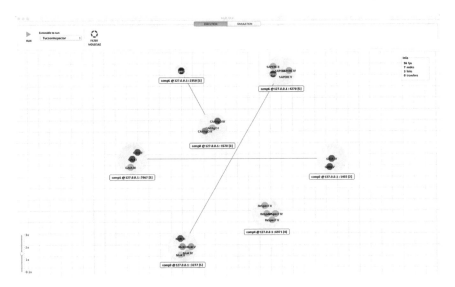

Fig. 9.2 Clustering result for cosine similarity measure

evaluation, are correctly assigned to the same cluster, that is, molecule, except for one molecule consisting of five papers tagged with term ReSpecT.

Furthermore, inter-molecule similarity connections are now linking molecules clustering papers belonging to different but strongly related topics, again according to experts evaluation, besides molecules aggregating papers belonging to the same topic—those tagged with term GAIA, as in Fig. 9.1. Namely, papers about SAPERE and MoK have a strong similarity due to many terms, such as "chemical", "coordination", "self-organisation", appearing with similar weights in both documents—the same for CArtAgO and ReSpecT papers, related by terms such as "coordination", "artefact", "environment", among the many.

However, here time taken to compute similarity for a single aggregation reaction application is ≈18 ms—doubled w.r.t. previous experiment.

9.1.3 Concept-Based Similarity

In this latter experiment, the refined approach is further sophisticated by

- modifying the matching function checking co-occurrences of terms, which has been extended so as to consider WordNet[3]-based *synsets* [5] in similarity measure—that is, synonyms, meronyms, hyperonymy, etc.
- modifying $\mathcal{F}_{MoK}$ function to implement the *concept-based similarity* measure defined in [2]

---

[3]http://wordnet.princeton.edu.

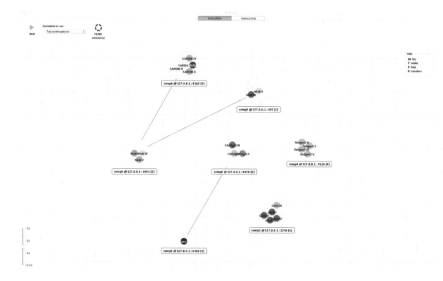

Fig. 9.3 Clustering result for concept-based similarity measure

Figure 9.3 shows no substantial improvement w.r.t. previous experiment, but only a different molecules configuration, suggesting that adopting more complex approaches, such as concept-based similarity and synsets-based matching, may not be worth the investment in computational complexity and execution time—depending on the application domain, of course. In fact, consider this $\mathcal{F}_{MoK}$ implementation takes $\approx$57 ms to perform a single comparison, way more than both previous experiments—mostly due to WordNet lookup.

Nevertheless, it should be noted that the lack of improvement may be depending on the application domain where $\mathcal{F}_{MoK}$ is put to test: all the papers involved in the experiment are from the computer science and engineering area, where synsets are not so meaningful and scarcely represented within WordNet.

> Besides comparing performance of a few widely adopted similarity measures, and evaluating the clustering capabilities of $\mathcal{MoK}$ aggregation reaction, the experiments confirm the feasibility of the chemical-inspired coordination-based approach to clustering envisioned in $\mathcal{MoK}$. In particular, it is worth to note that some sort of *semantic coordination patterns*, such as clustering of similar information, may be achieved successfully without resorting to full-fledged semantic reasoning facilities—e.g., ontology-based entailment and the like.
>
> This is especially relevant for $\mathcal{MoK}$, since it is expected to be deployed within knowledge-intensive sociotechnical systems, that is, business environments within which information is produced in massive amounts and at a very

fast pace. Therefore, being capable of *timely* detecting and reifying similarity patterns as soon as new information is available, may be crucial for the sustainability of the knowledge-management platform at hand.

Accordingly, the focus of the experiments has been about simplicity and efficiency of the approach, rather than on correctness and efficacy.

9.2 $\mathcal{M}o\mathcal{K}$-News

While $\mathcal{M}o\mathcal{K}$ is a general-purpose model for knowledge self-organisation, it can be tailored on specialised application domains, by refining the notion of atom—which in turn impacts the notion of molecule, too—and suitably defining function $\mathcal{F}_{\mathcal{M}o\mathcal{K}}$ exploited in $\mathcal{M}o\mathcal{K}$ reactions. Since news management provides a prominent example of knowledge-intensive sociotechnical system, a citizen journalism scenario has been chosen to deploy a $\mathcal{M}o\mathcal{K}$ system suitably tailored, so as to evaluate its capabilities to support the smart migration pattern envisioned as one of the two main $\mathcal{M}o\mathcal{K}$ goals.

Accordingly, in the remainder of this section $\mathcal{M}o\mathcal{K}$ is specialised for the news management business domain, starting from the most widely adopted standards for knowledge representation in the news management domain, and moving towards the definition of the $\mathcal{M}o\mathcal{K}$-News model specific for self-organisation of news.

9.2.1 Knowledge Representation for News Management

In order to specialise the $\mathcal{M}o\mathcal{K}$ model and make it domain-specific, two of the most relevant standards for news are taken as a reference for atoms refinement: *NewsML*[4] and *NITF*.[5]

NewsML is a news sharing format (or, tagging language) orthogonal w.r.t. media-type, aimed at conveying not only the core news *content*, but also data that describes the content in an abstract way; namely, *metadata*. In order to ease syntactical and semantical interoperability, NewsML adopts XML as the first implementation language for its standards, and maintains sets of *controlled vocabularies*, collectively branded as *NewsCodes*,[6] to represent concepts describing and categorising news objects in a consistent manner—similarly to what domain-specific ontologies do.

---

[4]http://iptc.org/standards/newsml-g2/.

[5]http://iptc.org/standards/nitf/.

[6]http://iptc.org/standards/newscodes/.

NewsML provides journalists the above features through four main abstractions:

News item—It vehicles both the news' content and its metadata, hence, information reporting about what has just happened, as well as information about the news itself—who owns the copyright, the topics covered, the target audience, distribution rights, etc.

Concept item—News are about events, persons, organisations, and the like. This information is worth to be tracked, reified, and referred to, along with the news content, to better identify, recognise, categorise it. Thus, a data structure collecting all this worth-to-be-remembered information is needed: the concept item, indeed.

Package item—It is meant to organise and convey a structured set of somehow related News Items—such as "Top 10 news of the week" and the like.

Knowledge item—It is a container for a whole taxonomy of Concept Items, acting like an ontology, which enables distribution of basic knowledge about all the terms the News Item refers to.

The News Industry Text Format, too, adopts XML to enrich the content of news articles, enabling identification and description of a number of features typical in journalism, among which the most notable are

- *who* owns the copyright to the item, who may republish it, and who it is about
- *what* subjects, organisations, and events it covers
- *when* it happened, was reported, issued, and revised
- *where* it was written, where the action took place, and where it may be released
- *why* it is newsworthy, based on the editor analysis of the metadata

NITF and NewsML are complementary standards. In fact, they perfectly combine to provide a comprehensive and coherent framework supporting management of the whole news life cycle: comprehensive, given that the latter cares about news overall structure, including metadata, whereas the former focusses on their internal meaning, to make it unambiguous; coherent, because they both exploit the same IPTC abstractions—e.g., NITF makes usage of NewsCodes, too.

To give a flavour of NITF capabilities, among its most used inline tags there are:

- `<person>` wraps personal names, both living people and fictitious. It could contain the `<function>` tag if the tagged person goes along with its public role
- `<org>` identifies organisational names. An inner tag (`<orgid>`) allows special codes to be added, such as codes from the Standard Industry Classification[7] list, or NewsCodes
- `<location>` identifies geographic locations and significant places. It contains either mere text or structured information including `<sublocation>`, `<city>`, `<region>`, `<state>`, and `<country>`
- `<event>` should be limited to newsworthy events, that is, events that carry news value for a journalist. Factors of news value are, for instance, significance, prox-

---

[7] http://www.sec.gov/info/edgar/siccodes.htm.

imity, prominence of the involved persons, consequences, unusualness, human interest, timeliness

- `<object.title>` could tag anything that no other tag could wrap

NITF tags like the ones above (and many others) can be spread throughout the text of, e.g., a web document,[8] to better characterise the semantics of its most relevant terms.

9.2.2 Incarnation of *MoK* Model

News representation standards can be used to specialise the *MoK* model for the news management business domain. There, journalists usually gain the knowledge they need to create news from diverse and sparse sources of information. Assuming that sources provide journalists with the required *raw information* already formatted according to the afore-mentioned IPTC standards—as in real-world news agencies typically happens—a simple yet effective mapping between models can be devised out.

In fact, a *MoK* atom has a clear counterpart in NewsML and NITF standards: the *tag*, which, along with the content it refers to, can easily be seen as what composes the "news-substance" of a news story. As a result, a *MoK*-coordinated news management system would contain `<newsItem>` atoms, `<person>` atoms, `<subject>` atoms, etc—that is, virtually one kind of atom for each NewsML/NITF tag.

Accordingly, a generic *MoK* atom of the form $\mathrm{atom}(src, Content, Meta\text{-}info)_c$ may become a specialised *MoK*-News atom as follows:

$$atom(src, Content, \mathrm{sem}(Tag, Catalog))_c$$

where:

> $src ::= $ *news source uri*
> $Content ::= $ *news content*
> $Meta\text{-}info ::= \mathrm{sem}(Tag, Catalog)$
>
> $Tag ::= $ *NewsML tag* | *NITF tag*
> $Catalog ::= $ *NewsCode uri* | *ontology uri*

Here, the content of an atom is mostly given by the pair `<Content, Tag>`, where `Tag` could be either a metadata tag drawn from NewsML or an inline description tag taken from NITF. The precise and unambiguous semantics of the news content (`Content`) can be specified thanks to the `Catalog` information, which could be grounded in either NewsML or NITF standards in the form of NewsCodes, or instead be referred to a custom ontology defined by the journalist.

---

[8]http://www.iptc.org/site/News_Exchange_Formats/NITF/Examples/.

MoK molecules and reactions—actually, any other *MoK* abstraction—are both syntactically and semantically affected by such a domain-specific mapping of the *MoK* model. Here, in fact, molecules can be re-interpreted as *ever-growing news stories*, and reactions as *autonomous news manipulators*. Thus, *MoK aggregation* reaction can now be interpreted as relating pieces of different news stories based on semantical relationships, either between NewsML/NITF tags or their tagged content. This *semantic matchmaking* capability may be straightforwardly assigned to $\mathcal{F}_{MoK}$ function, suitably extended beyond content-based similarity solely. *Reinforcement* reaction now increases relevance of those news pieces which are more frequently accessed, whereas, on the contrary, *decay* reaction makes obsolete, stale, or no longer considered information fade away as time passes by—recall *MoK* seeds guarantee later recovery, if needed. *Diffusion* then, is responsible of moving news toward the potentially interested journalists, leading to both *self-organisation* and *adaptation* of the spatial configuration of news pieces within the network of *MoK* compartments used as news stories repositories.

Another fundamental aspect of the *MoK* model perfectly suits the news management scenario: the notion of *concentration*. The three most characterising facets of a news are its *novelty*, *relevance*, and *usefulness*, that is, respectively: *(i)* how much new it is if compared to the actual environment and to time passing, *(ii)* how interesting it is perceived by other knowledge workers and target audience, and *(iii)* how useful it is to anyone according to some criteria—e.g., economic revenues, or new know-how it could provide. Concentration easily models all the three facets: the more a news—atom, molecule—is fresh, interesting, and useful to someone, the greater its concentration will be—hence, it will more frequently affect the dynamics of the *MoK* system, according to the biochemical coordination metaphor implemented by *MoK* compartments.

The specialised *MoK* model just presented, called *MoK*-News, is implemented and evaluated using the *MoK* prototype middleware described in Sect. 7.1. Next section reports on experimental results regarding information diffusion.

9.2.3 *MoK*-News at Work

In the news management scenario deployed for testing, NITF-tagged documents are exploited as *MoK* seeds, injecting news pieces atoms in compartments. There, journalists manipulate the information items living in their compartment for assembling their own news stories, transparently and unintentionally reinforcing relevant information pieces—through enzymes and reinforcement reaction. Reinforcement coupled with diffusion and balanced by decay, makes a smart migration pattern appear by emergence, guiding news pieces toward the (potentially) most interested journalists.

Figures 9.4 and 9.5 show how smart migration of news pieces can be realised within *MoK*-News. The depicted scenario is quite simple: a generator *MoK*-News compartment stores a collection of different news sources—talking about weather,

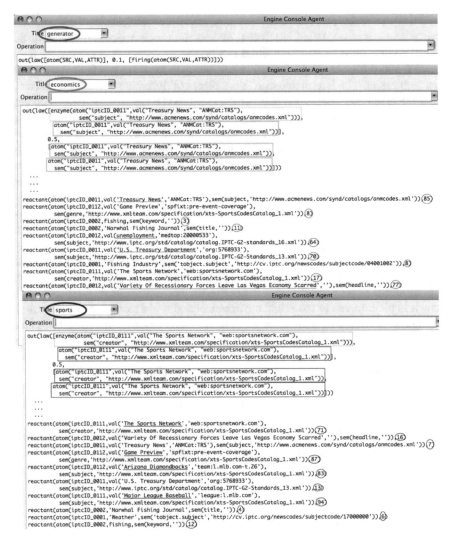

Fig. 9.4 Concentration values of atoms currently in a compartment belonging to an interested journalist are way higher than others [3]. Notice also that reinforcement 𝓜o𝓚 reactions appear as implemented within the TuCSoN prototype, after Step 2.*a* of the chemical engine—that is, reactants are sampled and products instantiated accordingly

baseball, and finance—and diffuses them to the neighbour compartments "economics" and "sports"—belonging to journalists/consumers interested to that particular topic.

Despite diffusion being implemented to be equiprobable towards each neighbour compartment, the observable effect is that users have within their compartment the most appealing knowledge chunks. What makes this *emergent self-organisation* phe-

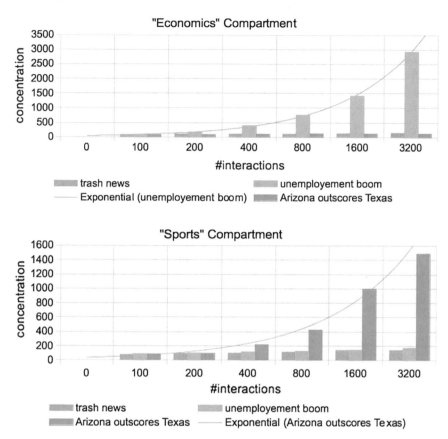

Fig. 9.5 The stochastic equilibrium between diffusion, reinforcement and decay laws, makes a smart diffusion pattern appear by emergence [4]

nomena happen is the (self-)balanced cooperation among two mechanisms typical of self-* systems: positive and negative feedback.

Positive feedback is enacted by *MoK* reinforcement reaction, that, in this implementation, takes an atom and the relative enzyme to produce two copy of the atom—thus increasing concentration by 1. Negative feedback stems from *MoK* decay reaction, which destroys 1 unit of atoms and molecules concentration.

The result of the competition between these opposite feedbacks is the *unstable equilibrium* depicted in Fig. 9.5, where compartments "economics" and "sports" are mainly populated by compartment-related atoms—thanks to the positive feedback—whereas concentration of "wrong" knowledge chunks are maintained relatively low thanks to both decay and absence of enzymes. Equilibrium is unstable because totally driven by users' interactions: as soon as the "sports" compartment is, e.g., re-assigned to a different journalist, interested in a different sort of news stories, *MoK* decay—thus negative feedback—would start prevailing, asymptotically homogenising concentration of news items in the absence of reinforcement—positive feedback.

As a last note it is worth to highlight how the number of fruitful interactions—that is, interactions involving information relevant to the interacting journalist—is fundamental to determine the speed of convergence. It should be noted also that the number of interactions displayed in Fig. 9.5 also includes $\mathcal{MoK}$ spontaneous interactions— e.g. through reactions and perturbation actions—not just users' actions—which is why it is so high.

The aim of this section is twofold: on the one side, showing how the $\mathcal{MoK}$ model can be easily *tailored* to specific application domains, by properly re-interpreting its general-purpose abstractions; on the other side, showing how $\mathcal{MoK}$ middleware prototype is able to achieve *high-level global* behaviours— in this case, smart diffusion of information—despite *simplicity* of the *local mechanisms* adopted—here, probabilistic diffusion and user-driven reinforcement. Focussing the latter aspect, a few things are worth to be noted.

First, the extreme simplicity of the local mechanisms adopted, that is, decay, diffusion, and reinforcement. In the deployed scenario in fact, decay simply removes one unit of concentration of the matched information piece, diffusion simply sends one unit of concentration of the matched information to a randomly selected neighbour, and reinforcement simply increases the concentration value of the information items manipulated by users. Being so simple, they are also efficient, and when coupled with the *scale* of the scenario—many users, many information items, many interactions—they lead to a meaningful emergent global behaviour despite their simplicity.

Then, besides scale, what enables the emergent behaviour is the presence of the *feedback loop* typical of self-organising natural systems—e.g., prey-predator ecosystems [1]: while decay asymptotically tends to homogenise concentration values, most likely decaying more concentrated information, reinforcement contrasts the process by promptly increasing concentration of selected information items—by users, implicitly. There, also, lies the beauty and elegance of the chemical metaphor for coordination.

References

1. Berryman, A.A.: The origins and evolution of predator-prey theory. Ecology **73**(5), 1530–1535 (1992)
2. Jadhav, M.A., Shinde, S.K.: A concept based mining model for nlp using text clustering. In: International Journal of Engineering Research and Technology, vol. 2. ESRSA Publications, ESRSA Publications (2013)
3. Mariani, S., Omicini, A.: Self-organising news management: The *Molecules of Knowledge* approach. In: Pitt, J. (ed.) Self-Adaptive and Self-Organizing Systems Workshops (SASOW), pp. 235–240. IEEE CS (2012). doi:10.1109/SASOW.2012.48. 2012 IEEE Sixth International Conference (SASOW 2012), Lyon, France, 10-14 Sep. 2012. Proceedings

4. Mariani, S., Omicini, A.: MoK: Stigmergy meets chemistry to exploit social actions for coordination purposes. In: Verhagen, H., Noriega, P., Balke, T., de Vos, M. (eds.) Social Coordination: Principles, Artefacts and Theories (SOCIAL.PATH), pp. 50–57. The Society for the Study of Artificial Intelligence and the Simulation of Behaviour, AISB Convention 2013, University of Exeter, UK (2013)
5. Miller, G., Fellbaum, C.: Wordnet: An Electronic Lexical Database (1998)

Part III
Conclusion

In the last part of this book, the final remarks about the book contents and purpose are provided.

Chapter 10
Conclusion

Abstract In this chapter, final remarks about the book contents and purpose are provided.

10.1 Conclusive Remarks

In this book, first of all (Part I) coordination of complex sociotechnical systems has been discussed focussing on different aspects: distribution in Chap. 2, self-organisation in Chap. 3, situatedness in Chap. 4, "humans in the loop" in Chap. 5. For each facet, state-of-the-art solutions to their peculiar issues have been presented and deeply described.

In particular, a chemical-inspired approach to coordination for self-organising systems, which relies on artificial chemical reactions with custom kinetic rates as coordination laws, has been discussed in Chap. 3. An architectural and linguistic approach to coordination for situated pervasive systems, which relies on a situated, distributed, programmable, and tuple-based coordination medium and language to implement situated coordination laws, has been discussed in Chap. 4. Finally, an approach to user-driven coordination for sociotechnical systems, inspired to behavioural implicit communication and relying on the notions of tacit message and perturbation action to drive the coordination processes enacted by the coordination medium, has been discussed in Chap. 5.

Then (Part II), the $\mathcal{M}$olecules of $\mathcal{K}$nowledge model and technology for self-organisation of knowledge in knowledge-intensive sociotechnical systems has been presented and deeply discussed, as a summation of the above described approaches.

The rationale motivating inclusion of the apparently distant research lines above described in the same book, as well as their integration in a single coherent and comprehensive coordination model, has been the following: engineering efficient and effective coordination for large-scale, data-intensive systems with "humans in the loop" is a very difficult task, which should be approached in a holistic way by considering both the model, the architecture, and the language level of a potential computational solution.

© Springer International Publishing AG 2016
S. Mariani, *Coordination of Complex Sociotechnical Systems*,
Artificial Intelligence: Foundations, Theory, and Algorithms,
DOI 10.1007/978-3-319-47109-9_10

Nature-inspired coordination models, in particular chemical-inspired ones, already proven their ability to deal with distribution, decentralisation, unpredictability, and scale in a simple yet expressive way, thus, in the very end, their suitability for the aforementioned engineering task. Then, the need for a suitable coordination infrastructure supporting chemical-inspired approaches naturally follows, while the need to readily account for users behaviour since the very foundation of the proposed coordination framework stems from the kind of systems (mostly) targeted by the book—that is, sociotechnical ones.

Moreover, the need for efficient and smart ways of preserving, managing, and analysing the astonishing amount of raw data, derived information, and high-level knowledge that any sociotechnical system produces everyday, is increasingly pushing researchers and practitioners.

Big data like approaches are more or less the state of art, mostly because they are good in finding hidden patterns in the data they are fed with. Nevertheless, they mostly neglect "humans in the loop", being the role of human users confined to analysis of ready-to-use results, produced by algorithms which are completely user-neutral and goal-independent. They also require ever-increasing computational power to scale up with the complexity of the problem at hand, which is something not all the organisations can afford.

For the above reasons, it may be appropriate to promote a paradigm shift toward self-organisation of information and knowledge, as promoted by the $\mathcal{M}$olecules of $\mathcal{K}$nowledge model, where

- user-driven adaptability of information mining and knowledge discovery activities is the main concern to deal with, and the foremost goal to pursue
- techniques supporting the mentioned activities natively account for users goals, as well as take advantage of the properties of the business domain at hand
- the overall performance seamlessly scales up and down naturally, as a result of exploitation of local information and fully decentralised mechanisms, rather than of *post-hoc* technical solutions

All the above is witnessed by the latest H2020 calls for proposals, increasingly demanding citizen-inclusive policy making, governance participation, user-centric knowledge sharing platforms, and the like—see, e.g., calls H2020-SC6-CO-CREATION-2016–2017,   H2020-EINFRA-2016–2017,   and   H2020-FETPROACT-2016–2017.